Critical
Ethnography

To Judith A. Hamera
and
Reighne Madison Dyson

D. SOYINI MADISON

University of North Carolina at Chapel Hill

Critical Ethnography

Method, Ethics, and Performance

SAGE Publications

Thousand Oaks ■ London ■ New Delhi

For information:

Sage Publications, Inc.
2455 Teller Road
Thousand Oaks, California 91320
E-mail: order@sagepub.com

Sage Publications Ltd.
1 Oliver's Yard
55 City Road
London, EC1Y 1SP
United Kingdom

Sage Publications India Pvt. Ltd.
B-42, Panchsheel Enclave
Post Box 4109
New Delhi 110 017 India

Printed in the United States of America.

Library of Congress Cataloging-in-Publication Data

Madison, D. Soyini.
Critical ethnography: method, ethics, and performance / D. Soyini Madison.
      p. cm.
Includes bibliographical references and index.
ISBN 978-0-7619-2915-4 (cloth) — ISBN 978-0-7619-2916-1 (pbk.)
    1. Ethnology—Methodology. 2. Ethnology—Field work. 3. Anthropological ethics. I. Title.
GN345.M324 2005
305.8—dc22

2004024118

This book is printed on acid-free paper.

09   10   9   8   7   6   5   4

Senior Acquisitions Editor:	Todd R. Armstrong
Editorial Assistant:	Deya Saoud
Production Editor:	Tracy Alpern
Copy Editor:	Stacey Shimizu
Typesetter:	C&M Digitals (P) Ltd.
Indexer:	Sylvia Coates
Cover Designer:	Janet Foulger
Cover Graphic:	Torkwase Dyson
Author Photo:	York Wilson

Contents

Acknowledgments

Dwight Conquergood, my precious friend and teacher, for exemplifying an ethics of ethnography, championing social justice, and inspiring generations of dedicated scholars, teachers, and activists.

The Department of Communication Studies at the University of North Carolina, with a special thank-you to Julia T. Wood, Della Pollock, and Beverly W. Long for your brilliance and your extraordinary support over many years.

Robin G. Vander, whose friendship helped make this book possible and who also makes the phrase "a friend in need is a friend indeed" a reality and a saving grace. Your integrity and wisdom never cease to amaze me.

Wahneema Lubiano, Kara Keeling, Sue Estroff, and Genna Rae McNeil, for your friendship, intellectual generosity, and for your eloquence in naming the most pressing matters that beset the world.

Judith A. Hamera, E. Patrick Johnson, Tony Perucci, Joni L. Jones, Elyse Lamm Pineau, and Lisa Merrill, for consistently deepening my understanding of the politics and alchemy of performance.

Michael Eric Dyson and Marcia L. Dyson, for your compassion and genuine commitment to public knowledge.

A special group of graduate students, scholars, and rising ethnographers who have taught me in more profound ways than I have taught them: Robert "Robb" Romanowski, Bernadette Marie Calafell, Elizabeth Nelson, Hannah Blevins, Renee Alexander, Phaedra Pezzullo, Annissa Clarke, Rivka Eisner, Deborah Thomson, Mathew Spangler, Nathan Epley, Chris Chiron, Tes Thraves, Leah Totten, Eve Crevoshay, Brian Graves, Kate Willink, Mark Hayward, Rachel Hall, and, with deepest admiration and gratitude, to Lisa B. Y. Calvente, who has been my rock and my light.

Arlene Jackson, Akua McDaniel, Treva Cunningham, and Walter Cunningham, for your enduring encouragement, friendship, and support long before I knew the power of ethnography.

Kwame William Obeng and Wisdom Mensah, for guiding me through the complexity of cultural codes and foreign territories.

Kingsley Kweku Acquah for helping me better understand the importance of world traveling and loving perception.

Abena Joan Brown, Val Gray Ward, and Useni Eugene Perkins, for over three decades of mentoring and enriching the lives of so many through committed leadership and community performance.

Staceyann Chin, for your excitement about this project, your respect for language, and your courage.

Lisa Aubrey, for your fearless commitment to truth and justice and for helping me to recognize the more complex translations required of politics "on the ground."

Todd Armstrong and Deya Saoud, for your patience, understanding, and extraordinary skills in helping bring this book into being, especially during the last days of completion when my fieldwork hurried me away to the other side of the ocean.

Tracy Alpern and Stacey Shimizu, for your pleasant rapport despite cyberspace and for being so good at what you do.

Adwoa Sarkoa Ulzen and Amber D. Turner, for your excellent research assistance and careful attention to detail under pressure.

Elizabeth Bell, University of South Florida; Amy Kilgard, San Francisco State University; Angela Trethewey, Arizona State University; Nick Trujillo, California State University, Sacramento; Kristin B. Valentine, Arizona State University; and John T. Warren, Bowling Green State University, for reviewing the manuscript.

Reighne Madison Dyson, born July 19, 2003, for motivating me to care more and more each day about the future of this planet.

Mejai Kai Dyson, for your precise mind, your belief in the significance of fairness, and for demonstrating that good character is a precious thing.

Torkwase Madison Dyson, for your extraordinary artistic talent and for exemplifying what it means to teach and to live graciously from the heart and soul.

Yosiah Daniel Israel, for reminding me that love is the greatest possibility.

1

Introduction to Critical Ethnography

Theory and Method

*Critical ethnography is conventional ethnography with a politi-
cal purpose.*

—Jim Thomas,
Doing Critical Ethnography (1993)

*We should not choose between critical theory and ethnography.
Instead, we see that researchers are cutting new paths to reinscribing critique in ethnography.*

—George Noblit, Susana Y. Flores, & Enrique G.
Murillo, Jr., *Post Critical Ethnography: An Introduction* (2004)

L ast summer, while attending an annual, local documentary film festival
in a small movie theatre with about 80 or more other interested people,
I waited with great anticipation for one of the award-winning documentaries
to begin. It had been highly recommended by a friend and the festival
description was intriguing. From what I could gather, the subject of the film
related to women's human rights in Ghana, West Africa. I was very excited
about seeing it. I was hoping the film was inspired by the work of indigenous

human rights activists in the developing world, particularly in Ghana, since it is a country for which I have deep affection. I lived there for almost three years conducting field research with local activists on human rights violations against women and girls.

As I waited anxiously for the documentary to start, I began to reflect back on my fieldwork and my days in Ghana working with and learning from Ghanaian human rights activists. I thought of the many sacrifices these people make in working for the victims of human rights abuses in their own country: by providing shelter and protection for them, by enlightening their countrymen and -women on the importance of human rights, and by their own political acumen in helping establish human rights policies. They are truly committed, openly condemning abusive cultural practices while simultaneously advocating for economic and social justice in the developing world. I witnessed so many of them being denigrated and condemned by members of their own communities; however, they forged ahead because of their belief in human dignity and self-determination.

The more I was exposed to the struggles of African men and women working in their own countries for peace, justice, and human rights, the more I realized how their work goes unrecognized by many of us in the West or global North. For many of us, the primary representations we see of developing countries, particularly Africa, are of tribal warfare, corruption, human rights abuses, and those desperately seeking asylum in the West. These representations do not tell the whole truth. The battle these local activists are fighting is one of immense proportions within their own communities that is made more difficult by the forces of global inequities. I remain inspired by the profound importance of their work. I welcomed this documentary as further credit to them.

The film began. A story was unfolding—a story being told by a young Ghanaian woman. My excitement grew. The camera focused on the young woman and shifted intermittently to particular sites in Ghana. As she told her story, she recounted the fear, helplessness, and desperation she felt when confronted by her father's demand that she undergo female circumcision (or what is variously referred to as *female incision, female genital mutilation*, or *clitoridectomy*). The portrayal was of a frightened young woman alone in a country where there was no refuge, no one to assist her, and no space of protection and safety. I was beginning to feel uncomfortable; there was something wrong with this story. The documentary came to an end, adapting a tone of hope and opportunity, as the young woman looked into the camera and poignantly expressed that she was finally safe: She had fled the dangers of Ghana. She is now in safe asylum in the United States of America.

The film ended with bold white letters written across the screen revealing the large numbers of women threatened by female incision. It told a tragic, compelling, beautiful, and well-crafted story of a young woman fleeing a dangerous country where there was no protection from the wrath of her father and the mutilation of her body; moreover, the enormous pain and injustice threatening this woman was all averted in the only option available to her: asylum—the safe haven of the United States.

I began to tremble with rage. The documentary was seriously misleading. It competed with countless other documentaries and it won; therefore, it was given a public viewing before hundreds of people attending the film festival. My blood was boiling. It was a gross and dangerous misrepresentation of Ghana and her people.

During the question-and-answer session, I could not contain my anger over the suggestion that there was no intervention or protection in Ghana for human rights abuses, thereby erasing the work of human rights activists in that country as though they were nonexistent. The filmmaker responded to my comments by stating that female incision occurs in the rural areas of Ghana, far from the city and out of reach from the work of the activists I knew. I sat there in utter disbelief. I had traveled throughout Ghana and knew first-hand of the work of activists in the rural area represented in the film. I witnessed their struggles against female incision.

I know the story of Mahmudu Issah, who with his organization of rights activists work in the same area where the woman in the documentary says she found no refuge. Muhamudu and his comrades are struggling with little resources to combat female incision and other human rights abuses at great risk to their lives and livelihoods. They provide safety and protection while making great strides to change the practice. Theirs is a far more compelling story that was absent in the film, leaving the viewer to assume they do not exist.

After it was all over and people were leaving the theatre, the filmmaker came up to me wishing to talk further about the film and the concerns I expressed. She spoke briefly of the region she visited and the woman who told the story. After listening to her speak and sensing her genuine concern around the issue of representation, it was clear to me that she was sincere in her efforts to create a documentary that depicted the experience of this woman and to make a statement about the cruelty of this traditional practice. I believe her intent was sincerely to help this particular woman and to bring attention to a cultural practice that imperils the freedom and well being of women. She was, for all intents and purposes, trying to "do the right thing."

So, why does my discontent with the representation of this woman's story still weigh so heavily that it occupies the opening pages in a book on ethics, performance, and critical ethnography? It is because with all the good intentions, excellent craftsmanship, and even with the reliability and eloquence of a particular story, representing Others is always going to be a complicated and contentious undertaking. I believe the documentarian to be ethical; yet the documentary, as with all products of representation, still raises ethical questions. These questions of ethics and representation are obviously not exclusive to this documentary. They arise again and again as I encounter ethnographic and qualitative projects and as I meet artists, researchers, students, and activists engaging the worlds and meanings of Others.

As I continue to think about the documentary, I must also be self-reflexive about my own discontent. After all, the medium was documentary; it was not a book or an article. The documentary does not purport to be ethnography, let alone critical ethnography. So why should I be disturbed? Why should the recounting of this experience occupy the opening pages of this book? The answer is that the film not only documented the lives and stories of real people the filmmaker came to know but also introduced those lives and stories to us. Representation has consequences: How people are represented is how they are treated (Hall, 1997). Whether *claiming* to be ethnography or not, the documentary *was* ethnographic in that the author or interpreter spent time in a location interacting with others within that prescribed space; furthermore, she interpreted and recorded what she found there and then, through her own interpretive standpoint, represented those findings to us. We meet the woman, learned of her experience and her culture through the idiosyncratic lens of the interpreter's interpretation. In this instance, as in most, interpretation held a great deal of power.

I recount the story of the documentary to illustrate what is at stake when you stand in as the transmitter of information and the skilled interpreter in both presenting and representing the lives and stories of others whom you have come to know and who have given you permission to reveal their stories. This illustration raises a multitude of questions; however, there are five central questions I invite the reader to consider:

1. How do we reflect upon and evaluate our own purpose, intentions, and frames of analysis as researchers?

2. How do we predict consequences or evaluate our own potential to do harm?

3. How do we create and maintain a dialogue of collaboration in our research projects between ourselves and Others?

4. How is the specificity of the local story relevant to the broader meanings and operations of the human condition?

5. How—in what location or through what intervention—will our work make the greatest contribution to equity, freedom, and justice?

These are questions we will engage throughout this book.

A few days after seeing the documentary, I expressed my concern to one of the judges of the festival who chose that particular documentary for viewing. She admonished me for believing that the film further entrenched the "backward view of Africa" and that it erased local human rights activists and their work. "After all," she said, "the film was only fifteen minutes long: There wasn't time to depict human rights. Anyway it is a documentary, and she is a filmmaker, not an anthropologist!" Whether in the form of a film or a book, or whether the recorder is a filmmaker or an anthropologist, or whether an account must be condensed to a paragraph or fills a 300-page monograph, we must still be accountable for the consequences of our representations and the implications of our message—because they matter.

Positionality and Shades of Ethnography

Critical ethnography begins with an ethical responsibility to address processes of unfairness or injustice within a particular *lived* domain. By "ethical responsibility," I mean a compelling sense of duty and commitment based on moral principles of human freedom and well-being, and hence a compassion for the suffering of living beings. The conditions for existence within a particular context are not as they *could* be for specific subjects; as a result, the researcher feels a moral obligation to make a contribution toward changing those conditions toward greater freedom and equity. The critical ethnographer also takes us beneath surface appearances, disrupts the *status quo*, and unsettles both neutrality and taken-for-granted assumptions by bringing to light underlying and obscure operations of power and control. Therefore, the critical ethnographer resists domestication and moves from "what is" to "what could be" (Carspecken, 1996; Denzin, 2001; Noblit, Flores, & Murillo, 2004; Thomas, 1993). Because the critical ethnographer is committed to the art and craft of fieldwork, empirical methodologies become the foundation for inquiry, and it is here "on the ground" of Others that the researcher encounters social conditions that become the point of departure for research (Thomas, 1993). We now begin to probe other possibilities that will challenge institutions, regimes of knowledge, and social practices that limit choices, constrain meaning, and denigrate identities and communities.

What does it mean for the critical ethnographer to "resist domestication"? It means that she will use the resources, skills, and privileges available to her to make accessible—to penetrate the borders and break through the confines in defense of—the voices and experiences of subjects whose stories are otherwise restrained and out of reach. This means the critical ethnographer contributes to emancipatory knowledge and discourses of social justice. The often quoted phrase "Knowledge is power" reflects how narrow perception, limited modes of understanding, and uncritical thinking diminish the capacity to envision alternative life possibilities; domestication will prohibit new forms of addressing conflict, and it will dishonor the foreign and the different. Knowledge is power relative to social justice, because knowledge guides and equips us to identify, name, question, and act against the unjust; consequently, we unsettle another layer of complicity. But, I must now confess: there is something missing with my singular emphasis on politics and the resistance of domestication.

The documentary, reflecting the aims of a critical ethnography project, took a stand against "suffering" and "injustice"—but it was not enough. I found its critique problematic. Therefore, I will argue that critical ethnography must begin to extend its political aims and augment its notion of "domestication" and "politics." Politics alone are incomplete without self-reflection. Critical ethnography must further its goals from simply politics to the politics of positionality. The question becomes, How do we begin to discuss our positionality as ethnographers and as those who represent Others?

Michelle Fine (1994) outlines three positions in qualitative research (p. 17):

1. The *ventriloquist* stance that merely "transmits" information in an effort toward neutrality and is absent of a political or rhetorical stance. The position of the ethnographer aims to be invisible, that is, the "self" strives to be nonexistent in the text.

2. The positionality of *voices* is where the subjects themselves are the focus, and their voices carry forward indigenous meanings and experiences that are in opposition to dominant discourses and practices. The position of the ethnographer is vaguely present but not addressed.

3. The *activism* stance in which the ethnographer takes a clear position in intervening on hegemonic practices and serves as an advocate in exposing the material effects of marginalized locations while offering alternatives.

Fine's outline is similar to the three positions of social inquiry set forth by Jurgen Habermas (1971) when he discusses the (a) *natural science model* of empirical analysis, in which the social world can be measured, predicted, and tested as life phenomena in the natural sciences through the invisible reportage of the researcher; (b) *historical and interpretive model*, in which social phenomena is described and its meanings and functions further elaborated through the balanced commentary and philosophical descriptions of the researcher; and the (c) *critical theory model*, in which social life is represented and analyzed for the political purpose of overcoming social oppression, particularly forms that reflect advanced capitalism through the overt polemics of the researcher. (See also Davis, 1999, p. 61.)

In the examples above, various positions of social science and qualitative researchers are *described;* however, George W. Noblit, Susana Y. Flores, and Enrique G. Murillo, Jr. (2004) take positionality a step further in what they refer to as *postcritical ethnography.* They not only describe positionality, but also comprehensively critique it relative to traditional notions of critical ethnography. Noblit et al. state that much of critical ethnography has been criticized for its focus on social change but lack of focus on the researchers own *positionality:* "Critical ethnographers must explicitly consider how their own acts of studying and representing people and situations are acts of domination even as critical ethnographers reveal the same in what they study" (p. 3).

Positionality is vital because it forces us to acknowledge our own power, privilege, and biases just as we are denouncing the power structures that surround our subjects. A concern for positionality is sometimes understood as "reflexive ethnography": it is a "turning back" on ourselves (Davis, 1999). When we turn back, we are accountable for own research paradigms, our own positions of authority, and our own moral responsibility relative to representation and interpretation. We begin to ask ourselves, What are we going to do with the research and who ultimately will benefit? Who gives us the authority to make claims about where we have been? How will our work make a difference in people's lives? But we might also begin to ask another kind of question: What difference *does* it make when the ethnographer himself comes from a history of colonization and disenfranchisement? Enrique G. Murillo, Jr., describes these identities in his revisioning of the term *mojado:*

> Mojado ethnography is how I have chosen to describe one node along my journey. Mojado (wetback) refers to Mexicans and other Latinos who cross the nation-state territorial border into the United States, and are socially, politically, economically (as well as legally) constructed as "illegal entrants," and "newcomers." . . . Mojado symbolizes the distrust and dislike experienced in *gringolandia,* as *la raza odiada,* "those damn Mexicans" *extranjeros,* which literally means "outsiders." . . . My experience as an educational ethnographer, to date, can sometimes be described as traveling those blurred boundaries when Other becomes researcher, narrated becomes narrator, translated becomes translator, native becomes anthropologist, and how one emergent and intermittent identity continuously informs the other. (Noblit et al., 2004, p. 166)

Murillo's positionality moves against the objective, neutral observer. Fieldwork research has a very long and early history of scientific empiricism and concern with systematic analysis that is testable, verifiable, and objective without the distraction or impairment of subjectivity, ideology, or emotion. What many early researchers, particularly during the colonial and modern period, did not recognize was that their stalwart "objectivity" was already subjective in the value-laden classification, meanings, and worldviews they employed and superimposed upon peoples who were different from them. The current emphasis on reflexive ethnography or postcritical ethnography and its critique of objectivity are in sharp contrast to the philosophy of a value-neutral fieldwork methodology that favors the analytic evaluation of the natural science model. But critical ethnography—or what some have called the "new ethnography" (Goodall, 2000)—must not only critique the notion of objectivity, but must also critique the notion of subjectivity as well. More and more ethnographers are heralding the unavoidable and complex factor of subjective inquiry as they simultaneously examine its position. Moreover, the current thinking is not that ethnographers can simply say or do anything they think or feel and pass it off as fact, but rather that they make sure we do not say "is" when we mean "ought"—or as Thomas (1993) writes, "We are simply forbidden to submit value judgments in place of facts or to leap to 'ought' conclusions without a demonstrable cogent theoretical and empirical linkage" (p. 22).

In various dimensions, this was done under the traditional banner of objectivity, when cultures and people were reinvented and redefined to fit inside the biased classifications and philosophical systems of the objective researcher. However, we are now more and more critical of the subjective researcher and how that subjectivity reflects upon its own power position, choices, and effects. This "new" or postcritical ethnography is the move to contextualize our own positionality, thereby making it accessible, transparent, and vulnerable to judgment and evaluation. In this way, we take ethical responsibility for our own subjectivity and political perspective, resisting the trap of gratuitous self-centeredness or of presenting an interpretation as though it has no "self," as though it is not accountable for its consequences and effects. Doing fieldwork is a personal experience. Our intuition, senses, and emotions—or what Wallace Bacon (1979) collectively refers to as "felt-sensing"—are powerfully woven into and inseparable from the process. We are inviting an ethics of accountability by taking the chance of being proven wrong (Thomas, 1993).

Dialogue and the Other

As we recognize the vital importance of illuminating the researcher's positionality, we also understand that critical ethnography requires a deep and abiding dialogue with the Other as never before. This means that our attention to ethnographic positionality still must remain grounded in the empirical world of the Other. In fact, it is this concern for the Other that demands we attend seriously to our position as researchers. Ethnographic positionality is not identical to subjectivity. Subjectivity is certainly within the domain of positionality, but positionality requires that we direct our attention beyond our individual or *subjective* selves. Instead, we attend to how our subjectivity *in relation to the Other* informs and is informed by our engagement and representation of the Other. We are not simply subjects, but we are subjects in dialogue with the Other. We understand that our subjectivity is an inherent part of research, but in critical ethnography it is not my *exclusive* experience—that is autobiography, travel writing, or memoir (or what some people call *autoethnography*). I contend that *critical* ethnography is always a meeting of multiple sides in an encounter with and among the Other(s), one in which there is negotiation and dialogue toward substantial and viable meanings that make a difference in the Other's world.

A more detailed explication of the relationship and dialogue with the Other is further elaborated in the corpus of work by Dwight Conquergood (1982a, 1982b, 1983, 1984, 1986a, 1986b, 1988, 1989, 1991, 1992, 1997, 1998, 2000, 2000a, 2000b). Conquergood frames dialogue as performance and contends that the aim of "dialogical performance" is to bring self and Other together so they may question, debate, and challenge one another. Dialogue is framed as performance to emphasize the living communion of a felt-sensing, embodied interplay and engagement between human beings. For Conquergood, dialogue resists conclusions. It is intensely committed to keeping the meanings between and the conversations with the researcher and the Other open and ongoing. It is a reciprocal giving and receiving rather than a timeless resolve. The dialogical stance is situated in multiple expressions that transgress, collide, and embellish realms of meaning. Dialogue is both difference and unity, both agreement and disagreement, both a separation and a coming together. For Conquergood, ethnographic, performative dialogue is more like a hyphen than a period. Dialogue is therefore the quintessential encounter with the Other.

Moreover, it is through dialogue and meeting with the Other that I am most fully myself. The wonderful paradox in the ethnographic moment of dialogue and Otherness is that communion with an Other brings the self more fully into being and, in doing so, opens you to know the Other more fully. Mikhail Bakhtin (1984) writes,

I am conscious of myself and become myself only while revealing myself for another, through another, and with the help of another. The most important acts constituting self-consciousness are determined by a relationship toward another consciousness (toward a thou). Separation, dissociation, enclosure within the self is the main reason for the loss of one's self. The very being of man is the deepest communion. . . . To be means to be for another, through the other, for oneself. (p. 287)

It is the dialogic relationship with the Other, this ongoing liveliness and resistance to finality that resists the connotation of timelessness commonly described as "the ethnographic present," that has adversely haunted traditional ethnography. The ethnographic present refers to the representation of a timeless account of the culture or people being studied. Charlotte Aull Davis (1999) states,

> The ethnographer moves on. [But] temporally, spatially and developmentally, the people he or she studied are presented as if suspended in an unchanging and virtually timeless state, as if the ethnographer's description provides all that it is important, or possible, to know about their past and future. (p. 156)

The Other inscribed as a static, unchanging, and enduring imprint in the ethnographic present is dislodged by a dialogic, critical ethnography. Dialogue moves from ethnographic *present* to ethnographic *presence* by opening the passageways for readers and audiences to experience and grasp the partial presence of a temporal conversation constituted by the Other's voice, body, history, and yearnings. This conversation with the Other, brought forth through dialogue, reveals itself as a lively, changing being through time and no longer an artifact captured in the ethnographer's monologue, immobile and forever stagnant.

Note: Brief Historical Overview of Critical Ethnography

The field of ethnography in the United States is primarily influenced by two traditions: the British anthropologist from the 19th century and the Chicago School from the 1960s.

Anthropology and British Functionalism

Anthropology was established as an academic discipline during the middle of the 19th century. In the beginning, the questionnaire was the main method the missionaries, traders, sailors, explorers, and colonial administrators used to obtain data from the population that inhabited their local outposts or stations. The questionnaires were then sent back to the colonial metropolis for the "armchair" ethnologists to interpret (Davis, 1999, p. 60). The most noted work of this period is James Frazer's *The Golden Bough* (1900).

Toward the end of the century, more ethnologists financed their own expeditions to "far off lands" for the purpose of conducting surveys. These surveys were generally based upon predetermined questions for the interests and benefit of the colonial empire (Davis, 1999, p. 68). The limitations, distortions, and superficiality of these accounts created a growing unrest and demand for more detail. As a result, in the early years of the 20th century there was a turn toward longer engagements in these locations. This was the foundation for long-term participant observation fieldwork and is associated with the work of Bronislaw Malinowski (1926, 1945) in Britain and Franz Boas (1928, 1931) in America and their students. As Davis (1999) writes about Malinowski and Boas,

> Both had come to recognize the complexity of the so-called primitive and to link this with both an attack on cultural evolutionism and a deep and genuine (if sometime naïve and unreflexive) opposition to ethnocentrism. . . . Both were concerned to recognize and include in their analysis the interconnectedness of each individual society's cultural forms and social structures; in British social anthropology, this came to be expressed theoretically by Radcliffe-Brown's structural functionalism; in American anthropology, its fullest expression took the form of an interest in culture complexes. (p. 69)

Structural Functionalism

A. R. Radcliffe-Brown's (1958) development of structural functionalism is concerned with defining and determining social structures and the interconnectedness within their own system of structures. It excludes any consideration of external influences; the focus was on the mechanisms that sustain the structure, thereby deeming human behavior as a function of the structures that guide and determine their culture and conduct.

The Chicago School

The Chicago School of ethnography developed in the 1920s in the Department of Social Science and Anthropology at the University of Chicago. Key contributors to the school were Robert Park (1864–1944), who turned the focus of fieldwork to the urban landscape; G. H. Mead (1865–1931) and John Dewey (1859–1932), who emphasized pragmatism; and Herbert Bloomer (1900–1987), proponent of symbolic interactionism. The Chicago School is credited for laying the foundation for "a vibrant and increasingly methodologically sophisticated program of interpretive ethnography" (Thomas, 1993, p. 11).

Positivism

Positivism is based on the idea that empiricism must reach the goal of positive knowledge—that is, prediction, laws of succession and variability.

Positivists believe genuine knowledge is founded by direct experience and that experience is composed of social facts to be determined while reducing any distortion of subjectivity (theology or metaphysics) by the presence of the ethnographer. Therefore, positivism is based on the following assumptions outlined by Norman K. Denzin (2001): (a) There is a reality that can be objectively interpreted; (b) the researcher as a subject must be separate from any representation of the object researched; (c) generalizations about the object of research are "free from situational and temporal constraints: that is, they are universally generalizable" (p. 44); (d) there is a cause and effect for all phenomena—there are "no causes without effects and no effects without causes" (p. 44); and (e) our analyses are objective and "value-free" (p. 44).

Post-Positivism

The post-positive turn—or what is variously referred to as the "performance turn," the "postmodern turn," the "new ethnography," or the "seventh movement" (Denzin, 2001, 2003)—has denounced the tenets of positivism. Positivism's goal for objectivity, prediction, cause/effect, and generalization has been replaced by the recognition and contemplation of subjective human experience, contingencies of truth claims, value-laden inquiry, and local knowledge and vernacular expressions as substantive analytical frameworks.

The Method and Theory Nexus

This book serves as a resource for qualitative researchers who wish to emphasize critical analysis, ethical considerations, and theories and practices of performance. In order to proceed, I must first stress that criticism, ethics, and performance require a level of *theoretical understanding*. Theory becomes a necessity, because it guides the meanings and the vocabulary for each of these three domains. Theory is embedded in their definitions and functions: Critical analysis is grounded in social theory, ethics is grounded in moral philosophy, and performance is both a practice and a theory. In accepting the significance of theoretical knowledge, it is equally important for us to comprehend the way in which theory is at times the same as method, and other times distinct from it.

How are theory and method the same and different? They are the same in that theory is used in ethnography as an *interpretive or analytical method*. We often rely on theory—whether it is Marxist theory, critical race theory, or phenomenology—to interpret or illuminate a social phenomenon. However, though theory may guide and inspire us in composing a lay summary, designing interview questions, or coding data, it is not theory but a methodological process that directs the completion of the task. The relationship between theory and method has a long and provocative history reflected in disciplinary boundaries and research traditions privileging one over the other, as well as defining them as exclusively separate spheres.

The researcher engaged in ethnography, ethics, and performance needs both theory and method.

This tension between theory and method can be addressed by emphasizing what is significant about each as separate spheres and as inseparable entities. According to Joe L. Kinchloe and Peter McLaren (2000), critical theory finds its method in critical ethnography. In this sense, ethnography becomes the "doing"—or, better, the performance—of critical theory. To think of ethnography as *critical theory in action* is an interesting and productive description. The following quotation from Jim Thomas (1993) underscores this point. He refers to critical theory as "intellectual rebellion." The passage is useful because, as it describes the approach of critical theory, it is also describes the aim of critical ethnography:

> The roots of critical thought spread from a long tradition of intellectual rebellion in which rigorous examination of ideas and discourse constituted political challenge. Social critique, by definition, is radical. It implies an evaluative judgment of meaning and method in research, policy, and human activity. Critical thinking implies freedom by recognizing that social existence, including our knowledge of it, is not simply composed of givens imposed on us by powerful and mysterious forces. This recognition leads to the possibility of transcending existing forces. The act of critique implies that by thinking about and acting upon the world, we are able to change both our subjective interpretations and objective conditions. (p. 18)

Critical social theory evolves from a tradition of "intellectual rebellion" that includes radical ideas challenging regimes of power that changed the world. As ethnographers, we employ theory at several levels in our analysis: to articulate and identify hidden forces and ambiguities that operate beneath appearances; to guide judgments and evaluations emanating from our discontent; to direct our attention to the critical expressions within different interpretive communities relative to their unique symbol systems, customs, and codes; to demystify the ubiquity and magnitude of power; to provide insight and inspire acts of justice; and to name and analyze what is intuitively felt.

If, as Kinchloe and McLaren (2000) suggest, critical theory finds its most compelling method in critical ethnography, then we must not only comprehend the necessity of theory but also its *method*. Enrique G. Murillo, Jr. (2004), states,

Theory is linked to methods, and methods to the scenes studied, grounding one's work. The methods rely heavily on direct observation (participant observation), open-ended interviewing, and textual analysis of human products. However, the degree and extent of utilization of each of these methods depend on the researcher's purposes, the guiding questions, theoretical framework, and the scene itself. (p. 157)

Although theory may fund the guiding principles of our doing, there is a necessary and distinct attention that must be given to the guidelines, techniques, and processes of that doing itself—our method. Theory, when used as a mode of interpretation, *is* a method, yet it can be distinguished from method (and indeed take a back seat to method) when a set of *concrete actions* grounded by a specific scene are required to complete a task. Murillo eloquently reminds us that methods are not simply isolated or immutable activities, but are contingent on our purpose, our fundamental questions, the theories that inform our work, and the scene itself.

* * *

I began the chapter with a story about representation. I will end this chapter by coming back to the story and the central question it raised: How do we represent Others and their world for *just* purposes? We have begun to address the question in this chapter by introducing the themes of *positionality, dialogue, Otherness*, and the *theory/method nexus*.

Summary

- **Positionality.** Positionality is vital because it forces us to acknowledge our own power, privilege, and biases just as we denounce the power structures that surround our subjects. A concern for positionality is a reflexive ethnography; it is a turning back on ourselves. When we turn back on ourselves, we examine our intentions, our methods, and our possible effects. We are accountable for our research paradigms, our authority, and our moral responsibility relative to representation and interpretation.

- **Dialogue/Otherness.** Dialogue emphasizes the living communion of a felt-sensing, embodied interplay and engagement between human beings. Dialogue keeps the meanings between and the conversations with the researcher and the Other open and ongoing. The conversation with the Other that is brought forth through dialogue reveals itself as a lively, changing being through time and no longer an artifact captured in the ethnographer's monologue or written transcript—fixed in time and forever stagnant.

- **Theory/Method.** Critical ethnography becomes the "doing" or the "performance" of critical theory. It is critical theory in action. Theory, when used as a mode of interpretation, is a method, yet it can be distinguished from method (and indeed take a back seat to method) when a set of concrete actions grounded by a specific scene is required to complete a task. We rely on theory—whether it is Marxist theory, critical race theory, or phenomenology—to interpret or illuminate a social action. However, in composing a lay summary, designing interview questions, or coding data, theory may inspire and guide, but it is a methodological process that directs and completes the task.

* * *

In the following chapter, an examination of methods is explored in greater detail. After the methods chapter, a series of hypothetical case studies are presented to illustrate how theory is applied as an interpretive method. Chapter 2 specifically discusses initial methods employed as the researcher enters the field, including such topics as "Starting Where You Are," "Being Part of an Interpretive Community," "The Research Design," "The Lay Summary," "Interviewing and Field Techniques," and "Coding and Logging Data." Chapter 3 comprises three fictional case studies or ethnographic stories that use key concepts from particular theoretical frameworks. Case One includes key concepts from *postcolonial* and *Marxist criticism*; Case Two includes key concepts from *theories of phenomenology, subjectivity, symbolism,* and *sexuality*; and Case Three includes key concepts from *critical race* and *feminist theory.*

Warm-Ups

1. Take an image—it can be from a photograph, a painting, an advertisement—and speak from the points of view of the various objects or characters within the image. How are they each expressing differently what it means to be within the frame or parameters of the image? How are they expressing their relationship to the other figures or images around them? In your various voicings of what is within the image, are you giving more emphasis to one or more images over others? Why or why not?

2. View the film *Rashomon* or observe a similar story that is constructed from several viewpoints that each tell their side of one story. How does the writer, filmmaker, or teller construct the narrative to give voice to the various characters? What devices are used?

3. Choose a current situation in world events in which two competing sides have been locked in enduring opposition and conflict. Speak from the position of each side with sincere, calm, and thoughtful persuasion and belief. Then, speak as the critical ethnographer in an effort to interpret the situation in order to make change.

Suggested Readings

Boas, F. (1928). *Anthropology and modern life.* New York: Norton.

Boas, F. (1928). *The mind of a primitive man.* New York: Macmillan.

Camaroff, J., & Camaroff, J. (Eds.). (2001). *Millennial capitalism and the culture of neoliberalism.* Durham, NC: Duke University Press.

Denzin, N. K. (2001). *Interpretive interactionism.* Thousand Oaks, CA: Sage.

di Leonardo, M. (1998). *Exotics at home: Anthropologies, others, American modernity.* Chicago: University of Chicago Press.

Fetterly, J. (1978). *The resisting reader.* Bloomington: Indiana University Press.

Hitchcock, P. (1993). *Dialogics of the oppressed.* Minneapolis: University of Minnesota Press.

Malinowski, B. (1926). *Crime and custom in savage society.* New York: Harcourt Brace.

Malinowski, B. (1945). *The dynamics of culture change: An inquiry into race relations in Africa.* New Haven, CT: Yale University Press.

Noblit, G. W., Flores, S. Y., & Murillo, E. G. (2004). *Postcritical ethnography: An introduction.* Cress, NJ: Hampton Press.

Peacock, J. L. (1986). *The anthropological lens: Harsh light, soft focus.* Cambridge, UK: Cambridge University Press.

Radcliffe-Brown, A. R. (1958). *Method in social anthropology; Selected essays.* Chicago: University of Chicago Press.

Thomas, J. (1993). *Doing ethnography.* Thousand Oaks, CA: Sage.

Willis, P. (2000). *The ethnographic imagination.* Cambridge, MA: Polity.

2

Methods

"Do I Really Need a Method?"
A Method . . . or Deep Hanging-Out

Human reality as such is an interpreted reality, a social construction given shape and meaning by the various cultural discourses/texts that circulate within it. Those texts that carry the weight of cultural authority as "reliable knowledge" or "objective information" (e.g., expert opinions or news reports) exerts powerful influences on how common perceptions are formed and common sense is made.

—Mary S. Strine, "Critical Theory and 'Organic' Intellectuals: Reframing the Work of Cultural Critique" (1991)

One day a student in my Performance Ethnography course raised her hand and said, "My advisor told me that *methods* are not necessary and that all you really need in the field is *deep hanging-out*." I had been teaching this course for more than 10 years, and I had recently come back from my fieldwork in West Africa. I have been asked all sorts of questions over the years related to the theory/method divide. However, I noticed that this particular student was more emphatic in her dismissal of methods. Although the course is offered in the Department of Communication Studies, students enroll from across the campus—students in sociology, education, history, folklore, and anthropology. The young woman came from another department outside the field of communication studies; she later expressed that it is only anthropologists who do "real" fieldwork. She was told to believe that self-reflection and intuition, good theory and politics, and in-depth knowledge of context and culture were all that was needed for "real" fieldwork. Another student in the course from sociology was completely irritated by her dismissal of methodology and adamantly expressed her discontent by stating, "If you don't have a methodology, you don't have anything! What do you think you are doing in the field?"

Over the years, it has become clear to me that certain disciplines have their own philosophy about the nature and definition of methods and their value. These tensions surrounding the disciplinary boundaries within and across the humanities and social sciences in defining the term *method* and its use have often resulted in a peculiar turf war: one side regarding fieldwork as more a matter of theory, subjectivities, and culture, with another side regarding it as more a matter of precision, validation, and evidence.

As stated in Chapter 1, method and theory are reciprocally linked yet necessarily distinguishable. At key moments in the ethnographic or qualitative process they are separable, and at other moments seamless. In my own work, there are moments when theory and method are at a discreet distance: for example, when it is time to design interview questions and log data. But it is theory that still informs the kinds of questions I will ask and the categories of data that take priority. Although I always have an overarching theory in my work that guides the purpose and direction of the study, when it is time to design questions, log data, and code information, I also rely more on concrete procedural models. These models are flexible and context specific, but they follow a basic formula and rather systematic technique. For example, when coding the mass of data on human rights from activists, stakeholders, field notes, and archival research, I employ a technique to order and categorize the morass of data from the general to the specific using a systematic method that is divided by domains, clusters, and themes.

Sometimes, theory will get in the way by actually obstructing method, but there are still other moments when the method is the theory. For example, in the interpretation and analysis of certain data, theory and method become one and the same. In my work with the personal narratives of indigenous human rights activists, a particular interview I examined required a method of analysis that articulated the connection between poverty and human rights abuses. My method of analysis was based on concepts from phenomenology, as well as from postcolonial and Marxist theory. Hence, my theory *was* my method, and my method was my theory. In terms of the theory-versus-method debate, the dismissal or privileging of one over the other raises important questions and considerations and is sometimes counterproductive. It is as counterproductive as the disciplinary turf battles that erupt over which disciplinary tradition is more "authentic" or "rigorous" in conducting fieldwork or which field is more "deeply" ethnographic.

This chapter serves as a practical reference guide. It is geared toward those undergraduate and graduate students who want to know more about *practical methods,* understanding that methods are a *set of procedures or a process for achieving an end, a goal, or a purpose.* In this chapter, I hope to address the question, What is an ethnographic method?

Corrine Glesne (1999) claims that methodological procedures for all qualitative researchers are basically the same: (a) state a purpose, (b) pose a problem or state a question, (c) define a research population, (d) develop a time frame, (e) collect and analyze data, and (f) present outcome (p. 4). James Spradley (1979) lists a methodological sequence that is similar to Glesne's: (a) select a problem, (b) formulate a hypothesis, (c) collect data, (d) analyze data, and (e) write up the results (p. 15).

This chapter will expand upon the methodological sequences outlined by Glesne and Spradley by elaborating upon the particular challenges for critical ethnography.

"Who Am I?": Starting Where You Are

Start where you are. The experiences in your life, both past and present, and who you are as a unique individual will lead you to certain questions about the world and certain problems about why things are the way they are. It is important to honor your own personal history and the knowledge you have accumulated up to this point, as well as the intuition or instincts that draw you toward a particular direction, question, problem, or topic—understanding that you may not always know exactly why or how you are being drawn in that direction. Ask yourself questions that only you can answer: "What truly interests me?" "What do I really want to know more about?" "What is most disturbing to me about society?" You might probe even more deeply and ask yourself, as in the words of the writer Alice Walker (2003), "What is the work my soul must have?" (p. 238), and go from there.

"Who Else Has Written About My Topic?": Being a Part of an Interpretive Community

When you have a general topic in mind, you are then ready to contemplate questions or problems that might relate to your topic. At this stage, in order to be most effective, it is important to read and examine other studies or models related to the topic. Be very careful that other studies do not become an uncritical or replicated model: be careful that you do not simply summarize or repeat what has already been researched and that you do not entirely reject the value of what has already been researched—avoid a blatant negation without careful consideration. It is important to be both critical of other studies and to be inspired by them. Find the balance between comparison and contrast. Extend and augment the studies you admire, don't simply repeat them. Consider what is useful from the studies you don't admire, even if their usefulness is by contrast. You may be surprised by what you will learn from your unfavorable models, as well as how such models will help you in sharpening your critical skills and refining your topical question or problem.

Other models, favorable and unfavorable, provide ideas about content, form, and method, and, most importantly, you will enrich your knowledge base. By considering other examples, you expand questions and contexts relative to your project and learn by comparing what you wish to adapt from studies you admire and what you wish to contrast and differentiate from those you do not. Moreover, you become part of an interpretive community writing on a subject, a community of other researchers with which you will be in dialogue. You will refer to their work, to enlighten and to critique, and your ideas and arguments will sometimes be in accord and at other times in discord with theirs. Keep in mind that it is also your responsibility as a critical researcher and as a member of a particular interpretive community to know what others are imparting about a subject and community that you have made a commitment to interact with and to learn with and from.

The Power of Purpose: Bracketing Your Subject

After you have identified a subject that you are drawn to and that is of unique interest to you, and after you have examined illustrations that will further guide you toward a more specific question or problem, you are now ready to begin to bracket your subject and contemplate your purpose. At this stage, you want to capture more fully and more specifically the phenomenon you wish to study. This requires that you bracket the population you wish to study (Denzin, 2001; Glesne, 1999; Lofland & Lofland, 1984).

As you identify or bracket in clear terms the population of your study, you are simultaneously developing your research question and your purpose. Take care that you are framing an *identifiable* question or problem, not simply a subject of interests that is general and amorphous. You must be more precise at this stage in identifying a question or problem as it guides you toward a path of inquiry and interest that is clear and directed. You will be more focused, self-assured, and motivated when you have a subject you feel strongly about and you can articulate for yourself and others. This does not mean that you are confined to this question and that there is no room for change, invention, or discovery along the way. In fact, in my experience, I have found that by clearly identifying a topic (while feeling free to alter and change), researchers feel more knowledgeable and skilled in changing or taking on different questions or problems, if necessary, than what their original questions or problems demanded. Once you get in the field, your question or problem may be enriched and augmented by what you experience on the ground. It may change into another domain completely or it may remain consistently vital and inspiring. What is important is to identify your question from the onset because, without a research question, your purpose will have less focus and certainty. Moreover, you will have less direction in formulating your ideas if you do need to alter or change the original question or problem.

The following steps serve to help you in the process of developing a specific research problem or question:

• After reviewing the literature and familiarizing yourself with other research models on the topic (including indexes, titles of references from bibliographies, quotations, etc.), note what sparks your interests and jot down titles, phrases, names, and places.

• Combine this list with your own interest and intuitive attraction toward an item, and then brainstorm questions about your subject of interest. Write, write, and keep writing. Take a break, and then write more questions.

• When you have exhausted writing down all the questions that come to mind, then consider the overarching themes that arise. This will take a bit of time, but enjoy the exercise. You will discover and learn from this step as you make connections and build clusters of ideas and meanings that surface and repeat themselves.

• For each cluster that you complete, create a topic sentence or a subject heading in the form of a question that best reflects the composite of questions within each cluster.

• After you have developed the summary or topical question for each of your clusters, you are now closer to the point of narrowing down your array of notes into a solid research question. Review your topical questions and contemplate how your research question will evolve from them. This is a process of prioritizing certain questions over others, eliminating overlaps, and blending questions together. Throughout the process, and most especially in this last step, keep in mind what it is that you, as a critical ethnographer, want to contribute or change for the cause of social justice. The formulation of your research question serves as an articulation of what it is you want to do and why.

Preparing for the Field:
The Research Design and Lay Summary

The Research Design

"Gaining access" is a major concern in qualitative research. There has been a great deal of attention paid to the challenges of what is understood as *entry*. As a qualitative researcher you must consider how you enter the terrain of your subjects in ways that are appropriate, ethical, and effective. As you begin your preparations to enter the field, it is often advisable first to complete a *research design*. This is a plan that outlines, step by step, what you hope to accomplish relative to your fieldwork process and methods. A research design comprises key points to be addressed. Please understand that you are not expected to address each of these points in precise or full detail at the beginning of your study and before you actually enter the field—some points you may address more fully than others. Your research design is to help you organize and plan what you are about to encounter in the field in order to provide more focus, direction, confidence, and sense of purpose.

The following points comprise a research design:

- A restatement of your question or problem
- A description of your (a) data collection methods as coperformer in the field or participant observer; (b) type, style, and techniques of interview; (c) field journal and data logging techniques; (d) data coding process; and (e) theoretical frameworks for data analysis and interpretation
- A delineation of your ethical methods in placing the welfare of subjects first by protecting their rights, interests, privacy, sensibilities, and offering reports at key stages to participants, including the final report
- A description of your research population in terms of (a) geographic location, (b) description of subjects, (c) norms and rules, (d) significant historical and cultural contexts, and (e) expectations for key informants or coperformers within the population
- An outline of your time frame for (a) entering the field, (b) data collection and/or performance process, (c) departure and/or public performance, (d) coding and analysis, and (e) completion of written report and/or public performance at home site

Please remember that it is perfectly fine if you do not have the answers to all of the questions included in your research design. It may not even be necessary for you to have the answers to them all. The research design is intended to serve as a starting point, a map, or a guide in organizing and specifying your project. It helps lead the way.

The Lay Summary

Remember, the research design is of primary significance to you; however, the *lay summary* is more for the benefit of the subjects you will be meeting. It serves to assist them in understanding who you are, what you are doing, and what their role will be in the process. The lay summary will also address specific questions; however, unlike the research design, the information provided in the lay summary will be relatively more precise and predetermined. However, it is important to keep in mind that your lay summary *draws from the information in your research design*, and several points of information that you will be sharing with participants are already articulated in that design. Also, keep in mind that the purpose of the lay summary is to explain your project to the people who are central to it; therefore, they have the right to know, and you have the responsibility to explain your presence in their lives.[1]

The lay summary should address the following questions:

• Who are you? What is your background and where do you come from? You will explain your institutional affiliation or sponsorship, and, if necessary, information that might be significant relative to your cultural, ethnic, or personal identity.

• What are you doing and why? Why are you in this particular place? What exactly do you plan to do here and for what purpose? You will explain to participants (a) what motivated or inspired you to enter into this particular space of their lives, (b) your research methods or how you will collect your data, and (c) your desired outcome and what you specifically hope to contribute toward social change. (Note: You may refer to your research design in communicating these points to participants.)

• What will you do with the results of your study? What happens to the information you gathered here after you leave? You will describe the end product of your fieldwork; that is, you will explain what form the information you gathered is going to take (a book, a performance, a policy report, a classroom assignment, etc.). You will also explain how, where, and to whom this information will be given or distributed.

- How were participants selected? What mechanisms did you use to gain access to the people in the field with whom you chose to speak and interact? You will explain your method and how you came to locate and meet them: for example, through an introduction from a key participant or community liaison, with assistance from relevant institutions and networks, through word-of-mouth, via the "snowball effect" or the "grapevine," as well as by "hanging out" at local sites such as churches, social gatherings, rallies, and so forth.

- What are the possible benefits or risks to participants? What will participants gain and/or lose by your presence in their lives? You will explain what you hope your project will do to serve and contribute to the lives or population of your study. This means you will express what difference your presence will make upon a situation or experience that relates to or affects them. You will also express with honesty and humility the possible consequences that your project may have upon the situation and/or their lives. As you describe all the possible negative consequences, you must also speak in clear terms regarding what measures you will take to try to prevent such consequences from occurring. (This point is elaborated with more detail and examples in the section on ethics.)

- How will you assure confidentiality and anonymity, when necessary, for participants as well as the site? You will explain your ethical stance and your methods by outlining step by step how your research data—specifically, names, places, encounters, and identities—will be changed, altered, and safeguarded from the general public, other participants, and your institutional colleagues. (This point is also elaborated with examples and detail in the ethics section.)

- How often and how long would you like to meet for interviews and observations? You will inform participants of why you may need to meet with them on more than one occasion and the possible duration of each meeting. You will also inquire about significant times to meet that will enhance the data and address more fully your research question. You will also keep in mind that how often you meet is contingent upon what is convenient and appropriate for participants.

- How and in what manner will you ask participants' permission to record their actions, experiences, and words? After you have described the project, particularly after you have informed participants of possible benefits and consequences, of what will be done with the data, and of the purpose of the project, the *means* by which the data will be recorded will more than likely be less invasive, foreign, or even suspicious. The means by which you record your data are through notes, tape recordings, photographs, and videotaping. You will obviously ask permission to record, especially for photographs and audio or video recordings. It is often good practice, particularly with video recordings, and for participants who are reluctant to meet a day or two before the more formal interview. If time allows, have a conversation about more general subjects that are innocuous or that are of interests to them in order to develop more familiarity and ease with the videotape. It is also effective when using video to make arrangements for these individuals to be part of a group interview and discussion before you videotape them individually. Being part of a group for the initial taping buffers the focus and concentration on them as individuals. It gives them an opportunity to interact with and respond to others who are also being taped and to witness by comparison or contrast how others respond.

The lay summary, like the research design, serves only as a guide or a map. Remember that every situation is different and context specific. It is important to feel free to adapt and adjust the need of the lay summary to your particular project and situation.

Interviewing and Field Techniques

> *Unlike survey interviews, in which those giving information are relatively passive and are not allowed the opportunity to elaborate, interviewees in qualitative interviews share in the work of the interview, sometimes guiding it in channels of their own choosing. They are treated as partners rather than as objects of research.*
>
> —Herbert J. Rubin and Irene S. Rubin,
> *Qualitative Interviewing: The Art of Hearing Data* (1995)

Interviewing is a hallmark experience of fieldwork research (Rubin & Rubin, 1995). The ethnographic interview opens realms of meaning that permeate beyond rote information or finding the "truth of the matter." The interviewee is not an object, but a subject with agency, history, and his or her own idiosyncratic command of a story. Interviewer and interviewee are in partnership and dialogue as they construct memory, meaning, and experience together. The primary aim of much social science research is to locate valid and reliable information, with the interviewer directing the questions and the interviewee answering them as truthfully as possible. This is not to suggest that validity and substantiation are irrelevant in critical ethnography, because they are indeed significant at many levels of inquiry. However, critical ethnography reflects deeper truths than the need for verifiable facts and information. The beauty of this method of interviewing is in the complex realms of individual subjectivity, memory, yearnings, polemics, and hope that are unveiled and inseparable from shared and inherited expressions of communal strivings, social history, and political possibility. The interview is a window to individual subjectivity and collective belonging: *I am because we are and we are because I am.*

The ethnographic interview may encompasses three forms: (1) *oral history*, which is a recounting of a social historical moment reflected in the life or lives of individuals who remember them and/or experienced them; (2) *personal narrative*, which is an individual perspective and expression of an event, experience, or point of view; and (3) *topical interview*, the point of view given to a particular subject, such as a program, an issue, or a process. It is important to note that these forms are not isolated from one another. They are separated here for definitional purposes, because they each have special albeit discrete characteristics from the others. But please keep in mind that each type will often and necessarily overlap with the others.

Formulating Questions

What is seen, heard, and experienced in the field, these are "the nuggets around which you construct your questions."

—Corrine Glesne, *Becoming Qualitative Researchers: An Introduction* (1999)

One of the most interesting and important challenges of the interview process is during the initial stages, when you are thinking about what questions to ask. There are those who have a natural talent for asking questions, while others are not so sure what to ask or how to ask it and need more guidance. Questions will naturally evolve the more time you spend in the field and the more experience you have with participants and with the context and culture in which they live or work. It is generally advised that researchers should have a basic level of understanding of the field—the general history, meanings, practices, institutions, and beliefs that constitute it—before they plunge full force into the actual face-to-face interviewing. Spending time closely listening, observing, and interacting in the field while compiling extensive field notes will provide a foundation of knowledge and experience upon which you may begin to craft your questions.

Greater knowledge and familiarity before you begin your interviews will inspire your questions. Your field notes will be an invaluable source and frame of reference as you contemplate your questions; however, it also helps to have a few tried-and-true models and guidelines. Below are two models I have found to be particularly helpful in developing questions. They are drawn from Michael Patton (1990) and James P. Spradley (1979). Following these models is a list of "tried and true" methods that I have found most useful over the years.

The Patton Model

We will examine the Patton model using the example of a qualitative researcher conducting interviews with black students about so-called black isolation on the campus of a major state university.

1. **Behavior or Experience Questions.** Behavior or experience questions address concrete human action, conduct, or ways of "doing." It is helpful to think about behavior as comportment or as action in some form, and to think of experience as being more mindful or reflexive of the meanings of the action or behavior. *"I notice that most black students stick together and claim their own spaces and groupings on campus. They eat together in the dining hall; they congregate among themselves outside Wicker Hall on the quad; they sit together in classes and so forth. This is behavior that is obvious and that most people can observe. Could you describe other ways or behaviors that are not so obvious where black students come together?"* Keep in mind that this question is not asking *why* these students come together, nor is it trying to decipher meaning. It is asking the interviewer for more information on *action* or *behavior*.

2. **Opinion or Value Questions.** Opinion or value questions address a conviction, judgment, belief, or particular persuasion towards a phenomenon. Although opinions and values are very closely related and often interchangeable, an opinion question is usually considered more individually idiosyncratic, while a value question leans more toward guiding principles and ideals emanating from formal or informal social arrangements. *"In your opinion, why do you think black students behave in this way?* And a somewhat different question is, *What do you believe is the value of this behavior? Does it even have a value?"*

3. **Feeling Questions.** Feeling questions address emotions, sentiments, and passions. The interviewer is concerned not with the truth or validity of a phenomenon, but with how a person feels about it or is emotionally affected by it. *"How do you personally feel about this behavior?* And to add another twist to that question, *How do you feel about the need to come together as black students in these ways?"*

4. **Knowledge Questions.** Knowledge questions address the range of information and learning a participant holds about a phenomenon, as well as where this knowledge comes from and how it is attained. *"What are the historical roots of this kind of behavior? How does the larger society influence the desire for these students to behave in this way?"*

5. **Sensory Questions.** Sensory questions address the senses and human sensation. How does the body hear, taste, touch, smell, and see a phenomenon at the purely visceral level in its contact with the phenomenon? *"How does your body, your senses, react in these moments of contact and allegiance with other black students? Do you see, hear, taste, smell, or touch in ways that are different at these times than other times?"*

6. **Background/Demographic Questions.** Background and demographic questions address concrete and practical information concerning the distribution, location, and size of populations including births, deaths, and other significant information related to population statistics. *"What is the population of black students on campus and what part of the country do most of them come from? Are there more men than women? What is the ethnic breakdown of black students on campus in terms of percentages of African Americans, Caribbeans, Africans, Europeans, and so forth?"*

The Spradley Model

We outline the Spradley (1979) model using the example of a qualitative researcher conducting interviews with food service workers on campus and after a recent strike.

1. **Descriptive Questions.** Descriptive questions ask for a recounting or a depiction of a concrete phenomenon. The focus here is away from ideas, abstraction, and emotion. Although we often employ descriptive questions to move toward abstraction and emotion, we are concerned here with delineating or rendering a picture or image of a real or actual circumstance or object. For Spradley, descriptive questions can be subdivided into "tour," example, experience, and native-language questions.

• Tour Question: Spradley (1979) writes, "Whether the ethnographer uses space, time, events, people, activities, or objects, the end result is the same: a verbal description of significant features of the cultural scene" (p. 87). Like a tour, a cultural scene unfolds in its many and varied elements. Spradley makes a distinction between grand tour questions and mini-tour questions. *"Can you describe an average working day in the cafeteria? Can you describe the space of the cafeteria itself, that is, the various rooms, cooking areas, and lounges providing a grand tour of the cafeteria building?"*

• Example Question: Example questions ask the participants to provide an example of a response that may need more specificity or clarity. Spradley (1979) states that example questions "most often lead to the most interesting stories of actual happenings which an ethnographer will discover" (p. 88). *"Can you recount an example of a particular working day that you will never forget?"*

• Experience Questions: Spradley (1979) suggests that experience questions "are best used after asking numerous grand tour and mini-tour questions" (p. 89). You are, in essence, asking the participants how they experienced the scene or subject just described. *"How would you describe the experience that day when you and the other cafeteria workers decided to go on strike? What did you do exactly and how did you feel about it?"*

• Native-Language Questions: According to Spradley (1979), "The more familiar the informant and ethnographer are with each other's cultures, the more important native-language questions become" (p. 90). With these questions, you are addressing the larger meanings, implications, and symbolic value embedded in the respondent's everyday language. *"How do you and the other cafeteria workers come up with the various terms like, 'snub nose,' 'hungry giant,' 'green pill,' and 'mean spot' to describe students and their different attitudes? How do you use these terms among yourselves?"*

2. **Structural or Explanation Questions:** Structural or explanation questions are not to be confused with inquires of actual societal or cultural structures, as in institutions or systems of power. By structural questions, Spradley (1979) is really referring to questions that require *explanation*. So, structural questions are really explanation questions that complement and should be asked concurrently with descriptive questions. Structural questions "explore the organization of an informant's cultural knowledge" (p. 131), and they most often require contextual information, because such information "aids greatly in recall and will avoid the problem of making an informant feel he is being tested with a series of short questions" (p. 125). *"Can you help me understand how the workers came up with the idea of a strike in getting the administration to pay attention to your demands? Can you explain how making up your own words for students is important? What is your role at the university?"*

3. **Contrast Questions:** Contrast questions evoke unlike comparisons. They often require contextual clarification from the interviewer in asking the questions and further explanation or elaboration from the interviewee after answering it. Spradley (1979) outlines three principles that give rise to contrast questions: (1) the *use principle*, in which "the meaning of a symbol can be discovered by asking how it is uniquely and distinctly used rather than asking what it means" (p. 156); (2) the *similarity principle*, in which "the

meaning of a symbol can be discovered by finding out how it is similar to other symbols" (p. 157); and (3) the *contrast principle*, in which "the meaning of a symbol can be discovered by finding out how it is different from other symbols" (p. 157). Contrast questions may take on a range of forms, from implicit or suggested contrasts to obvious and culturally understood contrasts. Questions may also constitute a contrast of two phenomena to several others, perhaps even referring to a listing of phenomena. *"How useful was the strike in getting people on campus to pay attention to the conditions and circumstances of laborers on campus? How did your campus strike compare to the strikes of other laborers, like the city garbage collectors two years ago? How was if different from the garbage strike?"*

Extra Tips for Formulating Questions

More Models

Other models for questions in addition to the series outlined above include the following:

1. **Advice Questions.** In searching for a point of view, personal philosophy, or disposition, you may ask advice questions as another choice for a model, using a formula such as, "What advice would you give to . . ." or "What would you say to others who. . . ." Advice questions are helpful in addressing some of the suggestions set forth by Patton (1990), such as behavior, feelings, knowledge, and opinion. *"What advice would you give to other campus laborers who are underpaid, overworked, and feeling disrespected by the campus community?"*

2. **Quotation Questions.** Repeating direct quotations from others and asking for a response is another effective model in addressing abstract issues, such as feelings and opinion. *"Someone once said, 'Rudeness is the weak man's imitation of strength.' What do you think?"*

3. **Once-Upon-a-Time Descriptive Questions.** Some descriptive questions aim for a narrated experience reflecting the drama of a story. These questions are most effective when the interviewer is relatively confident that the interviewee is capable of telling such a story, based on prior questions that reveal experiences, opinions, knowledge, and so forth. The interviewer referring to a context or situation already being discussed in the interview may then ask, *"Can you describe the time when . . ."* or *"Would you tell the story about the time when you. . . ."* *"Can you tell me about the time when*

you felt the most disrespected by a student and decided to let the person know how you felt?"

Initial Brainstorming

When you first begin trying to formulate your questions, a useful exercise is to reread your research question or problem over several times and then ask yourself, "If this is what I am to understand, then what is it that I need to know about it to answer the questions or address the problem?" You will then list everything of interests that comes to mind.

The Puzzlement

Lofland and Lofland (1984) suggest another helpful exercise to inspire questions: Ask yourself, "What is it about this thing that is a puzzle to me? What is it that I see before me?" List your questions about the puzzle: As you jot them down, you are "teasing" out the puzzlements (p. 53). Lofland and Lofland state that by sorting and ordering the puzzlements, "they take on general clusters and topics that have a global or comprehensive design" (pp. 54–55).

Attributes of the Interviewer and Building Rapport

Above and beyond techniques for designing interview questions and charting out the field study, one of the most important considerations is the ethnographer's own demeanor and attitude in the field. Much has been discussed regarding the importance of the ethnographic personality and what it means to look inward to refine and develop our own personal attributes as interviewers (Glesne, 1999; Patton, 1990; Rubin & Rubin, 1995). Below is a list of considerations relating to the interviewer that will help in building a harmonious or productive relationship with subjects in the field, or what is commonly referred to as rapport.

Mindful Rapport

It is important to keep in mind in the beginning that rapport is the feeling of comfort, accord, and trust between the interviewer and interviewee. Being mindful of rapport throughout the interview is essential in helping to create for the participant the feeling of being respected and of being genuinely heard. Keep in mind that being a good listener is an art and a virtue.

Anticipation

It is common to have feelings of anticipation that may range from joyful excitement to nervous apprehension. It is important to turn the energy of anticipation into positive planning—reviewing field notes, developing and brainstorming questions, and understanding that a level of excitement and anxiety are normal.

Positive Naïveness

The idea of the *knower and the known* is provocative in its implications of identifying who knows and who is striving to know. As ethnographers, our knowing is always leveraged by a level of unknowing that we struggle to fill by asking the knowers (Spradley, 1979). In the field, we will invariably come across to participants as unsophisticated, innocent, and easy targets for deception. Positive naïveness is acknowledging that you do not know and that you must rely with humility on others and trust upon the knowledge of knowers. Keep in mind that we are capable of grasping what we do not know with integrity, intelligence, and conviction.

Active Thinking and Sympathetic Listening

Although it is conventionally understood that the ethnographer is the interviewer and the participant is the interviewee, in critical ethnography the rigid back-and-forth replay of question-answer-question is replaced by a more fluid and reciprocal dynamic, in which the interviewee and interviewer become what Rubin and Rubin (1995) describe as "conversational partners." The conversational quality that evolves from the interview is substantively meaningful and a key factor of rapport that is generated by active thinking and sympathetic listening. You are listening with an open heart and kind reception to what is being said and expressed to you; you are not motivated by judgment, but by understanding. As you fully engage the art of listening sympathetically, you are actively thinking about what is being expressed; you are not just present in body, but deeply engaged in mind. The meanings and implications of what is being expressed are significant, and your mind is alert, active, and thinking. Again, we are engaged in the performative dynamic of dialogue.

Status Difference

It is important to be aware of power differences and status. If you are oblivious to or refuse to accept the power and privilege you carry with you as a researcher, you will be blind to the ways your privilege can be a disadvantage to others. If you cannot see or refuse to see the rewards of your status, you will also be blind to the complex inequities and veiled injustices of those whose status is unjustly subordinated. If this example of status difference does not apply to your project, and you are interviewing powerful people whose material and social status is greater than yours, you must still be aware of your status difference as a researcher. You have the power to tell their story and to have the last word on how they will be represented.

Patiently Probing

During the interview session, topics and questions will arise that will invariably lead you to feel that you need to gain a deeper or clearer understanding of what has been expressed. Perhaps an account seems contradictory and you feel you need to get at the veritable quality of the story. You need more information or a more lucid accounting, so you must probe further. Probing requires patience and understanding. No one likes to feel as though they are being tested or interrogated. Obviously, you are not a journalist or a judge; therefore, your probing must be done gently, with respect, and, when necessary, with assistance. Contextualize your probes with follow-up questions that aid memory and enhance dialogue.

The Gorden Model

In the awareness of our own attributes, we must also be circumspect about the attributes and elements that influence those we interview. Raymond L. Gorden (2003) makes an important contribution in his framing of "threats" that significantly affect those we interview. He sets forth a series of sociopsychological dimensions where participants generally feel threatened. Awareness of these dimensions and how they affect the interview are helpful to the researcher in understanding the subjective and idiosyncratic elements that shape responses. Each one will variously influence *what* is being said and *how* it is being said:

• *Degree of Ego Threat.* Gorden (2003) writes, "The respondent tends to withhold any information which he fears may threaten his self-esteem" (p. 159). Here is a situation in which the threat was not intended, but the response to the question brings feelings of embarrassment, shame, or belittlement. The participant may therefore avoid answering the question or respond in a manner that distorts reality in an effort to protect his or her self-esteem. When a threat to ego is recognized, the ethnographer may decide not to pursue the question or to buffer the threat with indirect words of comfort.

- *Degree of Forgetting.* It is important to keep in mind that memory is a factor in every interview, regardless of the topic or the identity of the participant. It is also important to understand that the purpose of the interview is often not simply to help the interviewee remember, but see *how* memory is expressed. In other words, it is not always the goal to get participants to remember facts and events correctly or as they "really" were. As critical ethnographers, we are not concerned with forgetting, but with memory itself and how individuals remember as they do. We honor the fact that each individual memory will be remembered in different forms and to different degrees.

- *Degree of Generalization.* As human beings, we capture experiences by generalizing them, as well as by specifying them. As researchers, we must be aware when generalizations take the form of "truths" that are really specific to a limited experience or are the result of a particular worldview. Just as generalizations are problematic in the truth claims they purport, specificity can be problematic in its oblivion to broader implications.

- *Degree of Subjective Experience.* As critical performance ethnographers, we are concerned with the construction and influences of subjectivity. We understand that the meaning of an event or circumstance cannot be devoid of the speaker's subjectivity, of the narration that brings the event or circumstance into being. What is significant for us is how experiences are expressed and enacted through the speaking subject. An experience or event that we wish to grasp as researchers will always be grasped through the degree of subjectivity encased in the expression of the telling (the participant's subjectivity), as well as the degree of our own subjectivity that is encased in our listening (the researcher's subjectivity). Subjectivity becomes all at once a vessel, lens, and filter of every telling.

- *Conscious Versus Unconscious Experience.* The unconscious is a powerful force in constituting what it means to be human. Consciousness comprises that which we are aware of and forms only an infinitesimal part of our psyche; the unconscious forms the greater part of our being. Freud (1927) compared the conscious and the unconscious to an iceberg, where consciousness represented the tip, preconsciousness was the medium between consciousness and unconsciousness, and the unconscious was the mass of the iceberg forming almost 90 percent of what is unseen beneath the water. It is helpful to be aware of the significance of the unconscious as we speak with participants. We are often witness to unconscious meanings, implications, and intentions as we actively and sympathetically listen. The power of the unconscious will be more forcefully recognized as you later begin to interpret and analyze the data. While it is important to keep the influence of the unconscious in mind, we must also keep in mind that our interpretations and questions are not meant to psychoanalyze the participant or to focus on deciphering consciousness from unconsciousness.

• *Degree of Trauma.* Deep fear, dread, and sorrow that leaves one traumatized by a past occurrence can manifest during the interview in the need immediately to shut down the questions or to respond to them in great length, detail, and emotion. Degree of trauma is further reason for the researcher to be prepared before scheduling the interview. Although degree of trauma cannot always be avoided, it is less difficult for both conversational partners to deal with trauma if the researcher is sensitive to and aware of the difficulties. This is an area that requires rapport; that is, dealing with trauma requires listening with sympathy, following the narrator's pace, demonstrating appreciation through eye contact and gestures of concern, explaining the reason for your question, and, if necessary, guiding the responses with gentle empathy.

• *Degree of Etiquette.* "Communication is given its form by taboos, secrets, avoidances, 'white lies' . . . and certain symbols and attitudes circulate only in restricted channels or between people in certain social relationships," says Gorden (2003, p. 163). When preparing for the interview process and in interacting in the field before you begin interviewing individuals, degrees of etiquette should be an important part of gathering information. There are elements participants will not express because of impropriety, and the reasons may be due to gender, race, age, or nationality, or to cultural civilities, habits, and taboos. It is important to understand when responses are affected or governed by norms of etiquette. What you think you are hearing as true to experience may actually be based upon how your gender or race is perceived in that culture or situation.

Interviewing is a dynamic process fundamental to ethnography. It is part technique, part ethics, part theory, part method, part intuition, part collaboration, and part openness to deep vulnerability. Della Pollock (1999) describes her positionality as interviewer and researcher on "birth stories" in her poignant book *Telling Bodies Performing Birth*:

> I made myself . . . vulnerable to being moved. Listening and writing. I saw myself as the register of someone else's power. Against the grain of current obsessions with the power of the researcher to shape, tame, appropriate, and control the worlds he or she investigates, in the course of talking with and writing about the many people who contributed to this project, I more often than not felt unnerved and overwhelmed, "othered," interrogated, propelled into landscapes of knowing and not knowing I would not otherwise have dared enter. (p. 23)

Interviewing does not *absolutely* require a set of predesigned questions and entering the field with an effective and detailed plan. It certainly helps a great deal (especially for the new ethnographer) if you do have them, but your project will not necessarily fail if you do not. What *is* required is genuine curiosity, sincere interest, and the courage to be "vulnerable" to another at the risk of being "the register of someone else's power."

You have walked down many paths and listened to many stories as an interviewer, and your most pressing questions are evolving into thickly described stories that are beginning to require some attention and deciphering. It's time to stop. What happens after the interviews have all been conducted? You now have an abundance of information and it all feels a bit unwieldy. You remember someone said something to you once upon a time about "coding and logging."

Coding and Logging Data

You are nearing the end of your fieldwork. You have conducted interviews, you have been listening and involved in the day-to-day processes that inform your research question, and you have a collection of data comprising field notes, interview tapes, and other relevant documents and artifacts collected and discovered during your stay. Now it is time to see what you have by bringing all the data together in some form or fashion of order. Coding or logging "allows you to recall the extra-ordinary complex range of stimuli with which you have been bombarded" (Lofland & Lofland, 1984, p. 46). What do you do with this mass of information? Keep in mind that every project and every researcher is unique, so it is expected that you will pick and choose, select and sort, and blend and combine what is useful for you. Coding and logging data is the process of *grouping together themes and categories that you have accumulated in the field.*

Glesne (1999) suggests that, when you select and sort, you build what she describes as "code clumps . . . [by] putting like-minded pieces together into data clumps, you create an organizational framework" (p. 135). The following model draws from a combination of various coding procedures to outline a step-by-step method that can be revised as needed to serve your particular project:

- It is generally understood that you order the mass of data by beginning with generic categories: interview tapes, places, and people, as well as prevalent topics or key issues. You may also think of coding as *high-level coding,* concerned with more abstract ideas, or *low-level coding,* concerned with more concrete data (Carspecken, 1996). However, you must also ask yourself before you begin, "What is the best way to group or cluster all this material so that it will help me focus more clearly on my analysis or how I wish to present this material?"

• The process of grouping is not only about putting similar categories together; the very selections and act of grouping is creating a point of view or statement: "Code with analysis in mind. . . . Themes emerge from your coding, these themes guide your analysis" (Carspecken, 1996, pp. 146–153). If you perform or adapt the data for the stage, you may also code with scenes for your performance in mind, and you may also think about coding with your audience or readers in mind. The point is that coding is not *exclusively* about grouping similarities—although this is the *priority.* You must consider factors of analysis, presentation, readership, and audience that may alter and guide your "clumps."

• The precision and detail of interviewing will guide your coding (Carspecken, 1996; Lofland & Lofland, 1984). Keeping this precision is very important: The more specific and thematic your interview, the less complicated it will be to group and order your data.

• As your clumps or clusters begin to form, you will then begin a process of further ordering:
   a. You will examine each specific topic within that cluster.
   b. You will then compare and contrast that particular topic within that cluster.
   c. You will continue to examine and note the topics within each cluster.
   d. You will discover overlapping topics, marked distinctions, and topics that should be moved from one cluster to a different cluster. You will also discover that some topics should be eliminated from the study completely.
   e. After the topics within each cluster have been examined, you will then make adjustments for comparisons and contrasts across clusters, thereby creating linkages and themes.
   f. The evolution of your themes has now become more apparent.

• When you have completed logging or coding your data—or if you feel you need more direction and clarity during the process—it is often helpful to create a graphic or picture of your organizational framework. You may want to create a tree, cluster, box, or table of what you have developed. These graphics can be invaluable, displaying the connections, hierarchies, and distinctions with more clarity.

Note: About Computers

The Internet has become an invaluable resource and methodological tool for many ethnographers. The Internet can be used to "conduct searches about a topic, analyze census data, conduct interviews by 'chatting' or videoconferencing, share notes and pictures about a research site, debate issues with colleagues on listservs and in online journals, and download useful data collection and analysis software" (Fetterman, 1998, pp. 72–73). For many researchers, the Internet is far more efficient in terms of time, detail, precision, volume of information, and speed than the traditional methods I just outlined above. Although the Internet is, in many ways, an invaluable and productive resource, we must remember that ultimately the information and data collected is determined by the eyes and ears, and the heart and mind, of the ethnographer who determines "what to collect and how to record it as well as how to interpret the data from a cultural perspective" (Fetterman, p. 84). The best approach I have found is to combine the hands-on methods of the researcher with the Internet's capabilities relative to the nature and context of the project.

There are three major categories available through the Internet that can be of help to the ethnographer:

1. **Search Engines.** Search engines tell you where you can find information on a topic. They list sites and resources available on the World Wide Web related to your question or topic. The researcher may use a search engine for most all their informational needs. Search engines provide a wealth of information, such as, maps, demographic information, historical dates, current events, cultural attributes, and so forth. Search engines may include Google, Yahoo, MSN, and Altavista, to name a few. Some search engines may also serve the same purposes as reference pages (discussed below).

2. **Reference Pages.** Reference pages guide you to a vast amount of sources and serve a purpose similar to that of a reference librarian. References pages, such as *The New York Times* Navigator, can link you to sources. For example, the Federal Web Locator can link you to agencies and departments affiliated with the federal government, and LookupUSA is a comprehensive directory-assistance resource that can provide information on telephone numbers and addresses of households and business all over the country. Search engines and references pages will also link you to specific Web pages of individuals, groups, institutions, and businesses that will then provide more detailed information for that particular site.

3. **Database Software.** There is a variety of software available for qualitative researchers. These programs have the capabilities to (a) record information in the field, thereby serving the purpose of a tape recorder. In addition, as it records, it can also (b) transcribe, sort, and highlight patterns and themes

within the data. Beyond highlighting key texts within the data, the software can (c) categorize and cluster themes and subthemes. Therefore, database software for qualitative researchers has the capabilities to compare and contrast data, to code and sort a wide range of information in less time than the traditional hands-on approach. However, it is important to keep in mind again that the computer and the software do not have the researcher's eyes, ears, mind, and heart. You may choose to transcribe, thematically cluster, and contrast the data beyond what the software program prescribes. There will always be nuances, translations, and idiosyncratic categories that the computer and software is incapable of processing. Some of us still do not use computer software in our work for this very reason. However, if you choose to use database software, make sure it serves you and you do not serve it.

If you do wish to complete your coding process by computer, but not rely on it as a major source, Carspecken (1996) suggests a useful method that is more meaning-based, more hands-on, less intrusive, and more conducive to ambiguity than many of the computer software programs that are marketed for qualitative and ethnographic data. You begin with the file comprising your fieldwork data and a blank file. From this point you proceed along the following course:

1. When an item is worthy of a code, toggle it to the blank file and type a number, a letter, or a name to identify or name the code.

2. Continue in this manner, developing new codes and combining like codes until all the items are identified, ordered, and given a code name. Along the way, you will discover and create subcodes.

3. Group codes together into major overarching themes. You may choose from among various possibilities. Carspecken suggests that you group codes according to the purpose and focus of your study.

* * *

This chapter served to provide concise and pithy tips on ethnographic methods for the beginner as well as the seasoned ethnographer. Therefore, this information may be new for some and a reminder for others. I have attempted to respond to the question of what constitutes an ethnographic method by organizing it as a *process* constituted of three parts. Part One encompasses identifying where you are now and choosing a subject. Part Two encompasses preparing for the field (the lay summary and research design) and formulating questions. Part Three encompasses building rapport in the interview and, finally, coding and logging data. Each of these three parts enhances and overlays the other: They are not isolated from one another. Please remember, your method is not simply a means to an end. It is a meaningful and conscious enactment of learning from and entering into an ethnographic domain of immense possibilities.

Warm-Ups

1. How would you respond to the claim, "We really don't need methods; all we really need is good theory, good intentions, and deep hanging out!"

2. Write a short biography. It can be in the form of a poem, a song, a visual image, or a narrative. What concepts, experiences, or points of view are more dominant in your personal history than others? What patterns or motifs seem to be repeated more than others? Then read your biography to yourself or another individual. Write questions of the biography on your own or in collaboration with another individual.

3. Choose a controversial figure in world politics. Conduct a brief search on the history and background of this individual. Then, write a series of questions for that individual geared to further expanding or engaging what is being discussed in the news.

4. With a partner, perform the sections on the attributes of the interviewer, both in ways that coincide and contrast with the points discussed. Formulate a series of questions based on a characterization of your partner from the models offered. Be creative by combining and overlapping the question models.

5. Write a sample lay summary and research plan based on your research project. Have your partner read it back to you for both of you to collaboratively critique.

Note

1. The list provided here of components that constitute a lay summary are a compilation of ideas from the following six researchers and their works: Corrine Glesne (1999); Norman K. Denzin (1997, 2001); Phil Francis Carspecken (1996); John Lofland and Lyn H. Lofland (1984); and James P. Spradley (1979).

Suggested Readings

Agar, M. (1996). *The professional stranger: An informal introduction to ethnography.* San Diego, CA: Academic Press.

Bernard, H. R. (2001). *Research methods in anthropology: Qualitative and quantitative approaches.* Walnut Creek, CA: AltaMira Press.

Bradbury, D. (1998). *The necessity of fieldwork.* Washington, DC: Smithsonian Books.

Carspecken, P. F. (1996). *Critical ethnography in educational research: A theoretical and practical guide.* New York: Routledge.

Emerson, R. M. (1995). *Writing ethnographic fieldnotes.* Chicago: University of Chicago Press.

Fetterman, D. (1998). *Ethnography step by step.* Thousand Oaks, CA: Sage.

Glesne, C. (1999). *Becoming qualitative researchers: An introduction.* New York: Longman.

Gray, A. (2002). *Research practice for cultural studies.* Thousand Oaks, CA: Sage.

Lofland, J., & Lofland, L. H. (1984). *Analyzing social settings: A guide to qualitative observations and analysis.* Belmont, CA: Wadsworth.

Mumby, D. (1993). *Narrative and social control.* Newbury Park, CA: Sage.

Patton, M. (1990). *Qualitative evaluation and research methods.* Thousand Oaks, CA: Sage.

Stockings, G. (1986). *Observers observed: Essays on ethnographic fieldwork.* Madison: University of Wisconsin Press.

3

Three Stories

Case Studies in Critical Ethnography

In this chapter, we meet three imaginary critical ethnographers, Joan, Robert, and Nia, who are each facing one of the biggest challenges of qualitative research: how to effectively and substantively interpret the relevant data and experiences encountered during fieldwork. They are each grappling with how to *theorize* and *analyze* the layers of meanings, symbols, implications, narrations, and possibilities they recorded, witnessed, and enacted. Both student and seasoned critical ethnographers confront this fundamental question: "How do I interpret what I have learned and discovered in the field?" As I have stated, in my view the ethnographer must have a certain command of theoretical knowledge in order to comprehend, critique, and communicate the worlds that were engaged with and inhabited in the field. Although our three ethnographers use a specific set of theoretical concepts for their individual projects, it is important to keep in mind that these concepts are not rigidly exclusive to any one project; indeed, they could be adapted between and among all of them to varying degrees and with varying emphasis. I have chosen to assign certain theoretical concepts to each case study based on how directly I felt they fit the nature and purpose of the project, not to determine or exclude their value for any particular subject.

In each of the three hypothetical case studies, the ethnographer faces a different set of issues and problems, but in combination the three stories represent difficulties most of us have had to confront in our projects in one form or another. I have imagined and created these three stories in order to encompass a wide range of problems and possibilities that the qualitative researcher might experience. We will follow Joan, Robert, and Nia through each section of the text as they variously struggle through the ethnographic challenges of critical theory, ethics, and performance.

Case One: Local Activism in West Africa

Key Concepts in Postcolonial and Marxist Criticism

Joan is a graduate student conducting an ethnographic study of a group of indigenous, global justice activists in a particular country in West Africa. These activists are working toward more just and fair policies for international trade and investment, as well as to reduce the proliferation and misuse in global arms trade. The group asserts that corporate investors constantly relocate and move money and jobs in and out of poorer countries at rapid speeds as soon as the companies turn a profit or the economy fluctuates. They do this with no warning or preparation for the locals, and as a result leave the local economy devastated and people out of work. The group argues that these global corporations are playing "global casino" with the lives of poor people. The activists also mobilize citizens in villages and in cities to demonstrate against free-trade policies. They state that poorer countries are forced to increase their exports all at once; therefore, there is an excess of goods, resulting in a fall in their prices and profits. Poor countries make little profit for what they export; at the same time, richer countries gain a surplus by selling the "cheap" goods of poor countries at higher prices. As a consequence, poor countries must export twice as much to earn a small surplus; therefore, what little surplus they do earn is used to pay off debts.

Joan worked with the activists in their campaign to assist local farmers, whose lives are distressed by free-trade policies, with tools, transportation, and equipment. One local farmer said to Joan in an interview,

> I can't compete with the big agricultural businesses, because they dump their imports like rice and cotton and the people suffer. How? I am a rice farmer with just a tractor and a hoe. I can produce only fifteen bags of rice. I don't have the technology to produce a lot of rice. I travel very, very far to the market—a full day—to try to sell my rice. But the big business can sell their rice cheaper than I can sell my rice and so the people buy their rice, because the people are so poor. I am a peasant farmer. I cannot compete with those big companies.[1]

The activists are also waging a campaign with international organizations against weapons trading. They maintain that firearms contribute to the devastating casualties of tribal conflict, civil war, massacres, torture, and assassinations; moreover, they assert that arms proliferation in the United States and Europe is profiting from more than half a million women, men, and children who are killed around the world each year. In collaboration with other international organizations, the activists send e-mails and information announcements to legislators and policymakers in richer countries with this quotation from Amnesty International, IANSA, and Oxfam (1999):

> The world's most powerful governments, who are also the world's biggest arms suppliers, have the greatest responsibility to control the global trade. The five permanent members of the U.N. Security Council—France, Russia, China, the U.K., and the U.S.A.—together account for 88 percent of the world's conventional arms exports; and these exports contribute regularly to gross abuses of human rights.

As the activists work locally and globally against the uncontrolled proliferation and misuse of arms and in mobilizing their countrymen and women to join the international fair-trade movement, Joan participated with and observes them at every level. She was a coperformer in meetings and planning sessions; in recruitment and petition drives; in teach-ins and demonstrations; in international correspondence and regional collectives. In addition, Joan conducted in-depth interviews and extensive oral histories with key members of the group. She is committed to fieldwork and dialogical engagement. However, with all her preparation and sincere dedication to fieldwork and ethics, Joan never ceased to be both unsettled and frustrated by the effects of globalization. One of the most striking discoveries for Joan was the power and significance of globalization upon her work and upon the lives of the people around her. Joan came to understand that local inquires, especially in the developing world, must be mindful of the fact of transnational economic interests: trade, investments, foreign exchange rates, technological access, foreign debt, labor, and the flow of capital. These multinationals guide economic realities, but they also guide the cultural and social realities of poverty and prosperity that, in turn, shape local knowledge and narratives.

Joan had not been prepared for the force of globalization upon the everyday life of the country. She came to understand that globalization is a critical factor for ethnographers, because it has transformed geographical boundaries, capitalist production, national sovereignty, and social structures in a way that deeply affects the rights and well-being of humankind across the planet. An important part of her research was coming to understand how the everyday affairs of local life and individual thriving are influenced by global power. As a critical ethnographer, she grappled with the dubious truths within the positives and negatives of economic globalization: the prosperity of the few at the expense of the many, a prosperity that simultaneously results in innovations in human communication, technological efficiency, and educational expansion. Joan has observed the positive side of globalization with its startling advancements in communication. People from all over the world are forming alliances and connections that have enormous effects. But, she also observed the negative side: natural resources upon which local citizens depend were being devastated for cooperate interests and profit, because local communities suffering under the dire circumstances of poverty feel they have no other choice but to destroy their natural environment to exist.

As Joan witnessed the effects of the global economy on the West African country of her fieldwork, she also witnessed what local activists were doing about it. First, the activists were steadfast in seeking nonviolent and creative measures to pressure and persuade multinational corporations to set fair standards for labor practices and environmental protection. Second, the activists formed alliances with other members of civil society who were working to develop international laws and trade agreements that would be enforceable by creating accountability measures of conduct for the establishment of fair-trade practices. Third, the activists also worked with other members of the international community in a campaign to more effectively democratize international financial institutions, such as the World Bank and the International Monetary Fund, so that developing countries would have greater representation and a stronger voice in decisions that guide the global economy.

The Final Stages

Joan was in the final stages of her fieldwork and was beginning to organize and log her data. As she gathered interview tapes and field notes from her journal, as well as newspaper clippings and other relevant documents, she began separating them into thematic clusters. Three main clusters developed from the morass of data. Joan realized that each one of the three clusters were central issues that most ethnographers conducting fieldwork on global justice in developing countries or the global South would examine: (a) *postcolonialism,* (b) *globalization,* and (c) *local activism.* These three major clusters would be further divided and refined into more discrete or specific themes. From each of these three themes, a number of subthemes (up to four or five) might evolve. However, it was these general or overriding themes that directed Joan to the particular theoretical methods that she needed to interpret her data and to build up her critical ideas. From the general domains of postcolonialism, globalization, and local activism, Joan employed theories related to materialism, specifically *postcolonial critique* and *Marxist theory.*

The second half of this story provides a general outline or definition of specific theoretical concepts, followed by examples that illustrate how these concepts may be applied in critical ethnography by using concrete examples from Joan's fieldwork.

Key Concepts in Postcolonialism

As Joan read the most current literature on postcolonial theory and tried to understand how the theory related to the time and space of her fieldwork, she discovered that the term *postcolonialism* refers to phenomena that are much more extensive than the particular time period after independence or imperial occupation. Postcolonialism, therefore, is not substantially a historical date, as in "post-colonialism" (after colonialism), but rather represents formations of meanings and practices. Postcolonialism refers to the multiple forms and locations of discourse, performance, politics, value, and the "everyday"—both past and present—that emanate from the history of colonialism (Appiah, 1992; Ashcroft, Griffiths, & Tippin, 1998; Loomba, 1998; McClintock, 1994; Young, 2001).

For Joan, as a critical ethnographer, the more useful term is *postcolonialism*, written without the hyphen to indicate the broader and more complex cultural politics that encompass the historical epochs of colonial rule and independence, as well as the contemporary era of globalization and postmodernity. She requires postcolonial theory to analyze her fieldwork experiences.

Postcolonial theory argues that in countries constituted by a colonial past—whether it is the Americas, Asia, or Africa—postcolonialism entails "all the culture affected by the imperial process from the moment of colonization to the present" (Ashcroft et al., 1998, p. 2). Therefore, when the critical ethnographer enters into a country with a colonial past, they also enter into a postcolonial present, with all the symbolic and material remnants passed down from the history of colonialism. Because postcolonial theory asserts that the aftermath of the colonial past exceeds the historical moment or transition from colonialism to independence, we examine how the colonial epoch—for better and for worse—profoundly affected education, language, geographic borders, religion, governmental structures, and cultural values that are carried forth to the present and will continue to be carried forth in the future.

While postcolonial theory examines various circumstances that constitute the present setting—settlement and dislocation, economic and material stratification, strategies of local resistance, as well as representation, identity, belonging, and expressive traditions—in order to more fully comprehend this present, postcolonial theory also examines and reenvisions history.

Note: Brief Historical Context

Globalization and colonialism begin with Christopher Columbus and the search for wealth and power. This continued for 450 years under European colonization. Colonialism developed during the 15th and 16th centuries from the quest for profit and explorations of discovery. Colonialism escalated in the late 17th and early 18th centuries with the settlements and exploitation of lands in Africa and Asia for the purpose of expanding the market for Western goods, controlling the natural resources of indigenous lands, and exploiting the labor of native people (Young, 2001).

Most of Europe sought colonies in Africa and the Pacific. In what is popularly called "the scramble for Africa," European nations partitioned the continent of Africa and carved-up the islands of the Pacific at the historic and notorious Berlin Conference between 1884 and 1885 (Young, 2001, p. 31). The result was that the Pacific Islands and almost every part of the African continent became a European colony. With advanced technology and military capabilities, Western nations easily conquered Africa and the Pacific. Western imperial domination was justified by the attitude that the West should control these areas in order to protect what Westerners viewed as weak peoples (Young, p. 50). According to Robert J. C. Young, the citizens of the imperial countries "supported this view especially because, with the exception of Japan's control of Korea, the power holders were white and their subjects were people of color" (p. 31).

Modernity and technology burgeoned as colonialism made Western nations rich through the extraction of labor and resources from colonized countries. "By WWI, imperial powers occupied or controlled nine-tenths of the territory of the globe," but this state of affairs began to change when, at the end of the second World War, "the Bolshevik Revolution emerged from chaos and destruction changing the nature of European class politics as well as the relationship between the colonized and the colonizer" (p. 59).

The 19th century is marked by a history of imperial appropriation, while the 20th century is marked by a struggle for independence (Young, 2001, p. 60). Colonialism came to an end as resistance movements began to emerge both within the imperial countries and even more forcefully within colonized territories. After World War II, these overpowering resistance movements made the colonial enterprise far too costly by "creating a barrier to Europe's own expansion" (Young, p. 43).

After colonialism ended, a new era of imperial domination was forming that is referred to as *neocolonialism*. The term *neocolonialism* was introduced in 1961 by the president of Ghana, Kwame Nkrumah (president of the first African country to win its independence from the British). Neocolonialism refers to the "imperial system of economic exploitation, in which the metropolitan center drains the resources of the periphery while at the same time encouraging it to consume its manufactured products in an unequal, unbalanced system of exchange" (Young, 2001, p. 47).

Postcolonial theory disentangles and critiques the social, cultural, and political implications of both the colonial epoch and the epoch referred to as *neocolonialism* (Nkrumah, 1966, 1968, 1969). Postcolonial theory examines the silenced expressions and subordinated practices that occur on the margins of power and brings them to the center of analysis. It debunks the taken-for-granted superiority of the metropolitan or imperial "center" that occupies not only the material institutions of power and dominance, but also how superiority figures into the imaginations of both the oppressor and oppressed (Ashcroft et al., 1998). For the critical ethnographer who is new to the literature, delimiting the complex and far-ranging inquiries that span postcolonial theory can be a challenging undertaking. Therefore, Joan chose to focus on four specific areas of inquiry in postcolonial literature: (a) language and hybridity, (b) place and displacement, (c) appropriation and mimicry, (d) neocolonialism and corruption.

Language and Hybridity

The language and hybridity area of examination is important in fieldwork because it addresses the profound importance of language relative to cultural identity and belonging as well as the multilayered implications when an imperial language displaces a people's native language. The results are a complex hybrid of meanings and cultural practices.

Conceptualizations of language and hybridity helped Joan interpret (a) how her learning the local language evoked trust and respect from her consultants, (b) how speaking the local language is an act of resistance and an affirmation of identity for local people, and (c) the significance of cultural symbols, codes, practices, and values in a country comprising of a mixture of traditions both from a colonial past and from multiple ethnic groups.

Place and Displacement

Place and displacement address the range of effects within the dynamic of migration from one local site to another, as well as migration from one homeland to the metropolitan center of the European world. This theme illuminates what it means to live and travel out of desire or necessity between the exploited and the exploiter, between the "third world" and the "first world."

Conceptualizations of place and displacement helped Joan interpret (a) how "freedom of movement" became so highly valued and desired, and how it often guides and determines everyday actions; (b) how identities and names are giving to those who travel and live abroad and the historical implications of such naming; (c) the relationship to region, land, and ethnicity among those migrating to and from other areas in the country; and (d) the cultural, social, and economic differences between rural life and city life.

Appropriation and Mimicry

The theme of appropriation and mimicry examines the internalization of colonialism by the colonial subjects. It is concerned with psychodynamics of the native who believes the discourse of superiority and believes that he or she is the "inferior native." It illuminates the various ways natives mimic the European to live in the illusion that they are "like him"—like the colonizer— or not like other natives.

The concept of appropriation and mimicry helped Joan in articulating (a) those who are accused of internalizing the racial and national inferiority perpetuated by their colonial "masters"; (b) the source and styles in the denigration of speech, dress, mannerisms, and economic status that is described as "white" or "European;" (c) the ambivalence toward the educated and rich among the population, the belief that they are complicitous with European life and values on one hand, and in opposition and defiance of them on the other; and (d) the strategies and motivation in adapting or appropriating "whiteness" for the purpose of turning back on it and both ridiculing and interrogating it.

Neocolonialism and Corruption

The concern in terms of neocolonialism is with contemporary power relations and global imbalances. It articulates how developing countries are manipulated and governed by remote control through the economic force of northern and economically advanced countries. It examines the inequities of poor countries, who must concede to the demands of the rich countries in the North, particularly in the form of trade and other economic factors. The theme of corruption explores the operations of the ruling elite in the home country and the consequences of their greed, duplicity, and corrupt practices on local suffering in terms of tribal wars, increased poverty, and human rights violations.

The concept of neocolonialism helped Joan in illuminating (a) the attitude of local people toward corruption in their country, (b) how the work of local activists is made more difficult by local authorities, (c) the connect in local suffering and global inequity, and (d) the levels of control the global North has over the economic futures of those in the global South.

Key Concepts in Marxist Thought

It is the Marxist doctrine that the development of human society is based on and determined by economic and social forces. Therefore, Marxism is concerned with how modes of production and class structure influence knowledge and the nature of existence. Marxism claims that it is not the consciousness of people that determines their being, but rather the opposite: Their social being determines their consciousness. In other words, poverty, exploitation, and wretched material conditions determine how one thinks and acts in the world. For Karl Marx (1976, 1983; Marx & Engels, 1999), it was the economic formation of a society and power arrangements that directed both social relations and individual awareness.

Joan chose the following key terms and definitions from Marxist theory in her research. These ideas were central in illuminating the complex webs of meaning that Joan encountered in a "developing world" context.

Capitalism

Capitalism is an economic system in which the private ownership of wealth (or capital) is structured toward the accumulation of more wealth (or surplus). Jan Aart Scholte (2000) defines capitalism, within the present global economy, by the following five processes. First, capitalism is a structure of production in which economic activity is oriented first and foremost to the accumulation of surplus. In other words, capitalist producers (who might be individuals, private firms, publicly owned enterprises, or other collective actors) attempt to "amass ever-greater resources in excess of their survival needs" (p. 95). Second, under capitalism, surpluses are invested in further production, "with the aim of acquiring additional surplus, which is then reinvested in still more production, in the hope of obtaining still more surplus, and so on" (p. 95). Third, capitalism offers "abundant opportunities to transfer surplus, especially from the weak to the powerful" (p. 95). Fourth, many other problems and conflicts remain dormant, because poor peoples in the South are unaware that much of their country's "limited surplus value is being transferred to the North through the repayment of global debts" (p. 96). Fifth, "today, the structural power of capitalism is such that most of the world's population regard surplus accumulation as a 'natural' circumstance and can scarcely imagine, let alone pursue, an alternative mode of production" (p. 96).

Joan could not avoid implicating the dubious nature of capitalism in her analysis of the global justice movement in West Africa. The literature on capitalism aided Joan in addressing questions regarding the inequities she experienced around her and how its roots and foundations can be identified.

The Circuit and the Hidden Abode

The circuit is the mechanism sustaining and generating capitalist production. The circuit is composed of varying levels that take the basic form of production, distribution, consumption, and reproduction. The circuit is continuously moving, while each condition of production is dependent on the other. The *hidden abode* refers to the condition of the circuit and capitalist production that is hidden in the everyday. Labor and the market are in many ways consciously "seen" and clearly experienced; therefore, this phase of production is apparent. However, there still remain hidden forces that translate and justify the circuit through behaviors, values, symbolic acts, and discourse that obscure and code certain operations that are not apparent (Marx, 1976) and often not seen.

The idea of the circuit and hidden abode aided Joan in articulating (a) how much of the work of the activist is in their attempt to bring to light the mechanisms of the global economy and arms trade that were hidden from the general public, (b) how trade rules are put into place and how profits are made and accumulated, and (c) how the machinery of production, distribution, consumption, and reproduction are working for the benefit of some at the despair of others.

Alienation

The product produced by the worker is now alien to him or her in exchange value; that is, the worker cannot afford to buy the very product he or she has produced; it stands opposed to the worker and is an objectification of his or her labor. The worker is also "unfulfilled" by this work. The labor does not belong to the worker, but to the capitalist owner. According to Marx (1976, 1983), the worker sinks to the level of a commodity. Laborers become "things" because their work does not belong to them—the worker feels alienated from his or her own work and then looks to the leisure time within the home community to feel free, human, and expressive.

Joan witnessed many entrepreneurs, farmers, and crafts people who took pride in their work and felt a sense of ownership relative to their labor. However, the concept of alienation helped Joan (a) name and decipher the others who labored for long hours of the day, but could barely make a living for themselves or their families; (b) articulate why their labor was not a source of pride, but rather an obligation and a dread; (c) express the sense of resentment on the part of laborers, who feel their wage was not equal to the labor they provided; and (d) articulate the absence of alienation when wage and benefits were equal and fair.

Class Consciousness

In Marxist theory, class constitutes divisions among groups of people in a society based on their economic resources and the values, opportunities, aesthetics, and social arrangements that evolve from these divisions. Those who accept uncritically the oppressive power arrangements of the world will form dominant or ruling class values and interests—although, according to traditional Marxism, they operate under a *false consciousness* (1976, 1983). However, when the proletariat or subordinate classes are aware of the inequity of the world from the need, value, and perspective of their class positioning, they reject the interest of the oppressive class and are then operating under class consciousness.

The concept of *class consciousness* was useful to Joan in (a) the manner the activists articulated class stratifications within their own country; (b) the manner stratification divisions operated based on education, cultural capital, and moral values; and (c) how the activists focused on poverty and the political economy in their efforts to enlighten local people of class divisions.

Commodity Fetishism, Consumer Lust, and Interpellation

The desire to consume is built into the society in order to sell products and keep the economy efficient. Commodity fetishism creates the desire to own and to possess an object—the commodity. A fetish has magical powers. Marxism asserts that commodities become a fetish because of our obsession to have them and because of the power they hold over us to consume or attain them. *Interpellation* refers to the manner in which representations and messages in culture—particularly media, art forms, advertising, commercials, and so forth—coerce, seduce, or call us forth to accept the ideologies and value that these forms project.

The commodity concepts aided Joan in interpreting (a) the influences, for better and worse, of popular culture and the media in interpolating or seducing people to buy what they cannot afford and to obsess over material objects such as cars, clothes, and jewels; and (b) how the activists expressed the challenges in combating commodity fetishism and the obsession some of their people have with the images and material objects represented in and advertised by American popular culture.

Hegemony

In its traditional definition, *hegemony* meant political control and domination of one state over another. The cultural critic Antonio Gramsci (1977, 1978, 1994) used the term differently to mean the manner in which dominant classes controlled and exploited subordinate groups by consent, thereby masking exploitation by convincing the exploited that their condition was natural to them, even good for them. Cultural institutions, at the level of superstructure, create ideas and images of acceptance and acquiescence to the *status quo*. The central feature of Gramsci's notion of hegemony is that it operates without force. We give consent because we are interpolated and prescribed to believe that the interest of the power bloc is really our interest. It becomes our worldview, and through hegemony we are in complicity with our own subordination.

The concept of hegemony helped Joan by addressing (a) the question of how people can act against their own best interest by causing injury and harm to their own people; (b) asking why some local people kept corrupt and brutal leaders in office; (c) examining how people are oppressed by consent and out of the direct control and view of the oppressor.

Praxis

Marx envisioned a world in which people were no longer divided by class and no longer alienated from one another or their own labor due to the capitalist mode of production. He envisioned an unalienated world through the idea of *praxis* (Marx, 1976, 1983). Praxis is the creation of alternative ways of being and courageous engagement with the world in order to change it.

The concept of praxis encapsulates the intensions and practices of the local activists. The concept of praxis helped Joan (a) articulate the dedication of the activists in their intervention upon poverty and injustice, (b) address the question of the British cultural critic Stuart Hall (1997): What can we do about the "problems that beset our world"?; and (c) adapt a vocabulary to help make the notion of "hope" more tangible and empirical.

Case Two: Secrets of Sexuality and Personal Narrative

Robert is an oral historian focusing on the personal narrative of three gay men who, at varying levels, are concealing their sexuality. Each of the three men has different reasons for not coming out, and each of them is from different ethnic and socioeconomic backgrounds. Robert chose an effective method to select the subjects for his study: He met with members of the gay and lesbian organization on his campus and spoke with them; he gave them a copy of his lay summary indicating who he is, what he planned to do, his research questions, the role of the participants, and the measures he would take to safeguard their anonymity and confidentiality. Robert asked the organization if they could advise him on where he might place announcements for his study, and if they would recommend individuals who might be interested in participating. He also asked if there were other support groups or organizations that might have access to such individuals. After reading the summary and listening carefully to Robert, the organization was convinced that he would protect the identities of his subjects and that his study would contribute to a heightened awareness and sensitivity to gay and lesbian concerns. They agreed to assist Robert in locating individuals and to provide a list of other groups that might be amenable to recommendations.

Through references from several organizations that are aligned with and supportive of the particular interests and issues that would affect the individuals Robert wished to interview, he was able to identify three men for his study. In the initial meeting and screening interview with the three men, Robert explained his method for anonymity and confidentiality. Because of his thoughtful and detailed explanation, the men felt secure and protected, and so consented to participate in the study. Robert developed a trusting and close rapport with each of them and conducted in-depth interviews over a period of one year. Introduced as a friend, Robert accompanied the men to various locations and events and met family members and close friends.

Each of the men embodies his own unique life story and reason for concealment:

Harry is a wealthy, middle-aged businessman with a wife and a three-year-old daughter. He is the chief executive officer of a large corporation. Harry has been married for five years; he and his family live in the Midwest. He has a stable marriage and he is a loving father. No one knows of his bisexual lifestyle except his support group and his male partner of two years.

Jim is a 21-year-old first-generation college student. He is on a football scholarship at a state university. He comes from a fundamentalist Christian family in a northwest rural community. Jim is in the early stages of his first homosexual relationship. Only two trusted friends know about Jim's relationship. He has no plans to tell his family.

Raymond is an 18-year-old African American high school senior from a highly educated and well-respected upper-middle-class family that has lived in the same southern town for four generations. Raymond is an art major. He received a full scholarship to attend an Ivy League university in the Northeast. He is the first in his family dating back to his great, great, paternal grandfather who did not attend a particular historically black university. Raymond has not disclosed his sexuality to anyone except a school counselor.

Over the year that Robert conducted his interviews with Harry, Jim, and Raymond, he was often struck by the differing degrees of alienation and fear each man expressed at the thought of openly revealing their sexuality. Each man referred to very specific individuals whom they felt would not understand and must never know. Harry observed that all three of the men carried this burden of secrecy with them in the day-to-day activities of their lives, not because they were afraid of discrimination or shame from society at large, but more because of the disappointment, scorn, or pain it would cause specific individuals: certain colleagues, family, and friends. They felt the secret was the only form of defense for themselves, as well as for those individuals who were integral in their lives.

However, Robert made an interesting observation. He realized that full disclosure for each of the men seemed to be both desirable and frightfully unimaginable: each man expressed a feeling of being forcefully pulled between internal need to tell and external demands to keep the secret. When Robert asked the men why they wanted to be part of his study, they each expressed, in their own terms, the feeling of a necessary and longed-for "freedom" that narration before a trusted listener in the naming and reflection of their fears and desires provides. The freedom through narration the men expressed reminded Robert of what the anthropologist Barbara Myerhoff (1982) called *definitional ceremonies*, where socially marginalized individuals "regularly seek opportunities to appear before others in the light of their own *internally provided interpretations . . .*" (p. 105). The constructed meetings of the in-depth interview become performed narrations and performative self-reflections in which the narrator is both the actor and the audience of his own life story and his own interpreted life meanings. It is during these definitional ceremonies that we may come into the fullness of our human capability—and perhaps human desire—to watch ourselves and enjoy knowing what we know (Myerhoff, 1982). Narrative is both the joy-filled freedom of expression and a confirmation. Harry, Jim, and Raymond were active narrators, appreciating the enduring consolation and the libratory experience their definitional ceremonies provided. As the study was coming to an end, each man expressed to Robert the value of the life history project in contributing to a greater sense of clarity and awareness of what it means to make certain life choices and the contexts that generate them.

Robert contemplated the power that narration as definitional ceremonies has to serve a purpose beyond organically healing and providing comfort; more specifically in the case of Harry, Jim, and Raymond, narration served to reveal the ways in which (hetero)sexuality is insidiously and covertly ingrained in human interaction and valued at most every level of social life, and helped to expose the multiple disguises and forms of homophobia, from quiet disproval to blatant aggression. Robert felt comfort in knowing that each narration put a human face on and added a particular history to the idea of the Other and social justice relative to what it means to be gay and to feel you must hold your life together by a secret.

Robert contemplated the method of interpretation that would best illuminate the meanings embedded in the stories told by each of the men. On the one hand, entering their narratives from their own point of view necessarily required an understanding of how subjectivity is formed and expressed. He would therefore turn to theories of *phenomenology*. On the other hand, entering their narratives from the point of view of the social and cultural universe that informs their point of view is deepened through theories of *semiotics* and *symbolic interactionism*. Moreover, examining the sexual politics that surrounds the personal and public domains in which each man must navigate is elaborated in the articulations of *queer theory*. Although each of these theoretical domains inherently overlaps at varying points and degrees, Robert's method of interpretation would more consciously and strategically embrace theories of subjectivity by combining queer theory with theories of phenomenology, semiotics, and symbolic interaction to address his research question.

* * *

We will now turn to brief descriptions of key concepts from theories that illuminate subjectivity: phenomenology, semiotics, and sexuality. Each theoretical perspective will then be applied by using examples from Robert's study.

Key Concepts in Phenomenology

Phenomenology encompasses multiple perspectives. It is not a "single unified philosophy or standpoint" (Moran, 2000, p. 4). There is transcendental phenomenology, existential phenomenology, hermeneutical phenomenology, and phenomenology that emphasizes Marxist theory, feminism, and semiotics. The basic premise of phenomenology is that the perceiver determines meaning, and therefore it is human perception, not external influences or objects of the material world, that is at the core of our analysis. Just as traditional Marxism argues that economic conditions determine our reality, traditional phenomenology argues that it is human consciousness that determines our reality. Whatever appears in the human mind as it manifests itself in consciousness is the phenomenological project. Therefore, interpreting everyday life experience, from a phenomenological view, requires a close analysis of how ordinary human consciousness perceives its day-to-day life world.

Although phenomenology encompasses a blend of perspectives and cannot be contained by one viewpoint, like in all schools of thought, criticism of its foundational elements still abides. Many Marxists claim that phenomenology remains inherently individualistic and regressive in its preoccupation with individual perception rather than the material forces of power, domination, and false consciousness that influence it in the first place

(Moran, 2000). Phenomenology is also at the center of the deconstructionist critique that rejects the possibility of a full presence of meaning; that is, meanings can never be fully present, apparent, or authentic in human consciousness—true meaning is always colored and filtered through the very consciousness that phenomenologists embrace. However, the deconstructionists and Marxists notwithstanding, critical ethnographers embrace phenomenology's orientation toward embodiment and perception, both in the telling and enactment of experience. We understand that human perception, on the one hand, reveals idiosyncratic meanings, contingent truths, and felt-sensing perspectives that are born from materiality, power, and the complexity of presence, and, on the other hand, uncovers what it feels like to experience all these elements up close and personal. As Moran writes,

> Phenomenology attempts to recognize and describe the role of consciousness in the achievement (*Leistung*) of *knowledge* and is not wallowing in the subjective domain purely for its own sake. Indeed, the whole point of phenomenology is that we cannot split off the subjective domain from the domain of the natural world as scientific naturalism has done. . . . What then is the enduring influence of phenomenology? It is frequently argued that the main contribution of phenomenology has been the manner in which it has steadfastly protected the subjective view of experience as a necessary part of any full understanding of the nature of knowledge. (pp. 15, 21)

As Robert examined the personal narratives of the three men, the following key concepts guided him in his analysis and search for meanings that spoke from the position or consciousness of the men themselves.

Bracketing and Dasein

Edmund Husserl (1999; Heidegger, 1961, 1962), considered the father of phenomenology, introduced the notion of bracketing. He felt that in order to reach pure perception (or *transcendental subjectivity*) it was necessary to bracket or put aside all scientific, philosophical, and cultural assumptions. For Husserl, the bracketing enabled a direct line to unadulterated perception or subjectivity without the messy interference of outside forces. However, many critics have disagreed with Husserl. The critic of phenomenology, Dermot Moran (2000), states, "Phenomenology is the story of deviation from Husserl; the history of phenomenology is the history of Husserlian heresies" (p. 3). Martin Heidegger (1961, 1962), Husserl's student, disagreed with the notion of bracketing the surrounding world of influences and asserted that we must consider the historicity and the facticity of living in time and space. There is never a "pure" interpretation. Therefore, we cannot bracket out the material, historical world for some ideal perfection of internal consciousness.

One of Heidegger's (1961, 1962) most significant contributions to phenomenology—one especially relevant to ethnographic interpretation—is his concept of *dasein* or "being." For Heidegger, *dasein* constitutes existence, and in German it literally means "there being" or "being there." The idea of *dasein* is that when *being* meets the world and discovers that there are Others with which *being* must share the world of existence, then anxiety, dread, and meaninglessness soon follow. The paradox is that *being* can only know itself through the Other and thereby through dread. Heidegger therefore asserts that *being* must find a way past anxiety and dread; thus, to live in the world with Others, *being* must find a way to care and make peace with the world. The main point of difference between Heidegger and Husserl was the intrinsic perception of the everyday world contaminated (for Husserl) by materiality versus the perception of the everyday world as inseparable (for Heidegger) from social, cultural, historical influences. In other words, they differed on the point of *transcendent consciousness*. But, true to the phenomenological investigation, they both were concerned with how the *world comes to appearances in and through human consciousness*.

Because Robert's introduction was to present the meanings and experiences he gathered in his data from the perspective or consciousness of the men themselves, he employed phenomenology as both a justification for embracing the standpoint of his subjects and as an analytical framework. The particular concepts of bracketing and *dasein* helped him address (a) the tension between individual and idiosyncratic meanings and descriptions that are based principally on the singularity of the perspective rather than the social forces that guide it; (b) how much of the narratives should focus on the singularity and uniqueness of the experience, rather than its political implications; (c) the question of living in a world with Others that creates dread and inhibition, as the men felt social pressure to hide their full identity; and (d) how the three men attempted to reconcile *dasein* by making peace in their particular spaces with Others.

Appearances and Bad Faith

Although Husserl (1999) and Heidegger (1961, 1962) laid the foundation for phenomenological analysis, there are three additional thinkers who are considered within the realm of existential phenomenology and whose ideas were particularly relevant to critical ethnography. First there is the existentialist and Marxist theorist Jean-Paul Sartre. It is Sartre (1973, 1993) who popularized the phrase "bad faith," meaning that people's recognition of their own freedom makes them feel anxious and afraid. Therefore, feeling the responsibility of their own freedom to be too terrifying, they turn away and run from it by imagining they are behaving under rules and norms by which they must abide (Sartre, 1993). In bad faith, one goes by the rules or follows the expected norm in order not to disturb the *status quo* or to rock the boat even if they feel it might be better to do so. As a result, they take "refuge from anxiety in 'bad faith'" (Magee, 2001, pp. 216–217). Sartre felt that phenomenology allows us to reflect more thoughtfully about our own affective, emotional, and imagined life as it could be more meaningfully lived.

Bad faith was an invaluable concept to Robert in (a) describing how these men chose within their own personal interactions not to disrupt the dominance of heteronormativity for fear of the consequences; and (b) providing a way of describing in more detail the fear, relative to social and familial rejection, that contributed to why they denied the truth of their identity.

The Body and the Other

The two other existential philosophers, Maurice Merleau-Ponty (1962, 1969) and Emmanuel Levinas (1987, 1996) concerned themselves, respectively, with notions of the body and the Other. Merleau-Ponty extended the relation of phenomenological consciousness to the human body. He most eloquently brought mind and body together by articulating how the living human body experiences and *takes in* the world. For Merleau-Ponty, the intersection between human beings and the world is a relation that comes into being through the personal, lived body. It is the body that brings us into the spatial world—experience is embodied as much as it is perceived. Merleau-Ponty (1969) states, "My body does not perceive, but it is as if it were built around the perception that dawns through it; through its whole internal arrangement, its sensory motor circuits, the return ways that control and release movements . . ." (qtd. in Moran, 2000, p. 424).

Emmanuel Levinas, arguably more than any other phenomenologist of his time, "wanted to redirect phenomenology from a self-centered subjectivity to a deeper understanding of Otherness" (Moran, p. 19). Levinas's special contribution to phenomenology was in his concern for ethics, particularly as they relate to the appearance of the Other in our subjective sphere. For Levinas, "Prior to any act, I am concerned with the Other, and I can never be absolved from this responsibility" (qtd. in Moran, p. 348). To be face to face with the Other, for Levinas, demands protection and loving justice: "Prior to any act, I am concerned with the Other, and I can never be absolved from the responsibility . . . to see a face is already to hear 'Thou shalt not kill'" (qtd. in Moran, pp. 43–44).

Robert's work very much wanted to connect perception of what appears in the mind with the felt-sensing body. The concepts of the body and the Other helped Robert (a) address the question of how the body is both affected by and also affects meaning and experience, (b) rescue phenomenology from accusations of self-centered musings on one's own detextualized life, and (c) show how phenomenology can intimately connect the self with the Other out of necessary obligation to responsibility and justice.

Key Concepts in Subjectivity and Symbolism

Phenomenology concerns itself with human perception or the *subjective view*, but we shall now go a step further by asking how this subjective view is formed in the first place. In order for there to be a perception or a subjective view, there must be a subject, and in turn this subject is composed of meaning and history. Therefore, subjectivity begins with an individual identity, a site of consciousness, and a thinking self. However, because the subject thinks and must then think from a body moving through particular spaces, subjectivity is not a pure free-floating consciousness, but comprises several factors: language, desire, sexuality, symbolism, and ideology, to name a few. This means that subjectivity is constituted by and within political, social, and cultural productions of meanings and practices. Therefore, it is important to see subjectivity as always historically produced within different contexts and not as a single, fixed identity. Robert's interpretive work with oral history and personal narrative drew upon aspects of phenomenology, but it also required an understanding of the specific dimensions of subjectivity. The following key concepts illuminate subjectivity as it relates to particular concerns regarding how symbols and sexuality serve in the making of the subject.

The Unconscious

Subjectivity is not only a factor of history and discourse; it is also elaborated most effectively in theories of the unconscious (Weedon, 1987). In psychoanalytic theory, the unconscious is central to the formation of the self, the subject, and subjectivity. Sigmund Freud (1963, 1980), the architect of psychoanalysis, set forth the idea that the psyche is composed of three fundamental levels: the conscious, the preconscious, and the unconscious. For Freud and other theorists of the unconscious, our dreams, myths, symbols, and that which is displaced, condensed, and repressed has the greatest influence upon what forms our being. From this view, consciousness is "infinitesimal" to the power and influence of the unconscious.

Carl Jung (1981, 1997) extended the notion of the unconscious to the idea of a *collective unconscious* found in all human beings and manifest in what Jung called archetypes or universal images found in dreams, works of art, myths, religions, philosophies, and so forth. According to Jung, archetypes are symbolic expressions communicated across time and space based on the instinctual behavior and natural inclinations of all humankind (Jung, 1981). According to Jung, we produce and are produced by the ubiquitous and universal archetypes that surround our existence.

The concept of the unconscious in Robert's work addressed (a) those moments in the narratives that were expressed, revealed, and brought to consciousness for the first time through the act of telling, and, in contrast, (b) why certain implications and origins for ideas and points of view are not addressed and why they are unknown to the narrator.

Language and Desire

Subjectivity is further layered by the contribution of the psychoanalytic theorist Jacque Lacan (1966) with his emphasis on language and desire. For Lacan, language is the very condition of the unconscious and therefore of subjectivity. Although the human subject cannot be reduced to language, according to Lacan there can never be a subject without it. Desire is inseparable in the formation of subjectivity, because it is desire that is the driving force in humankind's innate and unconscious need for completeness and recognition. In the struggle for completeness and recognition, desire is not simply sexual force, but a part of existence and what constitutes being human. Desire is the desire not simply for a body, but for the desire of the Other—the desire to be recognized, to feel free of lack and loneliness. It is the desire to be desired.

The concepts of language and desire helped Robert address (a) the question of how language, in the case of narration, orders and conceptualizes one's very being; (b) how language forms and discovers experience by making the unknown now known and manifest; (c) how the need expressed in the telling is beyond sexual need, how each man experienced the human and universal need for recognition; and (d) how our needs are compounded into a desire to reveal our true selves, particularly by the added need of not wanting to experience rejection.

The Sign and Symbol

A sign is a being or object that possesses information. Semiotics is an analytical technique examining how signs perform or evoke meaning and communication within a particular context (Barthes, 1975, 1987, 1988; Saussure, 1959). Every entity is a potential sign; therefore, semiotics may encompass entities as diverse as a piece of clothing, a photograph, a song, a building, food, machinery, or a road sign. An integrated system of signs becomes a social code. Signs comprise two primary parts: first, a mark that is written or spoken (that carries the message), called the *signifier*; second, a concept or thought (through which content is conveyed), called the *signified*. Semantics is understood as the meaning of signs and syntax and as the relational arrangements of signs to each other (Greimas, 1983). In addition, semantics and syntax combine to form deep structures and systems of meaning, as well as the making of meaning. Semiotics aims to uncover the dynamics beyond surface meanings or shallow descriptions and to articulate underlying implications. Semiotics also aims to discover the structures of events—that is, the sign system or rules that govern conduct. In studying the sign, you must examine the system of relations that enable the meaning to be produced.

Through the concepts of sign and symbol, Robert could contemplate (a) how the men, from their unique perspectives, are surrounded by symbols and signs whose meanings and value they lift from their empirical world and then rearticulate, represent, and thickly describe in their narration; and (b) how certain signs and symbols relate to objects that hold powerful meanings that shape behavior and how they influence the interactions and attitudes toward others.

Symbolic Interactionism

Growing out of philosophical pragmatism, the basic premise of symbolic interactionism is threefold: (1) It is the idea that we relate to objects and living beings based on the *meanings* we have for such objects and beings; (2) our meanings for objects and beings are derived from communication and relationships—that is, from social interactions with others; and (3) these meanings move between the social to the individual and are therefore shaped and guided by an interpretive process undertaken by an individual subject (Schwandt, 1997, pp. 148–149). Herbert Blumer (1969), influenced by George Herbert Mead (1938), describes several key dimensions that comprise symbolic interactionism:

> Let me remind the reader of the basic premises of symbolic interactionism: human group life consists of the fitting to each other of the lines of action of the participants; such aligning of actions takes place predominantly by the participants indicating to one another what to do and in turn interpreting such

indications made by the others; out of such interaction people form the objects that constitute their worlds; people are prepared to act toward their objects on the basis of the meaning these objects have for them; human beings face their world as organisms with selves, thus allowing each to make indications to himself; human action is constructed by the actor on the basis of what he notes, interprets and assesses; and the interlinking of such ongoing action constitutes organizations, institutions, and vast complexes of interdependent relations. (Blumer, 1969, p. 49)

Symbolic interactionism is therefore a method of analysis that describes human beings as both products and producers of symbols. These symbols are constructed and reconstructed, whereby meanings (and meanings of those meanings) form social processes that guide human behavior and experiences, and whereby the "complex interlinkages of acts that comprise organizations, institutions, division of labor, and networks of interdependence are moving and not static affairs" (Blumer, 1969, p. 50).

Symbolic interactionists insist that in order to understand the actions of a people it is necessary to conceive their objects as they conceive them. Although there are larger structures or system principals that govern social life (i.e., capitalism, sexual norms, ethnic hierarchies, ecological determinators, etc.), the symbolic interactionist places primary emphasis on the explanations and interpretations of these systems by social actors and the respective points expressed that describe the situation (Blumer, 1969, p. 58).

Symbolic interactionism provided a framework that helped Robert (a) articulate how the men both created and were created by their symbolic universe; (b) how names, descriptions, and judgments were given to objects and beings in the narrators' world that made the ordinary new and extraordinary; and (c) how meaning was brought forward that implied history, social interaction, and politics.

Key Concepts in Sexuality

The personal narratives in Robert's study of gay men and the significance of their nondisclosure concerned how these men as human beings, and therefore as symbol-making creatures, were particularly influenced, guided, and constituted by their sexual identity. Robert drew on the following concepts for his analysis.

Sexuality and Heteronormativity

The term *heteronormativity* refers to the view that heterosexuality is or should be the normal or legitimate sociosexual arrangement in society

(Hennessy & Ingraham, 1997). Heteronormativity therefore regulates any sexual practice that does not comply with dominant heterogendered practices by calling them "deviant" or "amoral." Where does heteronormativity begin? Where does it come from? Louis Althusser (1969, 1970) argues that our images and representations, along with our notions of what is called *the real*, marks the historical and material conditions of life. In other words, we are interpolated or pulled in by the symbols and representations that surround us and, as a result, construct what we believe to be real: "The heterosexual imaginary is that way of thinking which conceals the operations of homosexuality in structuring gender and closes off any critical analysis of heterosexuality as an organizing institution" (Ingraham, 1997, p. 275).

Heteronormativity may define heterosexuality as "natural," but many critical thinkers have argued that heterosexuality is neither natural nor inevitable, but is instead "contrived, constructed, and taken for granted" (Ingraham, 1997, p. 289). This means that biological *possibilities* are guided, sustained, and reaffirmed by economic, political, social, historical, cultural, and familial formations, symbols, and structures. Therefore, any one of us is potentially outside the norm of heteronormativity. Chrys Ingraham (1997) writes,

> Ask students how they learned to be heterosexual, and they will consistently respond with stories about how they learned to be boys or girls, women or men, through the various social institutions in their lives. Heterosexuality serves as the unexamined organizing institution and ideology (the heterosexual imaginary) for gender. . . . Most important in these theories is the absence of any concept of heterosexuality as an institutional organizing structure or social totality. (p. 288)

The conceptualization of sexuality and normativity provided Robert (a) a means to extend his symbolic and phenomenological interpretations more directly outward to systems, structures, institutions, and cultural politics relative to how the sexuality of these men were regulated in ways that were beyond their control, their own perception, and analysis; (b) a way to focus on the politics of sexuality in a critical analysis of the consequences and implications of each narrator's lifestyle and his choice in keeping it a secret; and (c) a way to combine structures and cultural politics, guided by theorists of sexuality and normativity, with a phenomenological approach that considered experience as told through the meanings and perspectives of the narrator.

Sex and Gender

Sexuality contains the complex and varied ways in which biological possibilities are shaped by social, economic, political, and cultural structures

(Wood, 2005). This means that both *sex* and *gender* categories are within certain sociocultural and sociopolitical contexts. This brings to mind distinctions between gender and sexuality. Sex is typically defined as "the biological identity of the person and is meant to signify the fact that one is either male or female" (Ingraham, 1997, p. 285), whereas gender is described as the socially learned behaviors and expectations that are associated with the two sexes (Ingraham, 1997, p. 284). Sex is distinguished as biology and defined as natural, while gender is viewed as nurtured—that is, learned or achieved. What is problematic about this well-received generalization is that distinguishing sex from gender in this way "reinforces the nature/culture binary, opening the study of sex to the domain of science and closing off consideration of how biology is linked to culture" (Ingraham, 1997, p. 286). Ingraham lends valuable insight to the gender/sex divide that is worth quoting at length:

> Sex as a category of analysis can never exist outside prevailing frames of intelligibility. By foregrounding gender as dependent on the male-female binary, the heterosexual assumption remains unaddressed. We need to question our assumptions about sex and gender as to how they organize difference, regulate investigation, and preserve particular power relations, especially those linked to institutional heterosexuality. . . . All of the institutions involved in the production of sex as a biological category defined as male or female, where each is distinct and opposite from the other, are participating in reproducing lines of power. (p. 286)

The distinction between sex and gender aided Robert in (a) clarifying the ways in which not only gender, but also sex, are classified and regulated by society; (b) how the concepts of sex and gender were signified in interpreting the narrators' own perception of gender and how these significations were further complicated and layered by homosexual desire; and (c) how the social construction of gender is further complicated when same-sex preferences do not comply with sexual dichotomies of male and female.

Queer Identity

According to the *World Book Dictionary* (1980 edition), the adjectives *queerer* and *queerest* mean "differing from the usual or the normal." As verbs, *queered*, *queering*, *queers* mean "spoil the effects or success of." The term *queer* is an appropriation of pejorative meanings, as in "peculiar," "bazaar," "strange," and so on, and therefore, like a wise and recalcitrant trickster, the queer movement has flipped and reversed the term to radically interrupt its negative meaning by breaking it open and remaking it into a symbol of resistance, inclusion, and advocacy. To be queer is to "spoil" discourses and practices based on exclusivity and oppressive normativity. To be queer is to claim difference as a necessity in the world. Queer theory has emerged as one of the prominent areas of academic scholarship that thoughtfully and fundamentally challenges notions of heteronormativity, bringing powerful insight to what it means to live, love, think, and act outside constructions of the norm. As Sue-Ellen Case (1990) writes,

> Queer theory, unlike lesbian theory or gay theory, is not gender specific. In fact, like the term "homosexual," queer foregrounds same-sex desire without designating which sex is desiring . . . [queer] works not at the site of gender, but at the site of ontology, to shift the ground of being itself. . . . Unlike petitions for civil rights, queer revels constitute a kind of activism that attacks the dominant notion of the natural. The queer is the taboo-breaker. . . . (pp. 2–3)

Queer identity inspired Robert and provided (a) another vocabulary with which he could make the leap from *this is the way it is* to *what if* (Denzin, 2003; Thomas, 1993); (b) an analysis, examples, and a vision for what it means to live your choices openly, without fear of rejection; (c) the vocabulary needed to suggest what to do about the problem of "coming out"; and (d) a means by which difference can be understood, embraced, and celebrated without shame or secrets.

Case Three: Community Theatre Conflicts and Organization

Nia's concentration is in organizational communication. She is interested in the *effects* of nonprofit community theatre organizations on lower income, ethnically diverse communities. Her central question is, What are the most effective methods relative to leadership and service that local theatre companies employ to assist and aid individuals in the development, renewal, control, and sustenance of their own communities?

Nia's present study focuses on the Cross Bridges Performance Collective, located in an economically neglected inner-city neighborhood in a major northeastern metropolitan city. Cross Bridges is composed of two main programmatic components. The first is the main stage production series. The series produces staged performances in which community members participate at all levels of the production process, ranging from publicity, hanging stage lights, building sets, and acting, to playwriting and adaptation. The second component is the performance educational workshop series. It comprises workshops in which improvisation, creative dramatics, puppetry, and image theatre are utilized to teach reading and communication skills; leadership and problem solving; and storytelling and oral history.

Nia has observed the company for two years. She has participated in the performance workshops and the main stage productions. After working with Cross Bridges, Nia has been impressed by how the young and the old in the workshop series are transformed through performance methods and techniques as they find pleasure in reading, as they envision new alternatives for solving problems, and as they imagine new ways of thinking about their community and their futures. Nia has also participated in two main stage productions and volunteered for the job of stage manager. She was inspired by the success of the company in bringing hostile factions of the community together through various staged performances. Nia witnessed how the most volatile and contested issues boiling among community members were dramatically transformed through the empathic force of performance into productive struggles for understanding. As the rehearsals progressed and as opening night drew closer, Nia was deeply moved by the bond that formed between cast members. The barriers of hostility and old resentments that harbor fear and unfamiliarity had gradually worn down during the rehearsal process through the coalescence of bodies and minds working and creating together. Rehearsals became the forum to imagine and to desire a new way of building relationships and community.

Nia's work with the company was a labor of love. She had become an enthusiastic supporter of community theatre and its power to make meaningful change happen. She admired the company members and was in awe of their commitment and their skills.

The season was nearing the end, and the company was getting ready for the last show on the schedule when the director asked company members if they would like to experiment with something new. For the final performance, the company made the decision to take part in a newly instituted experimental, cross-cultural program sponsored by the city's Urban Arts Exchange Project. The Exchange Project sponsored qualified individuals from certain areas of the city to participate as artists-in-residence in other communities that were located at a distance from their home community. The purpose was to create a cultural exchange of ideas, methods, and experiences, and to bring artists from different economic and ethnic backgrounds together that might not otherwise come into contact with one another. Cross Bridges was optimistic and welcomed the opportunity for this cross-cultural exchange.

Two individuals from outside the Cross Bridges community signed up as residents. The men were from a theatre company in the surrounding area of the city and each had considerable experience in acting, directing, and technical theatre. The members of Cross Bridges anticipated and appreciated the expertise these individuals would bring to the company, and the residents were excited about the ways these men would assist the company in helping to mount a successful production. Nia was delighted by the inclusion of artists from outside the local community of Cross Bridges, as it would expand the notion of "community" and "ethnicity"; moreover, it would broaden the reach of Cross Bridges by making outsiders aware of the significance and success of arts organizations in the inner city. But it would do something more: Nia's study now had policy implications for the future funding and implementation of the city's Urban Arts Exchange Project. The success of the artists-in-residence experiment at Cross Bridges would provide an exemplary case study for policymakers who are working to provide funding and to implement arts programs in economically disenfranchised communities throughout the city. The cross-cultural exchange held great possibilities.

Everything was now set. The residents had arrived. After just a few weeks, the residents had adjusted and settled into the culture and community of Cross Bridges, or so everyone thought. As the residents began rehearsals for the main stage production, everything seemed to go well in the beginning. However, as the rehearsals got underway, things slowly began to unravel. Nia noticed the men seemed aggravated and displeased during the rehearsal process. She noticed they were starting to make insulting comments about the director and were becoming more and more critical of her approach. She was aware that the artists-in-residence had their own particular style and method, one drawn from their local theatre company and performance orientation, and it seemed they were becoming more and more exasperated by this different approach by the Cross Bridges director. Moreover, they resented feeling forced to comply with the director's authority. The covert racial and sexual insults were making Nia very uncomfortable.

The residents subtly and indirectly began to express their discontent with the director to the other cast members through suggestions of incompetence and insinuations that she was exploiting their time and expertise. A few cast members were becoming uncomfortable with these harsh judgments and negative comments, and the cast members began slowly to separate along racial lines. For the sake of the show and for the unity of the cast, the director attempted to address levels of their dissatisfaction. When she learned that the residents felt she was too authoritative and that they wanted more input, she asked for their help with tasks she thought would genuinely make them feel included. But, she was immediately accused of exploiting them and their time. When she learned they felt exploited, she suggested that other members from Cross Bridges assist them with the work they felt was siphoning their time and energy. But, the residents became angry and accused her of belittling their talents and capabilities. By the time the rehearsals had finally come to an end and the show opened, the accusations and animosity felt by the two residents toward the director had become so obvious that, for fear of splitting cast relations any further, the director felt it best to withdraw a bit from interacting with the cast members. When this happened, she was accused of not caring about the cast and attempting to claim all the credit for the success of the show.

Although all the cast members remained loyal to the project, there was a general feeling of tension and unease. Those who felt a strong allegiance to the company and the director resented the animosity and the insults, which had racial and sexist undertones toward the black female director and which were experienced not only backstage, behind the scenes, but also in the open space of rehearsals. However, at the strongly voiced request of the director, they never confronted the residents and continued rehearsals without any disagreement surfacing. However, the tensions were deeply felt.

Nia was deeply saddened, because the exalting experience of working with Cross Bridges now turned into a nightmare. There was a clash of values and, for Nia, the very goal of the Urban Arts Cross-Cultural Exchange had abysmally failed.

When the show finally ended, the two residents left Cross Bridges and the director vowed never to work with them again or to participate in the Urban Arts Exchange.

Nia's challenge as a critical ethnographer and a student of organizational communication was to interpret the provocative tensions and layers of conflicts she witnessed within the organization. She decided that her interpretive method would primarily draw from *feminist theory* and *critical race theory*.

Key Concepts in Theories of Difference: Race

Theories of difference are concerned with the histories, consequences, and contexts of what it means to be unlike the norm, the majority, the comprehended, or to be outside certain registers of power. Theories of difference that encompass how race, gender, and sexuality operate confront the complexities of identity, belonging, and language by and within realms of politics—and I use "politics" in the same way Ingraham (1997) does, to mean "all those social, material practices in which the distribution of power is at stake" (p. 290).

Difference is full of complexity. There are obviously differences within difference. Those who are of the same race but a different gender—or of the same gender but a different race—complicate any notion of a clean or neat division of difference. The same can be said of sexuality and class. There are differences within differences, yet there are profound realities of sameness across different divides. A poor, black, gay woman born outside the United States is multiply "different," and each difference matters more than the others depending on the particular context or situation she must confront. Yet, in certain circumstances, she may feel more affirmed in a gay community than in a black community, and in other circumstances she may feel more at home in a black community than in a feminist community. Differences both intersect and diverge depending on specific contexts; however, to be different is always to be positioned against a norm.

Nia turned to theoretical conceptualizations of race and gender to help guide her through her analysis. The following terms were central to her understanding of the complex dynamics and frictions that erupted during her fieldwork research.

Race, Essentialism, and Social Construction

Critical race theory begins with the presupposition that race does not exist solely as a biological fact and is therefore less a product of nature and more a product of social classification and identification. Therefore, it is the social, political, and cultural processes of classification and identification that constitute race or racialization (Torres, Miron, & Inda, 1999). For essentialist thinkers, the body occupies a pure presocial and prediscursive space. The essentialist-versus-constructionist debate concerns what constitutes the *natural* and what constitutes the *social*: "While the essentialist holds that the natural is repressed by the social, the constructionist maintains that the natural is produced by the social" (Torres et al., 1999, p. 6). Constructionists, however, reject the idea that there is a natural human determinant or an essential fact of existence that precedes social, economic, and political processes. However, the term *strategic essentialism* argues that there is no pure order or essence in what it means to be human, but rather that, as a "rhetorical maneuver," essentialism has its place (Fuss, 1989; Spivak, 1988). Therefore, strategic essentialism asserts that the use of essentialism for useful ends depends on who is using it and how it is being used, as well as to what purpose. The postcolonial critic Gayatri Spivak (1988) reminds us that we are born into nature and we are born into history, therefore essentialism can be powerful for the dispossessed. Thus, interrogating essentialism does not necessarily entail dismissing it. The problem, according to Spivak, is when it moves from something provisional to something permanent.

The concepts of race and social construction guided Nia in (a) analyzing how race became a barrier in communication between the residents and the director, all of whom believed themselves to hold no racial prejudices and who prided themselves on their sensitivity to and engagement with difference; (b) analyzing the very nuanced, convoluted, and obscured ways racism operated in the company through unconscious habit, naturalized practices, and white supremacy; and (c) providing a framework for understanding how the director, company members, and the residents are constructed as racial beings according to certain assumptions about their own race as well as the race of others.

Race, Structure, and Image

Understanding racialization as process or construction leads us away from thinking about race as simply "natural" or biological and leads us to thinking about the *power dynamics*—ideology, images, and institutional formations that hold race in place. This means that physical appearances of what people may look like in racial terms, how we enact and react to these appearances—classify and identify them—becomes a legal, political, social, and historical reality (Guillaumin, 1999, p. 45). Therefore, race is a "human construct based on ideology with regulatory power within society" (Solomos & Back, 1999, p. 68). As the argument for racial construction is made, pulling it away from biological determinism toward a more radical discussion of social and political power, we see how race is formed and embedded by class and economic stratifications. Making the point that racial difference is a prevailing feature of American life that is inherent in structures of hierarchy, the critic Stephen Small (1999) states,

> Racialized structures are the institutional pillars of society. They are the routine, recurrent and organized features of contemporary life. The idea of "racialized" structures has two key components. First, it refers to the distribution of valuable resources such as political power, employment, education and housing. Primarily this aspect involves who owns what, works and lives where, and has good health. Secondly, it refers to the normal, recurrent and routinized procedures of institutions that shape and constrain our daily lives, from politics (voting and political representatives), economics (businesses, employment), education (universities, schools) health (hospitals) and other spheres of social life (family, media, music, sport). These behaviors and actions sustain the distribution of resources. (p. 50)

With these words in mind, we may agree that racial categories are produced and reproduced by everyday American activities of inclusion and exclusion (Ong, 1982, p. 267), and we may also add that the economic and political implications of race are always simultaneously operating through images, values, and desires that are racially oriented. Critical race theory analyzes the complex machinations of racialization in the various ways it is created, sanctioned, and employed, but it also illuminates the various ways race is an effect of our imagination and how racial symbols and representations determine our understanding and attitudes about race in the first place. These racialized images and ideologies turn back to shape structure, just as structures shape us. The cultural critic Cornell West (1991) reminds us that structures are not simply economic and political creations; they influence desire and value. It is images, not ideas, that dominate. Racialization therefore becomes a reciprocal circling of institutional process and individual ideology, each shaping and empowering the other. This is a complex and often hidden circling.

The concept of structure and image was an elaboration upon Nia's analysis of race as construction, and guided Nia in (a) understanding how construction actually works and what the forces and factors in society are that contribute to the construction of race above and beyond others, (b) analyzing how structure and image are conceptualized in critical race theory as a means out of which the subjects in her study operated, and (c) understanding how image was key in articulating how representation in performance and popular culture informs identities and how they are treated as a result of representation.

Whiteness and Privilege

We must keep in mind that critical race theory is not simply directed at the racialization of so-called minority identities or the social constructions of people of color; the construction of *whiteness* is also under examination. Critical race theorists point out that whiteness is often perceived as nonracialized; they argue, however, that whiteness is in fact a construction of race and that it forms a structural position of racial privilege. The most ardent theorist on whiteness states,

> In contemporary social settings, whiteness has been identified as a core set of racial interests often obscured by seemingly race-neutral words, actions, or policies . . . the phrase *white culture* is proffered to convey the material relations of social structures that reproduce white privilege and racism in this country, quite apart from what individual whites may feel, think, and perceive. (Frankenberg, 1993, pp. 196–205; qtd. in Hartigan, 1997, p. 185)

Critical race theorists argue that "whiteness is a taken-for-granted experience based on varying 'supremacist assumptions' that are sometimes critical, sometimes biological, sometimes moral, sometimes all three" (Bonnett, 1997, p. 213). The repeated phrase in much of the literature on race theory is that "whites have privilege whether they want it or not." White privilege is often masked as neutral social arrangements and institutional operations that seem to have no basis (Bonnett, 1997). Michael Eric Dyson (2003) states, "The genius of unarticulated, invisible whiteness is that it was able to impose its particularist perspective as normative" (p. 40). In other words, not only does the very invisibility of whiteness or its seemingly racial neutrality operate through machinations of privilege for a particular group, but these machinations are masked, distorted, and instituted as being normative.

The discussion of whiteness pointed Nia toward (a) the unmarked and unnamed ways in which the residents, in manner and attitude, were not simply constituted by racial privilege but were, more importantly, so uncritical of the privilege they inherited that they behaved with arrogance and entitlement when a racialized Other was placed in a position of authority/power over them; (b) how white privilege does not necessarily equate with white supremacy or racist acts and how white members of the company from the same community as the residents were an integral and active part of the company; and (c) an analytical framework upon which she could articulate the ingrained assumptions of white supremacy, particularly when supremacy becomes in tension with racialized Others where its own (unconscious) superiority is impeded.

Key Concepts in Theories of Difference: Gender

Nia also employed the next set of terms to unravel the very discreet but penetrating ways the problems of gender surfaced in her fieldwork.

Feminism and Power

Generally, feminist theory is concerned with power differences between men and women and how these differences impact the public and private domains of our lives (Butler, 1990; hooks, 1990; Warren 2003; Weedon, 1987; Wood, 2005). Feminist theory is concerned with gender inequities and "who does what and for whom, what we are and what we might become" (Weedon, 1987, p. 1). With the understanding that sex usually refers to biological differences between the male body and the female body, feminist theory focuses on how these differences are performed, hierarchically classified, and materially arranged in the social world.

Feminists have also been in tension over the struggle for representation and membership in dominant institutions at one end, and the struggle to dismantle or eliminate the very foundations of these institutions on the other. Many feminists feel the feminist movement lost its significance when it ceased in great measure to condemn patriarchal systems and focused more on the empowerment of a few women. This is certainly the case with certain feminist researchers, whose narrow understanding of empowerment does not consider broader implications for women who are not the same race, ethnicity, or nationality. Achola Pala (1977) states,

I have visited villages where, at a time when the village women are asking for better health facilities and lower infant mortality rates, they are presented with questionnaires on family planning. In some instances, when the women would like to have piped water in the village, they may be at the same time faced with a researcher interested in investigating power and powerlessness in the household. In yet another situation, when women are asking for access to agricultural credit, a researcher on the scene may be conducting a study on female circumcision. (p. 10; qtd. in Carby, 1997, p. 123)

The researcher's notion of empowerment does not comply with that of the women she is researching or their needs. Therefore, the researcher's notion of empowerment does not take into account the very institutional mechanisms that disempower the subject of her research. The controversy over women, empowerment, and what constitutes a feminist perspective that incorporates a broader and more useful agenda for women can be traced by what has been described as the three movements or waves in the development of women's rights. The first concerns itself with women's inclusion and access to institutions that had historically been denied women. In this case, the concern was for the liberty and freedom of women to enter the doors of these institutions and structures and to be represented in them, but not necessarily to change the structures themselves. The second movement or wave was also concerned about access and membership, but it was also concerned with the transformation of the structures themselves relative to discrimination practices at multiple levels (e.g., women, family, race, sexuality, economic inequities, and the environment). Second-wavers were interested in transforming institutions to make them more just, to build a more equitable society. The third wave, however, for many contemporary feminists is more global in perspective and more visionary in its concern for overlapping oppressions of difference. (I shall describe it below through the concepts of *material feminism* and *ecofeminism*.)

Feminist theory aided Nia in (a) addressing the interpenetrating domains of race and gender, particularly because the director was Othered by both race and gender; (b) analyzing discrimination, relative to the residents, as an intermix of race and gender; and (c) analyzing how patriarchal structures and practices position and discipline women with narrow choices—as a black female director, was she outside the domestic and patriarchal boundaries or women's work?

Material Feminism and Ecofeminism

The "material" in material feminism means the emphasis is on divisions of labor and the distribution of wealth both nationally and internationally, as well as how meaning and value (relative to freedom and opportunity) are constituted globally. Material feminism responds to pressing global issues of inequality and exploitation, as well as charges by so-called third-world feminists and people of color around the world that feminism in the West is out of touch with the struggles and debates outside the interests of white, middle-class, heterosexual women in the United States and Europe (Minh-ha, 1989; Mohanty, 1984). Chrys Ingraham (1997) states,

> This call for an international re-evaluation of western feminism intersected with the circulation of newly forming critical knowledges such as Afrocentrism, post colonial criticism, post structuralism, neo-Marxism, postmodernism, and brought about a rethinking of feminist concepts and politics. Throughout the struggles and debates within feminism over the past 20 years, materialist feminists have continually worked to develop an analytic capable of disrupting the taken-for-granted in local and global social arrangements and of exposing the economic, political, ideological conditions upon which exploitation and oppression depend. (pp. 276–277)

As a form of critical postmodernism, materialist feminism argues that the interlocking web of patriarchy, capitalism, heteronormativity, and racism are neither abstract nor isolated, but they are interpenetrating and ubiquitous as they interact at varying levels and degrees in regulating our everyday lives.

Ecofeminism

Karen J. Warren (2003), one of the leading proponents of ecofeminism, describes ecofeminism as feminism that employs gender analysis "to describe, analyze, and resolve the varieties of ways in which the unjustified domination of women and other subordinated groups of humans (human other) has historically been interconnected with the unjustified domination of 'nature' (nonhuman animals and the nonhuman environment)" (p. 5). Ecofeminism is both a theory and a social movement that is concerned with the very nature and practice of oppression in all its formations. The feminist communication scholar Julia T. Wood (2005) states,

> Ecofeminists believe that domination and oppression are wrong and destructive of all forms of life, including the planet. . . . For ecofeminists, oppression itself, not particular instances of oppression, it the primary issue. They believe that, as long as oppression is culturally valued, it will be imposed on anyone and anything that cannot or does not resist. Thus, women's oppression is best understood as a specific example of an overarching cultural ideology that idolizes oppression in general. (p. 71)

Ecofeminism is a more radical position than traditional forms of feminism in its emphasis upon social justice relative to multiplication of oppression and their interconnectedness. Again, Wood states,

> The goals of this movement flow directly from its critique of cultural values. Ecofeminists seek to bring themselves and others to a new consciousness of human's interdependence with all other life forms. To do so, they speak out against values that encourage exploitation, domination, and aggression and show how these oppress women, men, children, animals, plants, and the planet itself. (p. 72)

Although all ecofeminists do not agree, across the board, on points of emphasis and the urgencies given to certain oppressive practices over others, "all ecofeminists agree that many environmental issues have a gender dimension and that many gender issues have an environmental dimension" (Warren, 2003, p. 6).

As a critical ethnographer, Nia felt that she wanted to include a feminist analysis that also especially addressed issues of class and the political economy, because one of the missions of the theatre company was to inspire and promote economic justice in the community. Because the director was a black woman and because her performance dealt with issues related to the local/global nexus, it was important for Nia to include a feminist analysis that went beyond the racial and gender conflict with the residents to provide a deeper and more comprehensive examination of the feminist politics of the director. Nia was careful not to make the conflict with the residents the full story. Because the director played a significant role in Nia's research, it was necessary for Nia to understand the philosophy that guided the director's artistic productions. As a critical ethnographer, Nia understood she could not provide a substantive analysis if she did not study the theoretical principles that guided one of the central subjects of her study; therefore, examining gender and difference from a global perspective was important.

Warm-Ups

1. How might the theoretical concepts organized under each individual case study be applied and extended to the other case studies? For example, can Nia borrow certain concepts from postcolonial theory in her analysis of the community theatre company? How can Robert use Marxist theory in his project? Discuss how specific concepts may be especially relevant to your project and/or other interpretive questions relating to critical fieldwork.

2. What might be additional theoretical questions or key concepts from the case studies that interest you and therefore motivate you to do further reading in a particular theory?

Note

1. This excerpt is from an actual field interview I conducted in the winter of 2000 in Ghana, West Africa. The excerpt is from a political activist describing the position of local farmers in his village in Northern Ghana and their struggle with big agricultural businesses and fair trade.

Suggested Readings

Anzaldua, G. (1987). *Borderlands/la frontera: The new mestiza*. San Francisco: Aunt Lute.

Appiah, K. (1992). *In my father's house: Africa in the philosophy of culture*. London: Methuen.

Beauvoir, S. de (1952). *The second sex* (H. M. Parshley, Trans.). New York: Knopf.

Bhabha, H. K. (1994). *The location of culture*. New York: Routledge.

Blair, C., Brown, J. R., & Baxter, L. A. (1995). Disciplining the feminine. *Quarterly Journal of Speech, 81*, 1–24.

Dewey, J. (1948). *Reconstruction in philosophy*. Boston: Beacon.

Fuss, D. (1991). *Inside/out: Lesbian theories, gay theories*. New York: Routledge.

Gill, G. C. (1993). *Sexes and genealogies*. New York: Columbia University Press.

Grosz, E., & Probyn, E. (1995). *Sexy bodies: The strange carnalities of feminism*. New York: Routledge.

Ignatiev, N. (1995). *How the Irish became white*. New York: HarperCollins.

Jackson, J. L. (2001). *Harlemworld: Doing race and class in contemporary Black America*. Chicago: University of Chicago Press.

Johnson, E. P. (2003). *Appropriating blackness*. Durham, NC: Duke University Press.

Marx, K. (1983). *The portable Karl Marx* (E. Kamenka, Ed.). New York: Penguin.

Scott, J. C. (1990). *Domination and the arts of resistance*. Hartford, CT: Yale University Press.

Shome, R. (2003). Space matters: The power and practice of space. *Communication Theory,* 13:39–56.

Shome, R., & Radha, S. H. (2002). Postcolonial approaches to communication: Charting the terrain, engaging the intersections. *Communication Theory,* 12:249–270.

Spivak, G. C. (1999). *A Critique of postcolonial reason*. Cambridge, MA: Harvard University Press.

Warren, J. T. (2003). *Performing purity: Pedagogy, whiteness, and the (re)constitution of power*. New York: Peter Lang.

Wood, J. T. (2005). *Gendered lives: Communication, gender, and culture* (6th ed.). Belmont, CA: Wadsworth.

4

Ethics

If I had to choose, I'd rather sink with the atheists who say they don't believe in God, yet love God's children, and show it with the work they do and in their compassion for the vulnerable, than rise with believers whose view of God is shriveled and vicious, and who punish others, and themselves, ultimately, with hard-hearted moralizing, and a cruel indifference to the suffering of the unwashed that grows from the despotic ill-tempered of the self-righteous.

—Reverend Michael Eric Dyson,
The Michael Eric Dyson Reader (2004)

This section of the book provides a comprehensive examination of the complex and ubiquitous question of ethics. The three chapters in this section encompass three distinct frameworks for our entry into the domains of ethics. This chapter is an overview of key moments, ideas, and debates in Western moral philosophy as they relate to critical ethnography. This chapter also examines alternative views to Western moral philosophy and contemporary discussions of ethics with a particular emphasis on Maria Lugones's (1994) notion of *loving perception and world traveling.*

Chapter 5 turns from the philosophical examinations of ethics presented in this chapter to the more practical rules and guidelines for ethical practices that are outlined in the codes of ethics for the fields of anthropology, sociology, and folklore. After reviewing the history, definitions, philosophy, and institutional guidelines that constitute Chapters 4 and 5, respectively,

Chapter 6 will bring it all together by putting these discussions into practice and returning to our three fictional case studies. We will meet Joan, Robert, and Nia again, this time observing the ethical dilemmas they found themselves confronting in their fieldwork and how they worked to resolve them.

Defining Ethics

Ethics is concerned with the principles of right and wrong. Questions of morality and what it means to be honorable, to embrace goodness, to perform virtuous acts, to generate goodwill, and to choose justice above injustice constitute the study of ethics. To study ethics is also to contemplate norms and standards for human behavior, as well as to examine and classify the meanings and effects of moral statements and judgments. Part of being human is expressing beliefs and principles upon which we judge human action; moreover, most of us suffer when our principals are in conflict with our actions (Magee, 2001; Norman, 1997; Robinson & Garratt, 1999; Taylor, 1978). Being attentive to ethics is a challenging and compelling undertaking, because it evokes deeper questions about the *ends* or resulting ideal we as human beings desire for the ethical life or the ethical act: What does the ethical act really look like? How are my ethics different or the same as yours? What principles will guide the *means* or method for us to achieve the ethical ends that we desire? How do we determine what is ethical?

Understanding that ethics is both a subject of philosophical inquiry and a way of being in the world, we may connect the nature and properties of knowledge and discourse about ethics with the nature and properties of its actual existence and operations in the day-to-day. When we bring knowledge and existence together, we might ask which comes first. Are we good because we have a knowledge of goodness that directs us toward being good in the world? Or does bad knowledge distort the essential goodness within human nature, directing us to becoming morally flawed? Are we innately good—or innately bad, the bearers of original sin? Do knowledge and society make the good turn bad or the bad turn good?

Another perspective on ethics is the belief that our environment determines our behavior and directs us to behave rightly or wrongly. Are we all products of our society? But what, then, of free will? The counter view is that we are endowed with freedom to choose. We are autonomous individuals with the capacity to choose, even under dire circumstances, between good and bad. We are therefore responsible for our choices and must either pay the consequences or reap the rewards. Are we social objects or social beings? Karl Marx (1977) reminds us that people are always constructing their realities, but never completely on their own terms. Is it nature or nurture that guides ethical behavior?

To address the meaning of ethics as it relates to critical ethnography, we will now turn to a few more fundamental and enduring questions on the principles of right and wrong and the demand for moral action. We will discuss an *ethics of ethnography*, by which I mean how specific traditional and timeworn debates surrounding morality (e.g., human nature, justice, reason, the divine, and the Other) relate particularly to the ethnographic enterprise. An ethics of ethnography probes the question, What are the moral and ethical *implications* of conducting fieldwork?

Where Did the Notion of Ethics Begin?

Cultures all over the world embrace ethical principles and practices. The notion of ethics has its starting point all over the world and throughout time. Various ideas on ethics may be traced in the myths, religious traditions, and historical archives of cultures from East to West. In the West, one of the first thinkers to contemplate ethics and teach moral philosophy through a more systematic method was Socrates. Although Socrates was not the first human being in the world to ponder and to communicate virtue, morality, and ethics to others, his life and teachings have become a universal prototype when considering the foundations of ethics. Socrates may well have been one of the first critical ethnographers in the West.

On the death of Socrates, Plato (2000) wrote of his teacher in *Phaedo*, "This was the end [Socrates], of our friend; a man of whom we may say that of all whom we met at that time he was the wisest and justest [sic] and best." Socrates' famous adage that the *unexamined life is not worth living* is an ancient call for the necessity of an ethics of self-reflective questioning. For Socrates, ethics is *life* and its relationship to *goodness*—and thereby to virtue and justice—that constitutes the "good life" and that must always be engaged and valued through deeper and more complex questions. Although Socrates did not leave any written work, we know of his ideas through his circle of admirers and students—particularly through Plato (1999, 2000a, 2000b). We know he went about Athens asking all kinds of questions about morality, ethics, and politics, provoking conversations and debates to anyone and everyone who was interested. Examination for Socrates was dependent on the persistence and the capacity to ask unending questions, and all knowledge worth knowing proceeds from seminal questions. For Socrates, you ask questions to understand what is being asked; you ask more questions to determine what answers are the most satisfactory; you ask even more questions to understand the answers.

Although he is understood as the perennial questioner, Socrates still held certain immutable beliefs regarding ethics. First was his ethics of knowing. He believed that human beings do not *knowingly* do *wrong,* and if they know something is wrong, they will not do it; therefore, knowledge breeds virtue and goodness (Plato, 2000b, Bk. I–IV). To question is to be a seeker of knowledge and a seeker of "doing the right thing." Second was his ethics of the virtuous soul. He believed that human beings may suffer through unbearable hardships of devastating proportions, but that to maintain one's integrity through the despair is to maintain a beautiful and righteous soul. He believed it is the perpetrator of evil that must be pitied, not the victim, because it is the victim whose soul is pure (Plato, 2000b, Bk. X). Third, Socrates held that morality is present in the world and exists as part of the human soul. How we are to understand the existence and operation of morality is worth knowing for its own sake and for the sake of knowledge itself, because existence and knowledge are inseparable from the aim of *doing* good (Plato, 2000b, Bk. X).

While Socrates had a following of male devotees, to the state and to the majority of Athenians his incessant questioning of power, virtue, and justice made him a heretic and a disruptive influence, corrupting the youth and causing trouble. He was condemned to death in 399 BCE and charged with being "an evil-doer and a curious person, searching into things under the earth and above the heaven; and making the worse appear the better cause, and teaching all this to others" (Plato, 1909). Because of his belief in the integrity of the virtuous soul, when given the opportunity, Socrates did not abandon his teaching to save his life.

Socrates and an Ethics of Critical Ethnography

I begin with Socrates in our discussion of *defining ethics* because he represents one of the first ethicist to demonstrate through his life and teachings the power of *the question,* of *critical reflection,* and of *resisting domestication.*

The moral bedrock of fieldwork is always the question. To question, in Socratic terms, is an ethical endeavor, because the ethnographer employs the question, honestly, to acquire insight and valuable information and less to interrogate or judge other human beings. Yet the critical ethnographer's fieldwork question most often leads to the interrogation of and judgments about institutions and regimes of knowledge and power. The fieldwork question acknowledges with both humility and a direct(ed) interest that I do not know, and I am a "knower" in search of something "known." The fieldwork question is *provocative* and ethically responsible, because it has the potential to unsettle the taken-for-granted, to open critical awareness, and to remember what was forgotten.

If as Socrates said that the unexamined life is not worth living, one of the greatest attributes of the critical ethnographer is the need for critical self-reflection in our contribution to help make life worth living for ourselves and Others. To examine one's own life and intentions—to question and observe the self—in the process of questioning and interacting with Others is an ethical stance, because it requires consistent self-evaluation and monitoring relative to our integrity, effectiveness, and political commitment toward the end of helping make life more worth living.

Socrates and activists for justice in various corners of the world who resist those in power and the authority of state oppression resist domestication by questioning the legitimacy of the status quo and opening alternative possibilities for what ought to be and what can be. To understand our work as "critical" ethnography or "ethnography with a political purpose" requires a serious engagement with ethics and the recognition that politics cannot stand outside ethics. Socrates embraced the dynamic and radical force of the question above and beyond what can become the closed stagnation of the claim. Critical questions ignite thought and will, and as critical ethnographers we must ask to what ethical *end* and *means* does our work aspire.

What Constitutes an Ethical or Moral Act?

As critical ethnographers, we are compelled to act morally; in other words, we feel the responsibility to make *a difference in the world*—to contribute to the quality of life and to the enlivening possibilities of those we study. The emphasis on the "critical" in critical ethnography means that our inquiries and our intent will always already encompass moral action. Immanuel Kant (1724–1804) argued that the difference between a moral action and a nonmoral action was based upon a sense of duty. Morality is not reflected in the *inclination* to do good, but in the sense of *duty* to do good (Kant, 1991). Therefore, Kant is a deontologist, a believer in duty as the determination for morality. This means sacrificing what we *want* to do for what we *ought* do. In the search to establish fundamental moral duties or "compulsory moral rules," Kant believed we must employ reason. It is reason or the rational being that chooses to do what he ought to do rather than to act from inclination or self-interest. The purpose of reason is not to produce happiness, but to produce good will. Kant (1947) states,

> If adversity and hopeless sorrow have completely taken away the relish for life; if the unfortunate one, strong in mind, indignant at his fate rather than desponding or dejected, wishes for death, and yet preserves his life without loving it—not from inclination or fear, but from duty,—then his maxim has a moral worth. (pp. 12–14)

Kant's ethics of duty and reason include three additional moral principals: (1) human beings as *ends* and not *means*, (2) the *categorical imperative*, and (3) the *moral imagination*. First, Kant believed that human beings should never be used or maltreated as a means to an end, but should be seen as an end for their direct benefit and well being (Kant, 1947). Second, the categorical imperative is the universal application of the good deed; that is, just as universal law and reason govern the empirical sphere, so must universal law and reason govern the moral sphere. The categorical imperative demands that, in identical circumstances, the good deed that applies to you must apply to everyone. Third, morality for Kant is also dependent on a moral imagination. Kant suggests that when one faces a moral dilemma or questions the morality of an act, one may arrive at the answer by imagining oneself on the receiving end of the action. The immoral agent, therefore, should imagine himself being the victim of his own actions. Kant is suggesting that immorality may be due in part to a lack of imagination.

Kant and an Ethics of Critical Ethnography

For the critical ethnographer, Kant provides interesting challenges concerning reason and duty. The Western preoccupation with reason as a quintessential virtue has been widely criticized, and we will take up this critique later in this chapter. However, Kant's plea that reason must be at the service of good will is a useful point of departure for an ethics of ethnography.

We employ reason as critical ethnographers, but we do so with the good will in knowing that we must be circumspect and self-reflexive of the varying contexts that require and define different values and motivations for reason. To act with reason in one context may be to act without reason in another. To identify one category of human beings as having a special capacity for reason over other categories of humans is considered reasonable by some and harmfully unreasonable by many others.

Duty above all else is another controversial concept that has been justly criticized, yet it raises interesting questions for critical ethnographers regarding our ethical duty or our sense of duty for the greater good of the project and the individuals we study over our own personal interest, comfort, or pleasure. As critical ethnographers, our commitment to social justice becomes an ethical duty of the first priority based on social change and the well being of Others. Most of us part with Kant because it is not the virtue of pure duty or duty for duty's sake that guides our commitment, but rather the heartfelt desire to work for change. If I see a man mercilessly beating a dog, I do not stop him at the risk of my own safety because I feel it is my duty, but because of my inner compassion for the suffering.

An ethics of critical ethnography does not use human beings as a means to an end. We do not gain rapport and trust to simply get the data and then run in order to accomplish our own goals while leaving subjects vulnerable or feeling exploited. An ethics of ethnography considers the direct well being of the Other as the first priority. *Categorical imperative* and *moral imagination* are philosophical terms that may be appropriated to help us better understand and embody an ethics of empathy.

What Is the Relationship Between Religion and Ethics?

Religion serves to systematize, codify, and govern moral understanding. Human beings have universally turned to religion as the ultimate source for moral guidance and action. Much of the world does not believe that morality is invented or sustained by human will and consciousness alone, but that morality is contingent upon divine principles.

St. Thomas Aquinas (1224–1274), considered one of the greatest medieval theologians, adopted the philosophy that ethics are necessary for the common good of all, not just those in power or the elite. Ethics must reflect "natural law," which is bestowed on humanity by God (Aquinas, 1947). Aquinas maintained that government or secular law was necessary to ensure order and accommodate social life, but that it alone cannot inspire people to be good or do good. Furthermore, if secular law is not in accordance with God's natural law, people have the right and responsibility to disobey it. St. Thomas Aquinas (1947) wrote, "A Law, properly speaking, regards first and foremost the order to the common good" (1st Pt. of 2nd Pt., Q. 90, Art. 3). He goes on to explain why this is true: "Hence, the making of a law belongs either to the whole people or to a public personage who has care of the whole people; for in all other matters the directing of anything to the end concerns him to whom the end belongs . . ." (1st Pt. of 2nd Pt., Q. 90, Art. 3).

Aquinas sees ethics as a reflection of God's natural law, but what is important for the critical ethnographer is his or her position that (a) ethics must be based upon the common good for all, not just the elite, and (b) natural law or principles of ethics supercedes the law of the state: if common good is jeopardized, the state must be challenged. Another relevant moral philosopher merging ethics and religion who is helpful to the critical ethnographer is Benedict Spinoza (1632–1677). Spinoza works from the viewpoint that all that exists is within the realm of the godly. Everything that exists—man, animal, vegetable, mineral, and thought—make up the complex unity that is God. In his classic work *Ethics* (1999), Spinoza wrote, "God or in other words, Nature" (qtd. in Magee, 2001, p. 91). God, for Spinoza, is not outside the world of Plato's spaceless/timeless Ideal Forms, nor is God a force moving around in the world: God *is* the world itself. For Spinoza, existence is a single interconnected system that is synonymous with God. He is a pantheist, and his ethics dictates that God is boundless existence. Spinoza believes that human beings should not dwell on their personal problems, but should compare them to the totality of all things. Doing so will help us to bear them and to understand how insignificant they are to this totality. We should look at our own lives through the eyes of eternity. As part of an interconnected system, we cannot dwell on the self, but must learn and understand from this divine and intricate union with existence: "I have striven not to laugh at human action, not to weep at them, not to hate them, but to understand them" (Spinoza, 1999, chap. 1., sect. 4). Spinoza was the first Western philosopher to present a case for freedom of speech, and he maintained that "the true aim of government is liberty" (Magee, 2001, p. 95).

St. Thomas Aquinas, Benedict Spinoza, and an Ethics of Ethnography

Aquinas and Spinoza extend an ethics of critical ethnography to the realm of the divine and merge religion with politics. Both philosophers suggest a form of liberation theology, as they advocate for free speech and principles of democracy.

If the cultures, communities, and the lives we strive to understand are in some way divinely connected, we must keep in mind that what we witness will always have deeper, more layered, and broader implications, conse-quences, and contexts than we could ever grasp or interpret in the space of our lifetime. To assert that this interconnectedness is divine then opens the discussion of ethics and the need for thick description that moves from the secular to the possibility of the sacred. What does it mean for the criti-cal ethnographer to feel ethically compelled to understand the connected-ness of life and culture because this connectedness is viewed as a sacred phenomenon?

Set forth by these two men is the immensely powerful idea that, as Magee (2001) states, the "true aim of government is liberty." This assertion has been a cornerstone of ethical discourse and the ideal of the greatest good. Spinoza's charge of liberty and Aquinas's charge that laws belong to the people whom they are meant to rule are another command to us as critical ethnographers: What would the world look like if the true aim of all gov-ernments were freedom? How does our work contribute to the ideal of democracy in the various spaces and places where we work?

Do We Need Religion or a
Belief in the Divine for Ethical Behavior?
Is It the Nature of Human Beings to Be Good?

Religion provides mythic answers and master narratives for moral rules and their origin. However, philosophers have argued that religion alone cannot account for morality or ethical behavior. They believe that the idea of a set of rules cast down from a divine power to be faithfully obeyed does not address the potential for compassion and love harbored innately in the human soul, nor does it address the immense good deeds and benevolence of so many individuals who are not religious.

For Jean-Jacque Rousseau (1712–1778), human beings are naturally moral beings with the potential and capacity for goodness. Rousseau also goes against the prevailing enlightenment view of reason and logic as the foundation for progress and liberty. He states, "Man was born free, and everywhere he is in chains" (Rousseau, 1762, p. 2). Rousseau claims that man is the most perfect in his free, natural state, without the confines and contamination of civilization. He believes that it was civilization that distorts and corrupts man's morality and natural innocence; it is emotion and instincts that should prevail over reason in guiding one's life and life choices. For Rousseau (1762), "Man is naturally good. It is only institutions that make him bad" (Bk. 1). It was Rousseau who popularized the term *noble savage* to mean the purity, virtue, and innocence of primitive man against the evil restrictions of law, education, and civilization. Rousseau is also considered an avid anti-individualist. He is an advocate for the idea of a *general will*. His idea is that citizens should express their will as a collective body in order to form a social contract—a general will—that will take precedence over the individual will of its members (Bk. 1). He goes on to demand that, if there are individual objections, they must be subordinated to the general and collective will of all (Bks. 1–3).

Rousseau's views on emotion above reason form an interesting comparison to the moral philosophy of David Hume (1711–1776). Like Rousseau, Hume privileges emotions over reason and feels that reason is the slave of emotion. Also like Rousseau, Hume is not a supporter of organized religion. Rousseau (1762) feels that religion should come from the heart, not rules, commandments, or dogma (Bk. 2); Hume (1985) takes it a step further by claiming that there is no observable evidence or experience that God exists. Hume's contribution to moral philosophy is threefold. First, he argues, based on the empiricist premise, that no knowledge is valid unless it is based on observable experiences, whether it is our own or another individual's.

Second, he asserts that all that we experience—including and most importantly knowledge—comes through our senses, feelings, and emotions, and therefore we cannot use logic or reason to prove our moral beliefs are just or true. Hume (1985) writes, "Reason is and ought only to be the slave of the passions, and can never pretend to any other office than to serve and obey them" (Bk. 2, Pt. 3; qtd. in Denise, Peterfreund, & White, 1996, p. 165). What constitutes our moral beliefs and ethics, according to Hume, are psychological and opposed to logic. He states, "It is not contrary to reason to prefer the destruction of the whole world to the scratching of my finger" (Hume, 1985, Bk. 2, Pt. 3, sect. 3, chap. 63; qtd. in Denise et al., 1996, p. 165). Third, for Hume, the most productive use of understanding ethics is to study how we conceptualize and analyze ethics through meta-ethics—through a study of the meaning and function of moral language, how this moral language is employed to define, debate, and judge the meaning and value of morality.

Jean-Jacque Rousseau, David Hume, and an Ethics of Ethnography

Rousseau's idea of humankind as naturally good and virtuous without the interference of divine belief or religion, combined with his view of the noble savage existing without the contamination of civilization, law, and education, raises ethical questions for the critical ethnographer regarding human nature and institutional control.

An ethics of ethnography is consistently concerned with the influences of institutions on culture and human behavior. Rousseau and Hume are among the early thinkers who promote the idea of human behavior as innately good and human emotions as far superior to logic. What are the implications for ethics when ideas of human nature enter into our ethnographic accounts, particularly when human nature is held as being under constant threat of civilization, modernity, or even progress?

As an anti-individualist, Rousseau believes in the collective will. An ethics of ethnography is steadfast in efforts to weigh the importance of individual freedom with the general good. Rousseau presents us with the perennial question: Shouldn't the welfare for all supercede the welfare of one?

Hume's strict empiricism has been debated across the humanities and social sciences. The belief that knowledge is valid only when it comes from observed experience and direct observation and that all we experience comes from our senses, feelings, and emotions is a position that is still being promoted on the one hand, and contested on the other in varies forms. As ethnographers, we are by the nature of our work at home in the empirical domain. As critical ethnographers concerned with ethical practices we are faced with how we must critique, advocate, and communicate the multifarious forms presented in the empirical world that are not always experienced through our senses. How do we account for realities and "truths" in the field that we cannot observe or experience due to our own biases, lack of cultural knowledge, or insights? Does that mean those truths or realities do not exist simply because we do not see them?

Hume's emphasis on meta-ethics—that is, on studying the language and discourses relative to the subject of ethics—is the very purpose of this section. Meta-ethics constitutes moral philosophy and the wide-ranging implications and assumptions of goodness and virtue. I briefly present selected viewpoints and questions on ethics and morality in this chapter: do these viewpoints help you consider the ethical implications of critical ethnography?

Where Is Evil Positioned in the Idea of Ethics?

Niccolo Machiavelli's (1469–1527) *The Prince* (1914) serves as a prototypical examination of power and practical politics, or *realpolitik* (a German word for tough politics). It is an examination of how men behave in order to achieve and maintain political force and authority. Machiavelli writes of what men *actually do* in the face of both justice and injustice; he is less concerned with what they *ought to do*. In the *Discourse* (1985), he writes, "It is necessary for him who lays out a State and arranges laws for it to presuppose that all men are evil and that they are always going to act according to the wickedness of their spirits whenever they have free scope" (Bk. I, chap. 3; qtd. in Ashby, 1997, p. 271). Machiavelli asserts that to be a truly outstanding leader, immorality becomes necessary. The prince—the leader—must certainly be courageous and virtuous, but to rule necessitates betrayal, cheating, and even murder. In *The Prince*, he states, "Men should be either treated generously or destroyed, because they take revenge for slight injuries—for heavy ones they can not" (pp. 272–275).

Machiavelli's philosophy of government can be juxtaposed to the idea of the egoism articulated by Thomas Hobbes (1588–1679). Hobbes argues that man is motivated by his own self-love and self-interest. Therefore, man is naturally miserable, selfish, violent, and cruel. For the egoist, one must be moral only "because it is the best way to achieve your own long range interests" (Hobbes, 1996; qtd. in Taylor, 1978, p. 98). Morality must be imposed and, in order for this to happen, there must be an absolute and central authority whose responsibility it is to impose the law and to severely punish those that defy it. This sovereign power, according to Hobbes, must be established for the greater good of all. Morality for Hobbes was a means for the wicked but reasoning human being to avoid warfare and strife; therefore, human beings need a strong government to protect themselves from their own innate wickedness (Hobbes, 1996; also in Magee, 2001; Taylor, 1978). Hobbes believed that what people fear more than dictatorship is social chaos and disorder.

Machiavelli, Hobbes, and an Ethics of Ethnography

In contrast to Rousseau's and Hume's philosophy of innate goodness, Hobbes's and Machiavelli's views of humankind as innately "wicked" and "selfish" challenges an ethics of ethnography, arguing for an ominous or dubious power and acts of self-interests, both on the part of the ethnographer and on the part of the subjects. The perspectives reflected in the writings of Machiavelli and Hobbes are helpful to the critical ethnographer in contemplating ethics in the midst of malevolent actions and morally flawed situations.

If we believe the "true aim of government is liberty," but in the field we experience human beings exploiting one another through deceit, greed, acts of cruelty, or benign neglect, what part does an ethics of ethnography play in interpreting such behavior? The critical ethnographer may encounter field situations where power and abuse are sometimes rationalized as necessary evils, needed to contain chaos and control what is projected as the irrational nature of human beings. There are those who follow an ancient tradition of confining women and girls to labor in religious shrines against their will without compensation for their work, believing it is a divine sacrifice and God's will. As a critical ethnographer, what is your ethical responsibility in representing their beliefs? And what happens when the critical ethnographer observes herself inadvertently participating in acts that are not guided by the direct well-being of the Other, but by self-interest and personal gain? How is self-interest in the field even defined and identified?

* * *

A concentration on ethics is fundamental to critical ethnography, because we are involved in entering into the domains of Others and in the interpretive practice of both representing them and the multiple ways they construct their experiences and their worlds. And, because ethnographers are in the business of both crossing borders and representation, the power and the politics of their enterprise demands ethical responsibility. As stated in Chapters 1 and 2, what we say and write about Others has material effects. Therefore, as ethnographers, our acts and our words have implications beyond ourselves and are part of a larger web of human connections. Linda Alcoff (1991) reminds us that "the declaration that I 'speak only for myself' has the sole effect of allowing me to avoid responsibility and accountability for my effects on others; It cannot literally erase those effects" (p. 20). She then goes on to explain why this is true: "It is a metaphysical illusion that one can only speak for oneself: We are collectively caught in an intricate, delicate, web in which each action I take, discursively or otherwise, pulls on, breaks off, or maintains the tension in many strands of web in which others find themselves moving also" (p. 20).

Critical ethnography, in its very charge to enunciate and clarify the obscurities of injustices and then to thoughtfully offer just alternatives, must be deliberate in its ethical responsibility to carry forth that charge. Hall's (1992) caution regarding the material consequences of representation are manifest in the manner that our interpretations and representations may have implications at varying levels of public policy, community relations, accessibility to crucial resources, advocacy, and empowerment, as well as the protection and preservation of human dignity and life. When we enter the field, we enter the life world of Others, and we enter with the ethical intent to do good.

Critical Ethnography and the Ethics of Reason, the Greater Good, and the Other

In this section, we take up three points of provocation that present interesting challenges to an ethics of ethnography: the privileging of reason, the aspirations of the greater good, and the relationship with the Other.

Reason

One of the major criticisms of Western moral philosophy indicts Immanuel Kant and focuses on the definition and the designation of reason. Because in much Western moral philosophy, reason is the measure for human worth and value (some human beings by nature are capable of reason and other human beings by nature are not), reason becomes the justification for designating certain human beings as more worthy and more valuable than other human beings. Historically, rationality became the barometer of superiority and inferiority. Humanity, goodness, and justice were reserved for those who were seen as capable by nature of reason. Moreover, the idea of universalism was contingent upon the designation of reason.

Critical race theorist and philosopher Lucious Outlaw (1995) contends that universalism in Western moral philosophy in actuality operated under marginality and exclusion: "Universalism was reason-prepared, by both classical and modern Enlightenments, to handle diversity through reason-privileged hierarchy" (p. 315). The universal may imply everyone, but everyone is not equally human, as Outlaw further states: "The Aristotelian strategy, building on Socrates, Plato, and others, who identified reason as a definitive feature of human animals, proved decisive, particularly in defining human diversity as a function of different natures" (p. 311). He continues by asserting that this notion of the universal, which was not universal in the truest sense but based on "reason-privileged hierarchies," was to last through the centuries in the transformation of Europe and the founding of the United States:

> It was useful for some church thinkers during the Middle ages and was put to work during the Enlightenment . . . the strategy to universalism was elaborated into explicit accounts of human nature that were to contribute to major political transformations that revolutionized Europe and what became America during the seventeenth and eighteenth centuries. (p. 311)

Many of these philosophers, while preoccupied with contemplations of reason, morality, and virtue, were also blatantly contradictory. G. W. F. Hegel (1770–1831), who serves as an example, "was to become one of Germany's and Europe's most famous philosophers, and helped to nurture a complex of ideas that rationalized European racism" (Outlaw, 1995, p. 326). According to Hegel (1956),

> The Negro . . . exhibits the natural man in his completely wild and untamed state. We must lay aside all thought of reverence and morality—all that we call feeling—if we would rightly comprehend him; there is nothing harmonious with humanity to be found in this type of character. . . . At this point, we leave Africa, not to mention it again. For it is no historical part of the world; it has no movement or development to exhibit. Egypt will be considered in reference to the passage of her human mind from its Eastern to its Western phase, but it does not belong to the African Spirit. (pp. 91–99)[1]

Hegel's denigration of the "Negro" and Africa are not simply idiosyncratic to his individual thinking, but part of a system of thinking. This system of thinking is an element of the history and foundation of Western moral philosophy. Feminist philosopher Elizabeth V. Spellman (1988), in her assessment of Plato and Aristotle, states they were "inegalitarian to the core: they unapologetically wanted to justify the domination of men over women, masters over slaves, philosophers or intellectuals over manual workers" (p. 9). According to Spellman, Plato may be considered by some to be the first feminist in declaring that women may rule the state, but Spellman points out that her authority is permissible only if she acts like a man. Spellman argues that "Plato is treating souls as if they are gendered—that is, he argues that some kinds of souls are manly, some are womanly; manly souls belong in males, womanly ones in females" (p. 31). For Plato, one's soul is linked to the type of body one has and the type of behavior or activity one displays (p. 31). Spellman speaks to the hierarchical nature of the soul in Plato's way of thinking:

> Your bodily activity is not simply correlated with activity and states of your soul; your bodily activity is the necessary expression of the state of your soul. Doing what a cobbler does cannot be the expression of a soul contemplating the eternal Forms; thus the soul of a philosopher cannot be expressed in the life of a male cobbler. And though it can be expressed in the life of a woman, this is only so long as she acts in particular ways and engages in particular pursuits. (p. 31)

As Plato ranked the soul by its bodily manifestations, Aristotle ranked women, men, and slaves by their supposed nature. Spellman (1988) describes it this way: "The man is superior to the woman and so ought to rule her. Their relationship . . . is more equal than that of master and slave, but it is still far from being one between equals" (p. 40). The slave, however, ranks lower than the wife: Aristotle, in *The Poetics,* states, "While a woman is 'inferior' the slave is a 'wholly worthless being'" (qtd. in Spellman, 1988, p. 40). Spellman reminds us that whatever biological superiority male slaves have to female slaves, they are inferior to the wives of male citizens (p. 40). You will note that slaves within this context are not considered citizens, but only the property of their owners; moreover, what Aristotle considers to be "the prerogatives and functions and natures of 'men' and 'women' don't apply to males and females who are natural slaves" (p. 43).

In keeping with the concerns of Spellman and Outlaw, the critical ethnographer must be mindful of the rational, particularly in terms of the criteria, meaning, and value for the rational when applied outside its own context and domains.

Hegel argues for a system of thinking that is a complex blend of ideas that defend human dignity and freedom on one hand, yet dishonor and degrade the very notion of dignity and freedom as it relates to particular human beings and geographies. As critical ethnographers, we must ask ourselves, Where do our systems of thinking and theories come from? To what end are we employing certain regimes of knowledge, and who or what is being heard or silenced?

The Greater Good

The utilitarian idea is based upon the greatest good/happiness of the greatest number, and it is advanced by Jeremy Bentham (1748–1832) and John Stuart Mill (1806–1873).

Bentham, followed by Mill, developed the philosophy of utilitarianism, which is generally concerned with what Bentham called "the general good" or "the greatest happiness of the greatest number" (Bentham, 1988, p. 86). Bentham believed that human beings function between the opposing poles of happiness and pleasure. The human quest, therefore, is to avoid pain and acquire pleasure. For Bentham, then, the charge becomes, How do we make a society that offers more pleasure and less pain for the majority of its people? Utilitarianism is also concerned with how to measure and classify an act based on the amount of pleasure or pain it produces, while understanding that measurement of pleasure is oblivious to the intent or motives that constitute the act. What matters is the result, not the reasons guiding it.

Mill, however, took issue with Bentham particularly on the view of the majority. Mill was concerned about the "tyranny of the majority" and envisioned a moral universe where plurality and difference were welcomed and accepted even if they were not within the majority's interests; therefore, the majority would be required to protect and consider minority rights. Mill states, "I must again repeat, what the assailants of utilitarianism seldom have the justice to acknowledge, that the happiness which forms the utilitarian standard of what is right in conduct, is not the agent's own happiness, but that of *all* considered" (Mill, 1997, chap. II, pp. 26–28). Mill's utilitarian consideration for "all" also extends to his feminist philosophy. In his book *The Subjection of Women* (1997), Mill writes, "No slave is a slave to the same lengths, and in so full a sense of the word, as a wife is" (chap. II). In his letters, he suggests that the most important thing for women to do is to motivate and create fervor in themselves (Mill, 1910). Mill's utilitarian ideal that "everybody to count for one, and nobody for more than one" applies to the domestic sphere and women's rights, as well as legal, political, and social policies.

Pragmatism and John Rawls

As utilitarianism concerns itself with happiness, pragmatism concerns itself with the usefulness of knowledge and the ideal of democracy. The original pragmatists were concerned with knowledge as an instrument for survival and as an explanatory force for social processes, politics, and education. They wanted to bridge the gap between theory and practice, ideals and behavior, and ideas and action. The pragmatists underscored the belief that truth is relative, not unchanging or absolute, and therefore ethical rules of conduct are fallible and must change with time and context. Since humankind is a problem-solving organism, knowledge becomes the guide by which we make decisions and generate change. Because social life survives by change, our knowledge and ethics must adhere to change. John Dewey (1859–1952) states, "The conception of what is good must undergo change as society changes and as knowledge of the physical environment increases. The discrepancy between stated ideals and actual behavior in contemporary society can be understood as due in part to the persistence of obsolete values" (Dewey & Hurlbutt, 1997, pp. 330–340).

Through their thinking on the relationship of knowledge and change to the individual and society, Dewey and the pragmatists concerned themselves with the threat of obsolete values to the issues of progressive education and democracy. As utilitarianism and pragmatism both set out to form a political philosophy that attempts to combine individual freedom and happiness with social and collective welfare, thereby opening new inquires on democratization and ethics, John Rawls (1921–2002) enters the philosophical arena introducing another alternative to the ideals of justice and the social contract.

Rawls (1999) developed a theory of ethics and justice that rises out of the philosophical tradition of the social-contract theories of Hobbes and Rousseau. However, Rawls' social contract is a radical departure from Hobbes and Rousseau, particularly with its emphases on reciprocity. To begin, Rawls wants us to imagine a group of hypothetical individuals who come together in a kind of constitutional convention for the purpose of creating a just and fair community in which they and their children will live. What is most important for Rawls is that these individuals must come together under a "veil of ignorance." This means they are all totally unaware of what their future will be in this community—their financial means, as well as their social status are unknown; moreover, they all come together as complete equals without any advantages or disadvantages among them. They are then asked to invent rules and guidelines that will make the society just and fair for all its members. Rawls argues that beginning with the veil of ignorance will assure the ideal agreement, because it will provide the least privileged members of this imagined society with some form of protection. The most vulnerable members will be protected from the onset, because, not knowing their future conditions, everyone will want to safeguard themselves and their children from a life of struggle and poverty.

Rawls (1999) understood that in every society there will arise an energetic group of individuals with an entrepreneurial spirit that will become more economically successful than others; however, with the mandate for equality and with the veil of ignorance, the least well-off members of society are assured a minimum standard of living based on the original contract. It is collective acceptance under the conditions of imagined circumstance that guarantees justice for all, according to Rawls, not the utilitarian idea of the greatest good for the greatest number. Mutual acceptance or reciprocity is the foundation for a just and ethical society. Rawls states,

> It is this requirement of the possibility of mutual acknowledgment of principles of free and equal persons who have no authority over one another which makes

the concept of reciprocity fundamental to both justice and fairness. Only if such acknowledgment is possible can there be true community between persons in their common practices; otherwise their relations will appear to them as founded to some degree on force and circumstance. (pp. 255–256)

The ideal of a greater good, from the perspectives of utilitarianism, pragmatism, and Rawls's social contract, raises several key questions for an ethics of ethnography. As critical ethnographers, what problems may arise from the idea of the "greatest good of the greatest numbers" and what is implied in the notion of the "tyranny of the majority"? As critical ethnographers, how do we determine what is a useful knowledge of ethics? If truth and ethics are both fallible and context specific, can ethics ever be determined within the context of fieldwork? The notion of a social contract takes on various forms in moral philosophy. How does Rawls's social contract contribute to an ethics of ethnography?

The Other

Simone de Beauvoir (1952) correctly describes the ways in which Otherness has been traditionally named and produced: "Otherness is the same thing as negation, therefore, Evil. To pose the Other is to define a Manichaeism" (p. 123). De Beauvoir observes how this "Manichaeism" of Otherness resonates with the theological dualism of "the darker" or "evil" matter (the body) set against the "lightness" and "goodness" of the soul striving to liberate itself from the confines of the body.

For Emmanuel Levinas (1906–1995), in crossing into the territories of the Other and meeting the Other face to face, it is less about a clearer recognition of "myself" or "my relation to myself" and more about an ethics of responsibility (Levinas, 1987, pp. 78–79; qtd. in Moran, 2000, p. 321). For Levinas, the Other is not simply or exclusively defined by his or her relationship to me, but is outside of me demanding a response. It is the necessity of response and responsibility that is emphasized here. Levinas (1987, 1996) offers the idea of "face" to indicate the undeniable presence of another individual. To be face to face with another human being is both an experience par excellence and a moving beyond the self. Moreover, for Levinas, when the face of the Other is presented, it opens me up to the demands for justice. This is my quintessential responsibility, justice. Levinas (1987) writes, "Prior to any act, I am concerned with the Other, and I can never be absolved from the responsibility . . . to see a face is already to hear 'Thou shalt not kill'" (pp. 78–79). Ethics in this sense is to respond, and this response demands that I take responsibility for the freedom, welfare, and equity of Otherness.

In the following passage, Levinas poetically captures the understanding of Otherness from a perspective of critical ethnography:

> The human face is the epiphany of the nakedness of the Other, a visitation, a meeting, a saying, which comes in the passivity of the face, not threatening, but obligating. My world is ruptured, my contentment interrupted. I am already obligated. Here is an appeal from which there is no escape, a responsibility, and a state of being hostage. It is looking into the face of the Other that reveals the call to a responsibility that is before any beginning, decision or initiative on my part. (qtd. in Moran, 2000, p. 139)

For Levinas, to have a sense of the Other is to serve justice. It is to be responsible for the Other's life. For the critical ethnographer, the dynamics of justice, responsibility, and the Other are always reciprocally linked.

The ethics of critical ethnography have expanded and revised the long history that constitutes conceptualizations of the Other in central ways. First, the framing of the Other in de Beauvoir's description—as disenfranchised and outcast, constrained, degenerate, and objectified by dominating forces—is too limited a view. Critical ethnography problematizes the discourse of stigmatization beyond definitions of oppression and disenfranchisement where Otherness is inherently an object only to be free when it crosses the boundaries of its own Otherness to enter domains where it can become an active and aware subject (de Beauvoir, 1952; Sartre, 1993). The critical view understands that the Other is always already a subject in their own right, and it is the ethnographer who must cross the boundaries into the territories of Otherness in order to engage with the Other in their terms.

Second, critical ethnographers do not comprehend Otherness through Heidegger's notions of the inauthentic or anti-individualist masses of the "they" that are opposite to the ingenuity and creativity of the "self." Otherness is not objectified or dehumanized as a foreign mass of entities, but as felt-sensing individuals. Third, Otherness for critical ethnographers does not comply in the pure sense that self-consciousness needs or desires Other people to prove or validate its existence. In critical ethnography, the Other is neither or exclusively a foreign, objectified contrast to the self or an empowering mirror of self-awareness. Fourth, the Other is certainly a means by which I may understand and come to know myself, but the Other is not an end. Barbara Myerhoff's (1982) insight rings true: "Unless I exist in the eyes of Others I come to doubt my own existence" (p. 103). But Otherness is not only about coming to know myself more profoundly, because in this sense Otherness becomes more about receiving than giving.

Note: Postmodernism

In the 17th and 18th centuries, modernity comes to be associated with enlightenment. The secular enlightenment presupposes that history will unfold into an open, possibly limitless future. Technology and industrial development is associated with social change. Historical modernism actually begins in the 15th century and comes to characterize the Christian epoch (15th century, in the writings of St. Augustine). What falls apart in the modern era are the values of the 18th century, the age of *Enlightenment*, also known as the Age of Reason and the Age of Progress. In the 18th century, thinkers become optimistic that by using the universal values of science, reason, and logic, they can get rid of all the myths and holy ideas that kept humanity from progressing. They feel this can eventually free humanity from misery, religion, superstition, all unnatural behavior, and unfounded belief. Humanity would thus progress to a state of freedom, happiness, and progress.

An important difference, noted by Jean-Francois Lyotard (1984), between modernism and postmodernism is that modernism embodies a nostalgia for a lost sense of unity and also constructs an aesthetic of fragmentation; however, postmodernism begins with this "lack" or loss and celebrates it. Truth is based on radical contingency, and this "nihilistic" conclusion offers a way out of modernity and marks the birth of post modernity—truth is dissolved and the predominance of knowledge as contingent reigns.

Lyotard (1984) argues that postmodernism ought not to be understood in terms of a historical progression, which signals a present departure from past modernism, but should be characterized as a response to a set of concerns which are themselves already postmodern.

The social critic Fredrick Jameson (1991) demarcates three developments in modernism and postmodernism based on the global economy:

First Period (1700–1885): Market Capitalism

Second Period: Monopoly Capitalism/Age of Imperialism. National markets expand into world markets

Third Period: Postmodern. Postmodernism erupts on the world scene with the unrestricted growth of multinational corporations (this is the purest form yet to emerge)

Conceptualizations of the Other have a long and varied history articulated by Western thinkers and their critics around the world. This brief introduction to the key concepts in Western morality that have served to define an ethics of ethnography lays the groundwork for now turning to an extended and alternative view of ethics through the elaboration of "world traveling" and "loving perception," first articulated by Maria Lugones (1994). The emphasis on Lugones's notion of ethics will serve to bring the discussion of ethics into the discourse of those marginalized identities who are setting forth their own alternative moral paradigms and perspectives on the Other from their experience as outsiders. It will also serve to place our examination of ethics and the Other into a conceptualization of world traveling that is particularly relevant to the ethnographic project.

Maria Lugones: Contemporary Ethics, Ethnography, and Loving Perception

World Traveling and Loving Perception

A particular feature in being an "outsider" or "minority" of mainstream constructions of experience and reality is *code switching*, or what feminist philosopher Lugones (1994) calls "world traveling," where one must travel through worlds of difference, unfamiliarity, or alienation as well as the contrasting worlds of comfort, familiarity, and support by shifting codes from one world to the next. Lugones describes a world as "inhabited by flesh and blood people. . . . A World need not be a construction of a whole society. It may be a construction of a tiny portion of a particular society. It may be inhabited by just a few people. Some 'worlds' are bigger than others" (Lugones, 1994, p. 631). When outcasts travel to different worlds and perform differently in those worlds, they do so *not* out of deception, but out of appropriateness, civility, respect, or out of health and safety for their own survival. They are required to use space and language in a particular way that is constitutive of that particular world (p. 632). One may or may not be conscious that they are employing different gestures, language patterns, intentions, and personalities as they travel from one world to another.

Successful world traveling is a matter of skill and experience, and there are some who will be better word travelers than others, such as those who inhabit multiple worlds and feel at home, more or less, in all the worlds they inhabit. World traveling is a matter of learning the different rules and norms in these Other worlds and then choosing to play by those rules or not. It is also a matter of knowing what is expected and being able to anticipate it. It is a matter of knowing the language, the aesthetics and taste, the norms of civility, and the emotional landscapes. World traveling is a natural part of human interaction for all of us who live in a diverse social world where power and authority operate in diffuse and multicentered locations. However, for minorities or outsiders, where the levels and processes of disenfranchisement are more entrenched and deep-rooted, world traveling is a necessity that demands even more skill, effort, and experience when crossing the borders of different worlds. The more different you are, the more adept at world traveling you must be become. But there are some outsiders who have crossed into different worlds, and their presence in that world may not necessarily be based primarily on learning the norms or rules of that world, but more on learning how their identities are already constructed in it. These identities may inhabit that world by enacting the caricature or stereotype that that particular world projects upon them. Moreover, they may also refuse or simply not recognize themselves in the construction.

Stereotypes

For many marginalized identities and people of color, they are known in a particular world through caricature and stereotypes. A major problem is that the stereotypical projection of one's identity by other worldly constructions of who one is diminishes the complexity and humanity of one's individuality, as well as one's ethnicity or affiliated group. When in one world, I may animate that world's caricature or stereotype of the person they construct me to be. We all may fall prey to the expectations, images, and stereotypes that particular worlds hold for us. We actually enact the caricature, sometimes knowingly and sometimes unknowingly. We become a double self: the self of our "home place world" and the self that succumbs to stereotypical behavior that the particular Other world expects, sometimes demands, of us. We may realize we are playing the caricature—conscious of this construction as we perform it; but we are not always aware, we may not always understand:

> Some of the inhabitants of a *world* may not understand or accept the way in which they are constructed in it. So, for example, a recent Latin-American immigrant may not understand how she is constructed in White/Anglo worlds. So there may be a world that constructs me in ways that I do not even understand or I may not accept the construction as an account of myself, a construction of myself. And yet, I may be animating such a construction, even though I may not intend my moves, gestures, acts in that way. (Lugones, 1994, p. 631)

We may enact these stereotypes for several reasons. First, I may enact so you can engage or accept me into the construction you have of me; otherwise you will remain distant, fearful, or unfamiliar. Second, I may enact because I have internalized the caricature you project upon me when I am with you. Enacting the expected stereotype may be easier and more "natural" than breaking outside the expectations you have of me. Third, I may enact the caricature because the act is survival rich; I, like the trickster, am a plurality of selves in order to accomplish a particular end.

World traveling is a challenging endeavor. I am different in different worlds, and I can remember myself in both as I am in the other. "I am a plurality of selves" (Lugones, 1994, p. 634).

Being at Ease

Much of the way in which we all are required to code-switch or perform differently in different worlds is based upon what Lugones (1994) describes as "being at ease" in these worlds. One may be at ease in all the worlds one travels. However, for most marginalized individuals, they must travel to worlds where there are varying levels of ease. Lugones charts four ways of being at ease. First, to be at ease in a particular world is to be a fluent speaker in that world. To know the norms and the vocabulary of a location is to be at ease. Second, to be at ease, one must be normatively happy. You like the norms, you like doing what you are required to do there and what you think you should be doing. Third, one is at ease in a world where one feels "humanly bonded." You are with those you care for and they care for you—even when, and especially when, you are in a surrounding world that is hostile to you. Finally, one is at ease in a world where there is a shared history. For example, you may be among strangers and music is playing in the background. Someone you never met before says, "I remember when I first heard that song at Woodstock more than 30 years ago." There is little or no response from the others, but you are excited and say, "I was there too!" You both immediately make a connection in a way that memory can bring people together through the shared feelings and meanings of particular moments in time. You both enthusiastically share stories about being at Woodstock, unconcerned about the others around you.

Playfulness

With an understanding of *world, world travel,* and *being at ease in a world*, we will turn to Lugones's (1994) idea of *playfulness*. To be playful in a world means that it is both safe and appropriate for one to take risks, to be foolish and uncertain; to be playful means that one is free to not worry about competence and to abandon competition and self-importance. It means that in this particular world one need not fear harm or arrogance for being playful. In this world, one is secure, healthy, and totally at ease. Lugones writes,

Playfulness is, in part, an openness to being a fool, which is a combination of not worrying about competence, not being self-important, not taking norms as sacred and finding ambiguity and double edges a source of wisdom and delight. ... Positively, the playful attitude involved openness to surprise, openness to being a fool, openness to self-construction or reconstruction and to construction of the "worlds" we inhabit playfully. Negatively, playfulness is characterized by uncertainty, lack of self-importance, absence of rules or not taking rules as sacred, a not worrying about competence and a lack of abandonment or resignation to a particular construction of oneself, others, and one's relation to them. (pp. 634–666)

However, one must not confuse being at ease (and being competent) with being playful (Lugones, 1994, p. 635). To be playful in a world, you must be at ease in that world, but being at ease in that world does not necessarily mean you can be playful. For certain individuals, particularly outsiders, travel to Other worlds—even when at ease—does not mean they cannot necessarily be playful, because there are consequences. You cannot be playful in worlds where the norms, rules, expectations, values, and structures are not for playing. We do not generally consider a lecture hall, a courtroom, or a conversation with those who are unfamiliar to us or in authority over us as spaces for play. But we may be at ease in these spaces, even though we should not play. And there are the other spaces where we cannot play— spaces inhospitable to our identity and being.

Lugones (1994) reminds us there are "worlds we enter at our own risk, worlds that have agon, conquest, and arrogance as the main ingredients in their ethos" (p. 635). Moreover, we enter out of "necessity [those worlds] which we would be foolish to enter playfully" (p. 635). These spaces are not simply formal or competitive, but spaces that perceive difference arrogantly— with *arrogant perception*. In these worlds of arrogant perception, one must move with levels of competence, caution, awareness, and mastery. The nature of this world demands that one *must* be unplayful in it (p. 637). Therefore, for the outsider to be playful in a world that perceives you arrogantly is "foolish." However, as Lugones writes, "I am not a healthy being in the 'worlds' that construct me as un-playful" (p. 637). This does not mean that you can or should stop being a playful human being; you just cannot be playful in *that* world. We play in worlds that are safe and loving. As human beings we require the wholeness and abandon of play for delight, creativity, purpose, and good health. More important, we must also understand that in order to be playful, it is not the individual that must change but the unplayful world.

Arrogant Perception/Loving Perception

Maria Lugones (1994) brings forward Marilyn Frye's (1983) notion of "arrogant perception" as the failure to identify with someone that one views arrogantly or that one has come to perceive as the product of arrogant perception. Arrogant perception objectifies the Other and casts the Other as an inferior being. To perceive another arrogantly is to stand at a distance in opposition to an egalitarian relationship, thereby prohibiting any consideration for honest dialogue. Lugones (1994) writes,

> When I came to the U.S., I learned that part of racism is the internalization of the propriety of abuse without identification: I learned that I could be seen as a being to be used by White/Anglo men and women without the possibility of identification, i.e., without their act of attempting to graft my substance onto theirs, rubbing off on them at all. They could remain untouched, without any sense of loss. (p. 628)

An added connection is that between the failure of identification and the failure to love. Lugones (1994) sets forth a love of deep caring and responsibility. In perceiving others arrogantly and failing to identify with them, "We fail to love them in this particular deep way" (pp. 629–630). This particular "deep way" that Lugones sets forth is very similar to Martin Luther King, Jr. and his interpretation of the love found in *agape*:

> The Greek language comes out with another word which is the highest level of love. It speaks of it in terms of agape. Agape means nothing sentimental or basically affectionate. It means understanding, redeeming goodwill for all men. It is an overflowing love. . . . With this type of love and understanding goodwill we will be able to stand amid the radiant glow of the new age with dignity and discipline. (King, 1994, p. 564)

The critical ethnographer may understand loving perception as it echoes through the love of *agape* as a principle of ethics, but what does all this have to do with an ethics of ethnography and ethics as a method? It relates to an ethics of ethnography because Lugones is advocating for world traveling as a means to identify with Others and to perceive lovingly.

Summary

Although Lugones (1994) examines the experience of women of color in the United States, fieldworkers may learn a great deal from the strategies marginalized people employ as they world travel. Traveling to Other worlds is the ethnographic project. To travel to these worlds with the desire to do ethical work is an ongoing concern. To understand this ethnographic traveling to Other worlds through the particular kind of traveling or code switching that many minority populations must employ is the contribution that Maria Lugones brings to the ethics of ethnography.

Code Switching

To learn the skills of world traveling involves code switching: learning the language, rules, norms, and aesthetic conventions, of that world, along with what it means to inhabit that world. When one world travels, shifting codes becomes a skill of mobility and necessity, but it is also a matter of choice. There are consequences if I do not shift codes, but there are also consequences if I do. When I code-shift, I am behaving out of respect and appropriateness for that world, and because it is necessary (for a number of reasons: work, health, education, or fieldwork) to enter that world. In traveling to other worlds, when code shifting is necessary, a member of that world may express, "We are comfortable talking with this person and sharing what we do here, because this person knows and respects us." Yet there are other times when code switching may be resented: "She is trying to be like us and we don't like it," "He is not from here, and he doesn't belong here." Code switching for the world traveler is a delicate balance.

Stereotypes

In this Other world, you realize your identity is already constructed. You have a way of talking, gesturing, and valuing as that world constructs you as the outsider before you even travel there. Once you arrive and enter that world's construction of you, you may consciously or unconsciously animate the constructed identity or stereotype prescribed for you as the outsider, or you may resist it. We must also be aware that subjects will perform, in turn, the images, stereotypes, and caricatures they believe we hold of them.

Playfulness

For the ethnographer, the concept of playfulness is profoundly useful relative to ethics. We may both compare and contrast it to ethnographic world traveling. As ethnographers, we may be both playful and unplayful while recognizing and understanding when the subjects of the world we enter feel they can be both playful and/or unplayful with us and the worlds we represent.

Loving playfulness for the ethnographer is a playfulness that allows us to enter Conquergood's (1982b, 1998, 2002a, 2002b) dialogue with the purpose of understanding when we can be playful and when we cannot. To be deeply and honorably engaged with the world through Conquergood's concept of dialogic performance is to engage this balance. This is a turning back on the self with a loving and conscious self-reflection—a deeply felt dialogue that inspires you to extend and reach out to the Other who welcomes acceptable play. You are at ease, but, more importantly, through dialogic encounters you have changed and augmented another self, a plural self, that can be at play through your own permission and the permission of your subjects. Full play is protected by trust, loving perception, and different world constructions. It is here where ethnographers may learn from ethnic minorities who travel to different worlds all the time as a matter of course. To be playful is more than a matter of ease; it is a matter of being in a world that allows and encourages you to be playful, a world where it is healthy for you to play without threat.

Foolish Play

In foolish play, one ignores the rules of the world and becomes reckless, playful, and permissive, thereby projecting oneself toward a kind of folly and abandon that the world does not accept or understand. The ethnographer or subject acts in ways that are too familiar and too informal; therefore, others respond with insult, dismissal, or hostility. One is foolish to be playful in some worlds. For the ethnographer to play in these worlds is to disrespect certain boundaries of civility, privacy, and cultural norms.

World Traveling

As ethnographers, when we travel to Other worlds, we open ourselves to the greatest possibility of loving perception and dialogical performance, because (a) we witness and engage cultural aspects of the Other's world; (b) we witness and engage with Others' sense of self in their own world; (c) we experience how we are perceived *through Others' eyes*; (d) we are now bodies that must touch, see, and listen to each other because we are inhabiting a space in their world where distance cannot separate you; (e) we witness and engage the Other as a *subject* even as he or she may be subjugated, and, as a result, meanings of power and positionality begin to arise between us; (f) we are dependent on each other for the possibility of being understood. Traveling to another world threatens arrogant perception and makes loving perception possible. Loving perception evokes dialogical performance and sustains it. Loving perception is not sentimental or sappy, nor is it a romanticization of the Other.

Conclusion

By traveling to someone's world, we open a greater possibility for identification; moreover, we gain the opportunity to glimpse ourselves through *their* eyes. We see more than self-recognition with the Other, but the Other's recognition of us. It is this moment that leads the way to identification with the Other and the desire to be with the Other. Lugones (1994) writes,

> The reason why I think that traveling to someone's "world" is a way of identifying with them is because by traveling to their "world" we can understand what is to be them and what it is to be ourselves in their eyes. . . . Without knowing the other's "world," one does not know the other, and without knowing the other one is really alone in the other's presence because the other is only dimly present to one. . . . Through traveling to other people's "worlds" we discover that there are "worlds" in which those who are the victims of arrogant perception are really subjects, lively beings, resisters, constructors of visions even though in the mainstream construction they are animated only by the arrogant perceiver and are pliable, foldable, file-awayable, classifiable. (p. 637)

What Lugones is asking us to do is not always easy. We will meet people in the field that we general do not like. Some of these people may be victims of arrogant perception, but they are also arrogant perceivers: they may act in mean, repressive, and dishonest ways toward other Others. We have difficulty liking them or trusting them, let alone *loving* them. Loving perception, dialogic performance, and radical egalitarianism means that we must understand *every* individual as a valuable being worthy and deserving of understanding, fair judgment, and our caring attention. When this is of primary importance in our work, it also becomes the very reason that these individuals and their negative effects must be seriously contextualized and seriously criticized. Loving perception works to construct *agape* love and works to deconstruct its opposite.

Warm-Ups

1. Create three contrasting scenarios experienced by a specific identity that forms the character of a field researcher; that is, identify the sex, age, gender, class, nationality, or some other characteristic of the researcher and his or her research interest. The three scenarios should include a situation in which the researcher world travels to three contrasting worlds: one where the researcher is at ease but not playful; the second where he or she is playful in an unplayful world; and the third where he or she is playful in a world that

is safe and that welcomes play. Each situation must reflect a fieldwork environment. Please discuss the consequences or effects of each scenario.

2. Imagine that you are in a lecture hall explaining the concept of ethics, particularly as it relates to world traveling, to students who are divided into two different groups sitting on opposite sides of the room. On the right side of the room are students belonging to the Christian Right Coalition, and on the left side of the room are students belonging to the Young Socialist Party. Explain the theory and practice of ethics referring to the various thinkers and schools of thought outlined in this chapter.

Note

1. Outlaw (1995) states, "This work is produced from a lecture delivered by Hegel in the winter of 1830–31, though there had been two previous deliveries in 1822–23 and 1824–25" (p. 326). Outlaw also discusses the impact of Hegel's philosophy of European racism: "These ideas were expressed more than seventy years prior to the cannibalization of Africa by a person who was to become one of Germany's and Europe's most famous philosophers, and helped to nurture a complex of ideas that rationalized European racism" (p. 326).

Suggested Readings

Ashby, W. (1997). *A comprehensive history of Western ethics.* New York: Prometheus.

Clifford, J. (1988). *The predicament of culture: Twentieth-century ethnography, literature and art.* Cambridge, MA: Harvard University Press.

Conquergood, D. (1982). Performing as a moral act: The ethical dimensions of the ethnography of performance. *Literature and Performance, 5*(2), 1–13.

Hamera, J. (1995). Ethics and answerability: Critical theoretical perspectives on "The Storytellers" project. In S. Mason & E. van Erven (Eds.), *The Storytellers* (pp. 112–120). Utrecht, The Netherlands: Ocean Film Foundation.

Hord, F. L., & Lee, J. S. (Eds.). (1995). *I am because we are: Readings in black philosophy.* Amherst: University of Massachusetts Press.

MacIntyre, A. (1967). *A short history of ethics.* New York: Routledge.

Raphael, D. D. (1981). *Moral philosophy and social values.* Oxford, UK: Oxford University Press.

Spellman, E. V. (1988). *Inessential woman: Problems of exclusion in feminist thought.* Boston: Beacon.

Vardy, P., & Grosh, P. (1994). *The puzzle of ethics.* New York: HarperCollins.

West, C. (1991). *The ethical dimensions of Marxist thought.* New York: Monthly Review.

5

Methods and Ethics

A code of ethics cannot guarantee ethical behavior. Moreover, a code of ethics cannot resolve all ethical issues or disputes or capture the richness and complexity involved in striving to make responsible choices within a moral community. Rather, a code of ethics sets forth values, ethical principles, and ethical standards to which professionals aspire and by which their actions can be judged.

—National Association of Social Workers,
Code of Ethics (1999)

[Researchers] are not only responsible for the factual content of their statements but also must consider carefully the social and political implications of the information they disseminate. They must do everything in their power to insure that such information is well understood, properly contextualized, and responsibly utilized. They should make clear the empirical bases upon which their reports stand, be candid about their qualifications and philosophical or political biases, and recognize and make clear the limits of anthropological expertise. At the same time, they must be alert to possible harm their information may cause people with whom they work or colleagues.

—American Anthropology Association,
Code of Ethics (1998)

C hapter 4 raised a series of questions pertaining to the ethics of ethnography with very few answers. In this chapter, we will attempt to respond to the questions raised in Chapter 4 by reviewing the code of ethics and position statements from the American Anthropology Association (AAA), the American Folklore Association (AFA), and the National Association of Social Workers (NASW). From their specific disciplinary perspectives, each field contributes significant methodological considerations focused expressly on ethics. The disciplinary fields sometimes differ and contradict each other in viewpoints and approaches, particularly around issues of informed consent, confidentiality, and compliance with the Institutional Review Board (IRB). However, by examining a cross section of key positions, the codes of ethics from the various institutions will provide a foundation and a guide for an ethical method that adheres to different standpoints, contexts, and purposes.

Codes of Ethics for Fieldwork

In the following, I provide a summary of the codes from each field with an emphasis on the field of anthropology because of its detail and comprehensiveness. It is important to keep in mind that these various fields overlap in their ethical methodology more than they diverge. At points where a particular field differs from or has more of an extended perspective than another, it is noted and distinguished in italics.

Code of Ethics of the American Anthropological Association

The four points listed below serve as a summary of the core ideas in the AAA *Code of Ethics*, approved June 1998, and they also serve to summarize the central ideas in the AFS and NASW. They are taken from the "Briefing Paper on the Impact of Material Assistance to Study Population" (Luong, 2001, p. 2).

1. To avoid harm or wrong

2. To respect the well-being of humans and nonhuman primates

3. To work for the long-term conservation of the archaeological, fossil, and historical records

4. To consult actively with the affected individuals or group(s), with the goal of establishing a working relationship that can be beneficial to all parties involved

We will now examine in more detail the ethical codes related to (a) openness and transparency, (b) the study population, (c) the scholarly community, (d) remuneration, (e) reciprocity, (f) informed consent, (g) harm and negative impact, and (h) confidentiality.

Openness and Transparency

In proposing and conducting research to funders, colleagues, persons studied, and all those *relevant parties affected by the research*, all researchers must be honest and straightforward concerning the following:

1. Purpose(s) of study (The goals of the project or rationale for study).

2. General impact of study (Who or what will the project effect? What difference will it make on society?)

3. Sources of support (Who is funding or supporting the project?)

Study Population

The primary responsibility is to those studied (people, places, materials, and those with whom you work). This responsibility *supercedes* the goal of knowledge, completion of project, and obligation to funders or sponsors. If ever there is a conflict of interest, the people studied *must come first*. In addition, researchers must make every effort to ensure that their work does not *harm the safety, dignity, or privacy* of those with whom they work.

Researchers must make sure in the very beginning of the study whether or not the subjects choose anonymity. If this is the case, researchers must make every effort to assure the population their privacy. They must also make subjects aware that, despite their best efforts, there are no absolute guarantees.

Researchers must acquire informed consent in advance of the study, as well as intermittently throughout the study at key points of vulnerability or when gathering threatening or delicate information. Informed consent is a vital component of ethical inquiry and may in most cases take several forms both written and oral. Informed consent is also very controversial; we will discuss the problems that arise with informed consent later in the chapter. In most cases, informed consent does not require a written signature form. According to the AAA (1998), "It is quality of consent, not the format, that is relevant" (p. 4).

Researchers who enter into an enduring or binding relationship with their subjects must adhere to informed consent and *openness* or they must negotiate the *limits of the relationship*.

Although researchers gain professionally and personally from those they study, it is important not to exploit or respond in ways that are inappropriate.

Responsibility to the Scholarly Community

There will always be ethical dilemmas in every research project. Therefore, there should be a section in every proposal that indicates potential problems and the researcher's ethical concerns and guidelines. The following points, from the AAA *Code of Ethics* (1998, pp. 4–5), may serve as a guide.

Researchers belong to various research communities, bear a responsibility to those communities to represent them ethically, and are subject to the *general rules of conduct* for that community. They should also *not deceive or knowingly misrepresent* (i.e., fabricate evidence, falsify, plagiarize), *or attempt to prevent reporting of misconduct, or obstruct the scientific/scholarly research of others*. Moreover, researchers should support the research of future colleagues by preserving opportunities for them to *follow them to the field*. In other words, don't burn bridges; there are others who will come after you. Do not do anything that will close the door for them.

Researchers should apply their work and findings appropriately doing more good than harm and should make their data available to the scholarly and research community. Researchers should make every effort to preserve their fieldwork data for *use by posterity*.

Note: Hate Groups, Advocacy, and Responsibility

The following positions on advocacy and responsibility come from the *Commission to Review the AAA Statement on Ethics Final Report* (AAA, 1995, p. 8).

- Do researchers have an obligation to *promote the general welfare* of all populations studied? It would seem not, for example hate groups, terrorists, drug cartels, and like groups.
- Promote takes on many meanings through research: identifying a problem, putting a problem in context, and developing options for responding; by educating various audiences; and by advocating a particular solution or cause.
- In terms of advocacy, "The commission understands and supports the desire of some anthropological researchers to move beyond disseminating research results and education to a position of advocacy" (p. 8). This does not mean, however, that the researcher is *necessarily* to be an

advocate for or to be expected to *promote the welfare* of a group or culture studied.

The anthropological researcher, however, does have duties to the people studied, including doing no harm or wrong, providing full disclosure and informed consent, offering warnings of possible outcomes (good or bad) of the research for the people involved, and weighing carefully the risks and benefits of the study for the people being studied (p. 9).

Remuneration

What is fair compensation—"wages for labor" or "pay" for work and assistance (e.g., driving a car, helping with demonstrations or interviews, intellectual property rights or cultural knowledge, or traditional knowledge)—for members of the population studied? According to the AAA's "Briefing Paper on Remuneration to Subject Populations and Individuals" (Wagner, 2000), the ethical consideration of remuneration includes the following points:

* Appropriate and fair remuneration is culturally situated.
* Remuneration is an ongoing process negotiated by the researcher and guided by the population under study.

The international documents are clear that all people should receive equal pay for equal work. Likewise, they are clear about placing the ownership of heritage and the appropriate ways to handle issues such as remuneration in the hands of the people being studied (Wagner, 2000, p. 3). Article 23 of the Universal Declaration of Human Rights (Amnesty International, 1948) states, "Everyone without any discrimination, has the right to equal pay for equal work," and "Everyone who works has the right to just and favorable remuneration" (p. 4). Article 18 states that indigenous peoples deserve "fully all rights established under international labour law and national labour legislation" (p. 4). Furthermore, they should not "be subjected to any discriminatory conditions of labour, employment or salary." And Article 27 states that "everyone has the right to the protection of the moral and material interests resulting from any scientific, literary or artistic production of which he is the author" (p. 5).

Reciprocity and Material Assistance

As a form of reciprocity, researchers often provide material assistance to individuals with study populations who have assisted them in their work.

However, this raises questions about the consequences that well-intentioned reciprocity may have. Researchers may not be able to predict *the consequences of the material assistance to the study population.* The answers to questions regarding material assistance—when, how, why, and so forth—are not exact, but rather are contingent on the researcher's judgment and knowledge of the study population in its historical, social, and physical environments, as well as on careful consultation with other experts and with as many potentially affected individuals as possible (Luong, 2001, p. 2).

In conformity with the AAA *Code of Ethics* (1998), material assistance to the study population should do the following (Luong, 2001):

- Avoid exacerbating conflicts within the study population or conflicts of the study population with other populations.
- Avoid increasing the health risks of the study population or other populations.
- Avoid markedly disrupting social relations within the study population.
- Avoid damaging local archaeological, fossil, and historical records.
- Avoid negative impacts on the environment of the study population.

Informed Consent

It is understood that the degree and breadth of informed consent required will depend on the nature of the project and may be affected by requirements of other codes, laws, and ethics of the country or community in which the research is pursued. Furthermore, it is understood that the informed consent process is dynamic and continuous: The process should be initiated in the project design and continue through implementation by way of dialogue and negotiation with those studied.

According to the AAA's *Briefing Paper on Informed Consent* (Clark & Kingsolver, 2000, p. 2), the following is a list of characteristics researchers should seek to meet in obtaining the informed consent of participants. Researchers should

- Engage in an ongoing and dynamic discussion with collaborators (or *human subjects*, in the language of some codes) about the nature of study participation, its risks, and its potential benefits; this means actively soliciting advice from research participants at all stages, including planning and documentation.

- Engage in a dialogue with human subjects who have previously or continuously been involved in a particular study about the nature of ongoing participation or resuming participation in a study. This dialogue should include the nature of their participation, risks, and potential benefits at this particular time.

• Discuss with potential research subjects the ways study participation may affect them when research data are disseminated. For example, if photographs documenting their participation in a particular event or situation at a certain time could prove incriminating if viewed by a wide audience, this eventually should be discussed.

• Demonstrate, in the appropriate language, all research equipment and documentation techniques prior to obtaining consent so that research collaborators, or participants, may be said to be adequately informed about the research process.

• Inform potential subjects of the anonymity, confidentiality, and security measures taken for all types of study data, including digitized, visual, and material data.

• Seek to answer all questions and concerns about study participation that potential subjects may have about their involvement in the research process.

• Provide a long-term mechanism for study subjects to contact the researcher or the researcher's institution to express concerns at a later date and/or withdraw their data from the research process.

• Provide, if possible, alternative contact information in case a potential research subject or collaborator does not want to participate but does not feel able to communicate that directly to the researcher.

• Obtain official consent from the human subject to participate in the study prior to the collection of any data to be included in the research process. The form and format of official consent can vary, depending on the appropriateness of written, audiotaped, or videotaped consent to the research situation. Those granting the permission should be involved actively in determining the appropriate form of documenting consent.

• Write and submit forms pertaining to informed consent, and obtain approval by the appropriate committees and/or review boards prior to recruiting subjects, obtaining informed consent, or collecting data.

Due to the particular nature of folklore research, the AFA takes a more critical stand on informed consent. The "Documentation of Informed Consent" from the *Statement of the American Folklore Society on Research with Human Subjects* (n.d.) states the following:

Folklorists inform their consultants about the aims and methods of research. The nature of the relationships that folklorists build with their consultants, however, is such that a written, signed, legally effective document would be inimical to the relationship upon which folklorists' research is based. Folklorists cannot go as guests into people's home communities, build trust and friend-ships, and then present a legal document for signature. Nor can they ask for signatures to be witnessed.

Informed consent is given orally, and possibly can be recorded on audio or video, but introducing a written legal document into the folkloristic-consultant relationship would generally prove an insult to the consultant and bring folk-lore research to a halt. Institutional review boards should alter or waive the requirements for written informed consent in the case of folklore and other forms of ethnographically based research (p. 2).

Negative Impact

According to an AAA briefing paper on the potential negative impact of study work (Watkins, 2000), it is the researcher's duty

> to avoid harm or wrong, understanding that the development of knowledge can lead to change which may be positive or negative for the people or animals worked with or studied. . . . For example, because of the social stigma attached to cannibalism by Western society, a researcher might wish to consider the ways that such a statement concerning the practices of a marginal culture might be used to further marginalize the culture. (p. 2)

The following is a list of guidelines from the briefing paper to assist the researcher in considering the "potentially negative influences" their publica-tions of factual data may have on the populations they study (Watkins, 2000, p. 4). Researchers must

- Identify at the onset of any project the possible personal, social, and political implications that the publication of factual data concerning a study population may have on that population.
- Involve the study population throughout the entire process of the project (from the formulation of the research design through the collection of the data, the synthesis of data, and the publication of data) in such a way that the cultural context of the population under study is represented within the project to as much an extent possible.
- Weigh the scientific and anthropological importance of the data against the possible harm to the study population.
- Integrate the data in such a way that its role within the cultural context is fully explained.
- Present the data in such a way that sensationalism is minimized while the contextual comprehension of the data is maximized.
- Report truthfully any scientific or cultural biases that may be inherent in the presentation of the data.

- Explain the importance of the data under discussion both to the scientific and local communities in language understandable by each community and disseminate the information in both communities as widely as possible.

Moreover, although advocacy is a personal choice that each researcher must make, it is imperative that the researcher acknowledge the scientific need for balance in anthropological reporting.

Folklorists and social workers are both obviously concerned with issues of ethics, but the disciplines remain two different fields; that is, their purposes, relationships, contexts, and goals are not the same. The social worker will be concerned with issues of ethics and confidentiality that are not always or generally the same concerns as those of folklorists or anthropologists. The NASW *Code of Ethics* (1999) states,

> Social workers should protect the confidentiality of all information obtained in the course of professional service, except for compelling professional reasons. The general expectation that social workers will keep information confidential does not apply when disclosure is necessary to prevent serious, foreseeable, and imminent harm to a client or other identifiable person. In all instances, social workers should disclose the least amount of confident information necessary to achieve the desired purpose; only information that is directly relevant to the purpose for which the disclosure is made should be revealed. (p. 8)

The ethical responsibility regarding privacy and confidentiality is outlined in more detail in the *Code of Ethics* from the NASW (1999). Because social work, more explicitly, involves "particular attention to the needs and empowerment of people who are vulnerable, oppressed, and living in poverty," the challenges of privacy and confidentiality are of great importance (p. 1). Outlined below is a summary of central points on the issue of confidentiality in the NASW code that I have adapted for broader fields and areas of ethnographic fieldwork. Researchers should

- Respect consultant's privacy. Private information should not be solicited unless necessary for the research project.

- Not disclose confidential information to a third party unless given explicit permission to do so. Researchers should not discuss confidential information in any setting unless privacy can be ensured, and should "not discuss confidential information in public or semipublic areas such as hallways, waiting rooms, elevators, and restaurants" (p. 8).

- Protect privacy and identifying information particularly in the use of electronic mail, computers, facsimile machines, telephones, and telephone answering machines, when possible.

- Protect the confidentiality of deceased persons.

- Protect confidentiality and privacy in the event of the researcher's own dismissal, incapacitation, or death.

Note: Institutional Review Board

In 1974, the federal government mandated the Institutional Review Board (IRB) at all universities that accepted federal funding for research involving human subjects. This was instituted because it was understood that science is not value-free, nor does it always contribute to the greater good or well being of others. Past incidents where medical research resulted in physical and mental harm had devastating effects (such as the Tuskegee Syphilis Study, the Willowbrook Hepatitis Experiment, and the Milgram shock experiment).

Corrine Glesne (1999) outlines the five basic principles that guide the decisions of the IRB in their proposal review (pp. 144–145):

1. Research subjects must have sufficient information to make informed decisions about participating in a study.

2. Research subjects must be able to withdraw, without penalty, from a study at any point.

3. All unnecessary risks to a research subject must be eliminated.

4. Benefits to the subject or society, preferably both, must outweigh all potential risks.

5. Experiments should be conducted only by qualified investigators.

The IRB has come under a great deal of criticism by researchers who fall outside a biomedical model and by the American Association of University Professors (AAUP). The criticism may be summarized by the following points:

- Failure to recognize new modes of interpretive research that is more process oriented, collaborative, culturally located, and contentious (i.e., performance ethnography, autoethnography, oral history, and advocacy-/activists-oriented research).
- Infringement on researcher's First Amendment rights and academic freedom by surveilling inquiries within the humanities, such as research seminars and dissertation projects.
- The failure of the IRB to "recognize the need to include members who understand the newer interpretive paradigms" (Denzin, 2003, p. 254)

- The inappropriate and ineffective application of the IRB's Common Rule (i.e., the inconsistent judgments and measures of approval from one institution to another [p. 255]).

Too many researchers are choosing not to conduct research with human subjects because of the difficulties in some universities with the IRB. The board has been hotly criticized because it uses a bioscientific model that too often works against the kind of ethical concerns in the social sciences and humanities. Norman K. Denzin (2003) provides a clear and cogent critique of the IRB:

The IRB framework assumes that one model of research fits all forms of inquiry, but that is not the case. . . . The model also presumes a static, monolithic view of the human subject. Subjects and researchers develop collaborative, public, pedagogical relationships. The walls between subjects and observers are deliberately broken down. Confidentiality disappears, for there is nothing to hide or protect. Participation is entirely voluntary, hence there is no need for subjects to sign forms indicating that their consent is "informed." The activities that make up the research are participatory; that is they are performative, collaborative, and action and praxis based. Hence participants are not asked to submit to specific procedures or treatment conditions. Instead, acting together, researchers and subjects work to produce change in the world. (pp. 249–250)

Reviewing the codes of ethics from the fields included provides important guidelines in proceeding toward an ethical methodology. For each of the disciplines, formulating an effective statement took time, hard work, cooperation, and thoughtful deliberation by individuals committed to establishing guidelines for ethical fieldwork methods. For the complete documents and codes, you may download them on the AAA, NASW, and the AFS Web sites.

We will now examine how these codes are elaborated, complicated, tested, and challenged. The listing of codes may appear, on the surface, to be relatively easy to follow, but there will always be added dimensions and unexpected problems to consider. The next section will focus on three classic essays that extend the questions and topics covered in the above listing of codes to help us anticipate what other ethical dilemmas we might encounter in the field. Those essays are "Ten Lies of Ethnography: Moral Dilemmas of Field Research," by Gary Allen Fine (1993); "Conceptual Errors Across the Curriculum: Towards a Transformation of the Tradition," by Elizabeth Kamark Minnich (1986); and "Performing as a Moral Act: Ethical

Dimensions of the Ethnography of Performance," by Dwight Conquergood (1982b).

Extending the Codes

Moral Dilemmas

In Fine's (1993) essay, he lists the challenges ethnographers face in meeting three overarching ethical conventions of fieldwork. He describes them as "classic virtue," "technical skills," and "the ethnographic self." He provides counter examples for each of these ideals that I will discuss in this section. For classic virtue, the notions of (a) "the kindly ethnographer," (b) "the friendly ethnographer," and (c) "the honest ethnographer" are tested by certain concrete situations. First, you strive to be *kind,* but your kindness is not always realized or appreciated. You may unintentionally insult those you meet or you may end up being thought of as a "fink" or a traitor. Second, you are *friendly* and value friendliness as a virtue, but there are people you meet that you genuinely dislike. Third, you try to be *honest* as you propose your study and describe your intentions, but you do not always know with certainty or cannot say with complete honesty what the details or discoveries will be for your project until you are actually in the process of completing it. In each case, classic virtues are questioned; however, ethics demands that although you may not like some of the people that you meet, although your intentions may be questioned and misunderstood, and although you cannot always with complete honesty represent your project before it has begun, you must remind yourself that it is not a perfect world and working with human subjects will always be a complicated and contradictory enterprise; therefore, you continue to strive for the ideals of kindness, friendship, and honesty while anticipating the challenges.

For technical skills, Fine (1993) argues that the aspirations of (a) "the precise ethnographer," (b) "the observant ethnographer," and (c) "the unobtrusive ethnographer" become difficult in the following situations. First, you understand that possessing technical skills as an ethnographer often suggests that one must be as *precise* as possible in interpreting the lives of others; however, precision falters when we realize that all of our interpretations are filtered by our own subjectivity and interpretive paradigms, as well as by our own idiosyncratic writing styles. Sometimes, ethnographers have more in common with playwrights than with scientist. Second, we understand that one of the cornerstones of ethnography is the ability to be a keen *observer*; however, we can never grasp or present the whole picture (Fine, 1993). There is always something that will be left out, and there will always be elements of observation that are vitally important to one ethnographer's sensibilities and less important to another's. Third, in most of the literature on qualitative research methods, one of the most important attributes is for the ethnographer to be as *unobtrusive* as possible in order not to disturb the natural surroundings of the site or to divert attention away from the innate actions within the field toward actions that are influenced by the "approval" or "disapproval" of the researcher. Try as we must, our presence does make a difference; sometimes, it can be of little importance, and at other times it may drastically affect the fieldwork site.

Technical skills are a part of the methodological process, but they are also an ethical concern, because precision, observation, and ethnographic presence necessarily carry with them moral judgments, interpretive implications, and the responsibility of representation. As we aspire to fine-tune our technical skills, we will not perfect them, because we are not perfect beings, but we strive to do the very best we can.

The final category, the ethnographic self, focuses on the positionality of the ethnographer and when the aspirations to be (a) "the candid ethnographer," (b) "the chaste ethnographer," (c) "the fair ethnographer," and (d) "the literary ethnographer" become shaken. First, you make every attempt to be forthright and *candid* about all that you see, hear, and experience in the field; however, you may need to decipher what must be stated from what need not be stated. There will be times when you make mistakes, when you feel foolish, fearful, or awkward, and when fieldwork encounters are threatening, embarrassing, or intimate. Candor is desired, but it has limits. It is important to reflect upon the consequences of candor. Gratuitous candor that does not benefit anyone, and where there are no real lessons learned, frankness can read like crass indulgence or shallow sensationalism. You might ask yourself what purpose does candor serve? Am I putting myself in jeopardy for the sake of a candor that rubs against personal and professional respect, intimacy, and vulnerability? How does my need for candor affect and represent Others?

Second, chastity is another virtue in the field; although there have been particular accounts where the researcher reports moments of intimacy, they are rare and often denounced. Intimacy, desire, and sexual encounters in the field do happen, but, again, one must consider the consequences in terms of power relations, cultural insensitivity, safety, and the potential for emotional harm. You must be ever-so self-reflexive and contemplate your intentions and the possible effects of making public those private encounters and personal moments in the field. Sometimes the personal and the private are profoundly important and provide the greatest impact for the reader in understanding larger, more universal realities and implications. The question becomes why should we care about private matters? Where do they lead us?

Third, if we can attribute certain rules to ethnography, the attribute of *fairness* would be one of them. We are reminded as qualitative researchers again and again of the importance of being fair. Fine (1993) states,

> What does it mean to be fair? Is fairness possible? The label "fair" can consist of two alternative meanings: that of *objectivity* or that of *balance*. Each is problematic, and each is far from universal in qualitative research narratives. Some suggest that they should not even be goals. Qualitative researchers need not be warned about the difficulty, if not impossibility, of pretending objectivity. Objectivity is an illusion—an illusion snuggled in the comforting blanket of positivism—that the world is ultimately knowable and secure. Alas, the world is always known from the perspective, even though we might agree that often perspectives do not vary dramatically. . . . Few ethnographers accept a single objective reality. (p. 286)

Fourth, the ethnographic self is conventionally known and presented through writing; therefore, all of us who present our work in the form of writing become the literary ethnographer. Writing is a domain in qualitative research and ethnography that has become a topic of much deliberation about the descriptions it offers (e.g., poetic, impressionist, performative, interpretive). The challenges and demands of writing will be taken up in more detail in the next section; however, Fine's (1993) comments are worth mentioning as an initial consideration of how some ethnographers may be more preoccupied with the writing craft; that is, they are conscious of writing styles and devices to the point that the encounters and actualities of the ethnography become overshadowed by language use, metaphors, and poetic devices. Fine suggests that "the writing can hide lack of evidence. . . . The writing carries too much meaning, and inevitably meaning gets shuffled and is imprecise" (pp. 288–289).

The ethical implications related to the ethnographic self in terms of candor, chastity, fairness, and writing are based upon the fact that it is the ethnographer who becomes both the transmitter and the interlocutor for a world that is largely shaped by his or her positionality. Our candor, chastity, fairness, and writing are always contingent on the unique situation; however, these elements must always be aligned with basic codes of ethics that are part of self-reflexive and conscious deliberations.

Conceptual Errors

Adding to the challenges offered by Gary Alan Fine, the feminist critic, Elizabeth Kamark Minnich (1986) outlines four overriding perceptions or conceptual errors that have dominated Western epistemology relative to its erasure of difference and the Other. Minnich's analysis will assist the critical ethnographer in unveiling and recognizing certain taken-for-granted practices, particularly in the academy, that cut against the grain of an ethics of ethnography as it relates to notions of Otherness. For the purpose of parity and justice, Minnich's work brings us to a deeper recognition of the relationship between knowledge, power, dominance, and the Other.

The first conceptual error that Minnich (1986) describes is *faulty generalization.* This is where differences and distinctions become ignored and discounted. In faulty generalization, one type or category of human being represents all others. According to Minnich, faulty generalizations take for granted or naturalize one kind of human being as the universal human while claiming that this singular category represents everyone else.

A common example of faulty generalization is the meaning and use of *man* and *mankind* as a universal signifier for everyone. In many forms of usage, these terms literally and intentionally refer to males at the exclusion of all other human beings (i.e., women and children). This is obviously a faulty generalization in reasoning, intent, and usage. However, these terms, when *intended* to include *all* human beings, remain an inherited faulty generalization that fails to critically disrupt the historical reasoning and intent of its own traditional exclusion.

The second conceptual error is *circularity.* This is where value judgments and ideas of rationality are derived from one particular tradition and then used to prove why other traditions or other concepts of rationality are unreasonable or unworthy. Circularity does not account for the fact that value and reasoning from any one individual, cultural tradition, or intellectual perspective is partial, idiosyncratic, and constructed. Minnich (1986) describes it this way: "In all fields, we find somewhere the intellectual equivalent of redheads defining red hair as a necessary possession of humans, and then using their definition to prove that it is true that only redheads are properly human" (p. 12).

An example of circularity is the proclamation by one religious doctrine that it in and of itself is the one and only doctrine that holds the absolute Truth. In other words, religions A, B, and C have different doctrines, and within each different doctrine they all claim to represent the absolute Truth while claiming the others false. This is circular thinking, because it is equivalent to making the claim that only C is a good religion because C makes the claim that it is the only good religion.

The third conceptual error is *peculiar theoretical constructs and inadequate paradigms.* This is where "ideal" models or illustrations suggest universal applicability without explicitly stating that they do. In other words, "metaphors, normative notions that make no claim to be generalizations from any real sample," are employed in such a manner that they stand in as a general truth (Minnich, 1986, p. 17). Minnich retells a classic example to make this point:

> The story of the blind people and the elephant is a Jain story: the elephant that felt to one like a rope; to one like a tree trunk; to one like a barrel; to one like a fan; to one like a tube is all of those things. Together, the blind people knew the elephant; one by one, they were partly right, and only wrong if they thought they were wholly right. (p. 17)

The fourth conceptual error is *falsification of the status of knowledge*. This is where scholars and teachers "confuse the subject matter as constituted by the particular history of their field with the subject matter itself" (Minnich, 1986, p. 23).

One example of falsification of the status of knowledge is when European and Euro-American artists are the only artists included for a course in the study of art history. One may surmise from this that Europeans and Euro-Americans are the only people that have a history of art. When only one kind of people is represented in a course of study, that representation is often mistakenly understood as the field of study itself. Another example occurs when the *construction* and *interpretation* of knowledge, rather than knowledge itself, is taught as reality. Minnich explains it this way: "When historians confuse the past as it has been recorded, interpreted, and studied by historians with the past itself, [an] error has been committed. By that view, until recently indeed women and most men had very little if no history—and hence, no past" (p. 24).

These conceptual errors as articulated by Elizabeth Minnich describe the manner in which dominant regimes of knowledge marginalize, ignore, and devalue other ways of knowing and being that are outside that prevailing regime or culture. When applied to an ethics of ethnography, they direct us at several levels toward the following ethical contemplations. As ethnographers, we should strive

• to be more self-reflexive and self-critical of our own value-laden perspectives and not take our own perspectives for granted; to questions ourselves and to think honestly about the attitude and disposition we hold for the subjects of our study before we enter the field. Subjects demand that we articulate and make known our own subjectivity, partiality, and biases as we interpret and represent Others.

• to be more mindful of where our theories and paradigms come from and to ask ourselves what voices, representations, and experiences are being excluded on one hand and too quickly universalized on the other.

- to be more precise concerning both our theoretical and methodological choices. Do we need to explore other frames of analysis that may be more applicable to the uniqueness of a particular context? We must ask ourselves if the analytical and methodological frameworks are relevant and appropriate. Interpretive analysis is not a one-size-fits-all proposition.

Minnich (1986) concludes by assuring us that "the errors are not necessary, not by nature, not by requirement of rationality, not by anything" (p. 29). She then introduces a call to action of sorts by stating that these errors, in the past, "were committed by a particular people in particular times, and they can be undone by a kind of critical thinking that is directly related to action" (p. 29).

Dialogic Performance

We will turn to the action of ethnography in the work of performance scholar, ethnographer, and activist Dwight Conquergood. In his popular essay "Performing as a Moral act: Ethical Dimensions of the Ethnography of Performance" (1982b), Conquergood presents five stances relative to ethics, four of which are fundamental problems or offenses to ethical fieldwork in varying degrees and circumstances. However, the fifth stance of *dialogical performance* contributes to an ethics of ethnography that provides a methodological approach that resists conceptual errors based on exclusivity and repressive paradigms of knowledge.

The first ethical offense is what Conquergood (1982b) calls *the custodian's rip-off*. This is where fieldworkers enter the field for the single purpose of "getting good material" to further their own self-interest and ambition. Human beings are used as raw material that must be acquired or collected to successfully get the job done. In the custodian's rip-off, researchers are only concerned with getting what they want for themselves and for their projects, with little or no consideration of how their presence affects the dignity, safety, traditions, order, economy, and health of the people they meet.

The custodian's rip-off occurs when the researcher enters the field without respectful regard for subjects, but measures the time and trust given to him or her by the success and effectiveness of the research project. In her very fine study of domestic workers, Judith Rollins (1985) describes a researcher who asked for a family recipe that her interviewer, an elderly domestic worker, cherished deeply. The recipe had been in the elder woman's family for generations and it was a symbol of the history of love and caring the women in her family enacted through the art of cooking and domesticity. It was a special recipe that was created by the lineage of her mothers with their writing and imprints on the original copy. The recipe was one of her most valued possessions, a remembrance of her youth, the women who loved her, and early years of protection and joy. The researcher pressured the older woman to please let her borrow the recipe as an artifact to interpret for her research. Although the elder was very reluctant, she wanted to help the young woman who insisted that she understood the value of the recipe and vowed she would return it. Wanting to help, and believing the researcher's promise that she would take great care of the valued recipe and return it, the elderly woman let the researcher borrow it. The researcher took the recipe to analyze for her project and forgot to return it to the woman. The elderly woman never saw her recipe again. She expressed to Rollins the sense of loss, pain, and deep regret over the broken promise.

The second offense, *the ethnographer's infatuation,* is where the field-worker succumbs to romantic infatuation and superficial identification with the people of the study. The ethnographer is enamored with the Other in a shallow reverie over "aren't we all the same." Conquergood (1982b) states, "Although not as transparently immoral as the custodian's rip-off, this performative stance is unethical because it trivializes the Other. The distinctiveness of the other is glossed over by a glaze of generalities" (p. 6). The Other becomes an object of the researcher's admiration without a will or voice of its own. The ethnographer, secure in his or her own "protective solipsism," obviates differences and negates the possibility that the Other can reverse positions and become the judge, critic, and interpreter of the researcher or ethnographer.

The ethnographer's infatuation occurs when ethnographers go into the field imposing their own romantic lens over difficult realities. The ethnographer will overlook deep-seated contradictions, detailed symbolic meanings, and troubling questions in the field for glorifying appearances and shallow romanticism. For example, the researcher may encounter terror, poverty, human rights abuses, or social injustices, but then overlook the details and consequences of their severity and replace them with palatable banalities and general clichés about a common humanity. For example, I equate infatuation in my own fieldwork with those researchers I have observed who elide the complexities of human rights abuses only to excuse certain practices, such as various types of servitude or female incision (what is pejoratively referred to as "female genital mutilation"), as characteristic of the culture's intriguing uniqueness. Some will take the radical relativist stance that every culture has the right to its own idiosyncratic practices—always fascinating and permissible—without criticism, particularly from outsiders.

The third offense is the *curator's exhibition.* Whereas the enthusiast is enthralled by a shallow identification and sameness, the curator is fascinated by exotic difference and distance. We move from the shallow to the sensational. Conquergood (1982b) states, "This is the 'Wild Kingdom' approach to performance that grows out of a fascination with the exotic, primitive, culturally remote. The performer wants to astonish rather than understand" (p. 6).

In the curator's exhibition, the researcher becomes so enamored with difference that subjectivity and meaning is erased. While living in Ghana, a mask carver told me a story of a researcher who was enthralled with the "exotic" artwork of West African carvings. He was so ready to mark difference that he misinterpreted the meanings of a particular genre of carved masks and wrongly defined them as fetish symbols used in ceremonial witchcraft to bring destruction upon one's enemies. The carver, who is Catholic and doesn't believe in witchcraft, said the masks are actually carved to represent contemporary life in Ghana, largely for the purpose of selling to tourists.

The fourth offense is the *skeptic's cop-out*. The skeptic remains detached and determined that he will not enter domains of Otherness. With cavalier certainty, he claims he cannot embody or engage an identity outside his own. This stance forecloses engagement. Conquergood (1982b) states, "The skeptic's cop-out is the most morally reprehensible corner of the map because it forecloses dialogue. The enthusiast, one can always hope, may move beyond infatuation to love. Relationships that begin superficially can sometime deepen and grow" (p. 8). Conquergood compellingly describes the skeptic as "detached and estranged, with no sense of the other, sits alone in an echo-chamber of his own making, with only the sound of his own scoffing laughter ringing in his ears" (p. 8). The skeptic's cop-out shuts down the potential for engagement with the Other; therefore, we are left with no evidence or example of their entry into domains outside their own.

It is the fifth stance, located in the center of the four offenses outlined above, that to Conquergood (1982b) now becomes the ethical alternative. Conquergood describes this stance as *dialogical performance*. The four extreme corners of the map, from *detachment* to *commitment* and from *identity* to *difference*, reside in tension outside the frame that centers and focuses upon dialogical performance. Dialogical performance and genuine conversation are at the center and superimposed over the single connecting point where the offenses each meet. Commenting on "the strength of the center" where dialogical performance is situated, Conquergood explains that this center of dialogue "pulls together mutually opposed energies that become destructive only when they are vented without the counter balancing pull of their opposite" (p. 9). Dialogical performance becomes the centerpiece, representing the moral ground that keeps the counter-balancing pull in operation:

The aim of dialogical performance is to bring self and other together so that they can question, debate, and challenge one another. It is a kink of performance that resists conclusions. It is intensely committed to keeping the dialogue between performer and text open and ongoing. Dialogical understanding does not end with empathy. There is always enough appreciation for difference so that the text can interrogate, rather than dissolve into, the performer. That is why I have charted this performative stance at the center of the moral map. More than a definite position, the dialogical stance is situated in the space between competing ideologies. It brings self and other together even while it holds them apart. It is more like a hyphen than a period. (p. 10)

Conquergood (1982b) provides for ethnographers clear modes of ethical considerations. Each mode is a further call for reflecting upon our own positionality as it relates to ethical methods. We may determine that it is the nature of our work to be dialogical; therefore, the other four stances outlined here are too extreme. Would any thoughtful ethnographer really commit any of these stances? The significance of this mapping, as Conquergood states, is for us to consider the quintessential offenses as well as the relative offenses that commonly occur along the frames of each. We may not always assume we are incapable of committing such offenses, but we must instead be humble enough and circumspect enough about the power and privilege that we hold as researchers and about our own positionality along the axis of the five stances.

Warm-Ups

1. An inexperienced fieldworker is conducting fieldwork at a senior citizen daycare center. She has been working at the center for more than two years. After providing informed consent at the beginning the project, her primary consultant has just informed her that he does not wish to be included in the study. He asks that all interviews and other relevant data relating to him be excluded from the study. If the student does not include data from this consultant, most of her research will not be of use. She will not be able to complete her research in time for graduation. What should she do?

2. Referring to the Fine (1993) discussion, what would be the three most challenging lies for you in the field? What do you anticipate would be the consequences?

3. According to the Minnich (1986) discussion, what conceptual errors have you internalized and enacted the most during your academic experiences? What have been the consequences?

4. According to the Conquergood (1982b) discussion, what are the moral transgressions that you have witnessed the most and most. Which ones do you feel you most want to avoid and why?

Suggested Readings

Davis, C. A. (1999). *Reflexive ethnography: A guide to researching selves and others*. London: Routledge.

Gray, P. (1991). The use of theory. *Text and Performance Quarterly, 11*, 267–277.

Jackson, M. (1989). *Paths toward a clearing: Radical empiricism and ethnographic inquiry*. Bloomington: Indiana University Press.

Latham, A. J. (2001). Postmodernism, poststructuralism and post(critical) ethnography: Of ruins, aporias and angels. In P. Atkinson, A. Coffey, S. Delamont, J. Lofland, & L. Lofland (Eds.), *Handbook of ethnography* (pp. 477–492). London: Sage.

Lather, P. (1986). Research as praxis. *Harvard Educational Review, 56*(3), 257–277.

McLaren, P. (1992). Collisions with otherness: "Traveling" theory, post-colonial criticism, and the politics of ethnographic practice—The mission of the wounded ethnographer. *International Journal of Qualitative Studies in Education, 5*(1), 77–92.

Noblit, G. W., & Hare, R. D. (1988). *Meta-ethnography: Synthesizing qualitative studies*. Thousand Oaks, CA: Sage.

Rosaldo, R. (1989). *Culture and truth*. Boston: Beacon.

6

Methods and Application

Three Case Studies in Ethical Dilemmas

I n this chapter, we will return to our three case studies from Chapter 3 and address the ethical dilemmas that each of the researchers struggled to resolve. At the beginning of each case study are a series of ethical questions that the researcher encountered during his or her fieldwork. At the end of each case, the questions are addressed based on methodological procedures presented in the example.

Case One: Local Activism in West Africa

Advocacy, Representation, and Voice

- How can I be an effective advocate without compromising my intellectual integrity and critical objectivity?
- How do I represent complex problems without negatively misrepresenting the subjects of the study?
- How can I prevent my voice, as researcher, from overpowering the voices of the subjects themselves?

By the end of her second year, Joan had developed a close and trusting relationship with the group. They had become friends and extended family; she was a natural part of social events and family gatherings. At the beginning of her fieldwork she was the ethnographer; at the end, she was simultaneously ethnographer, advocate, friend, and extended family.

Two years have come and gone. It is time to go back to the United States and begin writing. The transition from fieldwork to writing *about* the field is not an easy adjustment. Although one is always writing through various processes of the field experience, when it is time to write the ethnography, there is a shift in modalities from the openness of the field to the enclosure of the writing space. Joan is also experiencing return anxiety. She feels as though she is crossing two vastly different terrains: one that is geographic, and the other that is emotive. On one level, the once-foreign world that evolved through time into richly accustomed sights, sounds, and meanings is now suddenly displaced by a one-way plane ride into a different world, the world of "home," which is, after two years, both vaguely familiar and unfamiliar. On the second level, the transition from the felt-sensing interactions within the day-to-day rhythms of Others with whom she lived and traveled with empathy and loving perception is now suddenly displaced by the quietude of writing and by the solitary reckoning that after two years of *knowing her face through the face of the Other,* she is alone now to write and to determine who gets the last word. Joan feels the weight of both loneliness and responsibility.

Several weeks pass. Joan completes the first steps in an ongoing process of organizing data, coding/recoding notes, and working through themes. Joan is journeying into writing, and the memories of her experiences in the field are slowly becoming more acute, more ordered, and tangible. She is realizing that writing is also evoking new discoveries and meanings. Return anxiety is gradually beginning to diminish. She is slowly starting to feel inspired again. The writing is becoming a kind of re-creation and reenactment of her fieldwork, as well as a laudatory testimony to indigenous activism in the developing world. Joan is also becoming more and more adamant in her own position as an advocate for arms control and global justice. She is more determined than ever that her study must meaningfully contribute to the strength of the movement. She is finally making the adjustment to being back home and to the solitude of writing. Her writing begins to flow.

As she continues to write, she works passionately to describe the deeply layered and sensual dimensions of the field and even more passionately to convey the politics that motivates the work of her friends and consultants in West Africa. She is mindful of her own rhetorical arguments and her commitment to social justice. As a critical ethnographer, honoring her subjects by advocating for a global Arms Trade Treaty and fair trade is paramount. As the writing progresses, Joan is becoming more driven by her political beliefs: Arms trade fuels poverty and death for the weak and profits for the strong; easy access to weapons is contributing to the destruction of too many innocent people—someone is killed every minute by imported arms. Joan is on a mission and the writing continues to flow.

Joan has now completed the first draft that serves to introduce key members of the group: their vision, their purpose, and specific incidents and experiences that illustrate the courageous sacrifices they have made to end the violence in their country. Joan wants so much for her readers to recognize their work, to be inspired by their struggles, and to support their cause. These are African people and many of them are very poor with few resources. Joan understands that much of the world looks upon the poor, the black, and the foreign with what Maria Lugones (1994) calls "arrogant perception." She is passionate in creating a representation that is truthful to their courage and their struggle, a study that will oppose and rebuke the arrogant perceivers in the world. Joan recollects the treatise on African people that the father of modern philosophy, G. W. F. Hegel, professed and that contributed to a system of ideas that rationalized European racism: "The Negro . . . exhibits the natural man in his completely wild and untamed state. . . . There is nothing harmonious with humanity to be found in this type of character" (qtd. in Hord & Lee, 1995, p. 314).

Joan thinks, Hegel never traveled to Other worlds, literally or figuratively. Could his history and disposition ever imagine the intelligence and moral character of her friends and consultants throughout the continent of Africa, a continent that according to his moral philosophy and the legacy of too many others is void of "humanity"? Joan becomes more determined than ever to tell the stories of African people who are putting their lives on the line for their principles: to stop the free flow of weapons that leads to mass destruction. These men and women say they must never allow a return of the fighting that took thousands of innocent lives and made armed violence the terror of everyday life in their country. Joan records the stories told to her of children witnessing their parents gunned down by the soldiers; of the torture and massacre of villages; of hospitals, churches, and schools shattered with blood and bullets. These African people are taking their destiny in their own hands to teach peace and forgiveness in their country and to stop the race for weapons. For them, the painful memories of the past invoke a steadfast determination to build a new future. Joan's ethnography champions a cause, but it is also a record of the collective memories of brutal violence and the collective hope of sustained peace.

Joan has read the draft over several times, but something is beginning to change. She is coming to realize what she had never realized before. She is suddenly struck by the implications of the very memories she recounts. Why couldn't she see this before? Her confidence and passion are beginning to turn into an uneasy feeling. She reads the draft again. She is confused. Feelings of doubt are creeping in. She begins to question the implications of her work: In her efforts to detail the incredible courage of her friends, was she actually detailing memories of a past that portrayed African people as brutal, savage, and barbaric? Does the study actually perpetuate Hegel's philosophy of African *inhumanity?* Will recounting the brutality overshadow the African *humanity* of consultants and their commitment to resist the violence perpetuated by their own countrymen? Is she producing yet another item for mass consumption in which the brave and benevolent Westerner travels to the "Dark Continent" to "save" the unenlightened Africans from their own destruction? More doubts now begin to surface as these questions lead to deeper questions concerning her own intentions. Is she another example of Conquergood's (1982b) *curator's exhibition?* Does her study properly honor the dignity and courage of her friends and their cause for global justice, or is it really just advancing her own career? After all, she left Africa to complete her dissertation on the backs of their struggle. She will be commended by colleagues and friends for "brilliant" work and admired for living the "hard life" in Africa for "so long." Joan thinks about this last sentiment and knows that her two years could not compare to the lifetime of dedicated work that comprised the day-to-day existence of her friends. She left West Africa to get her degree: They remained to continue the struggle.

Joan is now at a discouraging stopping point in her work. She feels immobilized by the ethical implications of her project. She immediately makes an appointment to see her advisor, Professor Acquah. She needs help and advice.

When Joan arrives at Professor Acquah's office, she expresses her doubts. She fears that recounting the stories of armed violence and the perpetrators of the destruction would contribute to the already stereotypical view of African people. But the dilemma is that these stories are stories of profound memory, memories that are the source of their inspiration and their determination. Can she *not* tell the stories of their brutal past? Can she simply erase context and history by not recounting the war? Yet, if she does tell their stories of murder and torture, won't she be reinscribing the awful stereotype? Joan feels that she had fallen into an ethical trap. She then turns to Professor Acquah and confesses that she is also feeling the guilt of academic imperialism. She has begun to feel that she will be rewarded for work that comes from the blood and sweat of Other people's suffering.

Professor Acquah listens carefully. He reminds Joan that she kept referring to her consultants as "friends." He asks her what she thought her friendship meant to them. Joan thinks for a moment, and then says that she believes it meant she had listened well, that she understood, that she cared, that they trusted she would do what they needed her to do—what she promised them she would do. Joan says it meant they have been together through various trials and tribulations. They have grown close. They feel she will do the right thing by them.

Professor Acquah asks, "What makes you think this way?"

Joan says, "Because it is what they told me and what they showed me."
He then asks, "What does the friendship mean to you?"

Joan answers without hesitation. "It means that I can't let them down. I feel a responsibility, as well as a desire, to do what I promised I would do, because I've spent time with them. I've been together with them, and I lived out so many stories with them."

Professor Acquah tells Joan that she has just described in her own words the first principles of ethical fieldwork: "Our primary responsibility is to the people we study. When there is a conflict of interest, these individuals must come first." He continues, "This means that it is their story and their struggle that must be told even at the risk of being misunderstood and unfairly interpreted, because they gave you their time, their trust, and opened their lives to you with the expectation that you would report their experiences and interpret their stories justly. It also means that your *angst* and *guilt* about your benefits cannot eclipse or cloud your *responsibility* to do meaningful work." He then surprises Joan by asking another question that seems unrelated and offbeat. "What is your method?"

Joan looks puzzled. "Method? I don't know. Do I have a method?"

"Yes, you do."

Method and Advocacy

The methodological process that will constitute Joan's work and the work of much advocacy research requires a primary focus on *power structure* and *context*.

Method One

You become aware of an issue through your research or you become more deeply committed to the issue as a result of your research. Method requires that you address meanings and descriptions of the issue: How would you describe what you are advocating for and against? Is the advocacy position described or defined differently in relation to varying context and power dynamics? Keep a journal on how this advocacy position is defined and referred to within your working context and other competing contexts. As you include background research on the topic, comparing and contrasting it with your fieldwork data in order to gain an understanding of the history, debates, and key strategies that constitute the issue, begin to decide whether or not you should discuss with your consultants how you should name or define yourself as an advocate specifically in relation to them.

Illustration

Joan knew very little about arms trade and proliferation when she began her fieldwork. She asked her consultants for titles and references for background research, as well as to gain an understanding of the kinds of readings that helped to inform their work. She also used her resources as a college student and as an American to do extended research of more titles, thereby offering them a remuneration of a wider variety of resources (i.e., bibliographies, articles, books, videos, reference books on funding, etc.). Also, Joan continually asked for clarity and as much accuracy as possible and appropriate in understanding and recording the terms and concepts used by her consultants. Key definitions and descriptions were from the (emic) perspective of her consultants.

In her role as an advocate, she followed the lead of her consultants. She did not take on a leadership role except in specific situations where she and her consultants determined it was necessary. Her role as advocate was continually evolving and taking on various dimensions. Joan took great care in respecting the authority and wisdom of her consultants. She understood the importance of humility and not crossing the line to become the "take charge" American. Her advice and suggestions were always within the realm of dialogic performance (Conquergood, 1982b), rather than orders or directions.

Method Two

As you conduct your fieldwork and perform varying activities, as well as witnessing varying dimensions of "being there" that are both large and small, determinations will be made that will at varying moments guide how you will balance the role of researcher with that of advocate. This is a delicate and complex balancing act that should be done in collaboration with your consultants.

Illustration

There was a situation in which Joan was asked to travel and represent the organization for a meeting in a nearby village. The trip was a routine visit and not central to her research. However, it was scheduled at the same time she was to attend a conference that was, in fact, key to her research. Joan decided to travel to the village because, although it was routine for her and not integral to her research, it was a strategic and vital meeting for the organization and for the strength of the movement. The balance between researcher and advocate was always in negotiation. There were other times when it was necessary for Joan to prioritize her research over her role as advocate. Her choices depended on the answers to these questions: Which domain has *more to lose* if I choose one over the other? In which role would I be *more effective* in accomplishing something relative to this specific task? With which role is it more important for me to be identified at this particular moment in my service as an advocate? With which role is it more important for me to be identified at this particular moment in my service as an academic?

Relating to the last two questions, Joan paradoxically found that it was of more value in certain academic situations to emphasize her role as advocate. Conversely, in her fieldwork among her consultants and others, they often requested under certain situations that she emphasize her role as an academic.

Method Three

As you conduct your research, you must be ever mindful of anonymity and confidentiality, always checking and rechecking for permission and consent in the disclosure of names and information.

Illustration

Where it may have led to some form of harm or difficulty, as determined by herself and her consultants, Joan coded names of particular people, places, and events through a combination of colors, numbers, and symbols. The majority of her consultants found the IRB Informed Consent Form suspicious and inappropriate. The majority felt more comfortable giving consent on the tape-recorded interview or verbally in their conversations with Joan.

In the ongoing process of checking and rechecking for permission to disclose names and information, to record data, or to take photographs, it became such a natural part of the process that often times Joan's consultants would say before she even asked, "You may record this" or "Do not take photographs here." Joan had developed a rapport where the question of permission was anticipated and ingrained in the fieldwork research.

Method Four

In instances where your advocacy position or the position of your consultants places them or Others in a questionable or negative light, you must consider the context of their lives in relation to structures of power that constitute their actions, culture, and history.

Illustration

When recounting the war and the brutality of the movement, Joan took great care to explain the politics and history that lead to and contributed to the fighting: the history of colonial rule; the complex relation between poverty and violence in the specific locale of her fieldwork; the machinations of local corruption and global inequity; and, most important, the abundance of weapons pouring into the country. An emphasis on *causes* leads to an understanding of the roots and reasons of their *effects*.

Method Five

Your positionality as an advocate must be acknowledged through self-reflexive reporting. As an advocate, your standpoint cannot be veiled by an invisible identity or by third-person omniscient narration. You must make transparent your advocacy position or else it becomes a question of disguise and therefore of ethics.

Illustration

Joan clearly has a strong position against arms trading. She does not make an effort to appear objective. Her predilection is transparent and she is honest in acknowledging her political bias to the reader. Her readers are aware that she writes from a certain ideological standpoint; moreover, it is clear that she writes from a subject position constituted by the composite of identities and socioeconomic and political factors that inform her voice. By acknowledging her position, Joan is taking responsibility for the claims and interpretive descriptions that she makes, rather than making it appear as though they come from the "facts" set forth by an omniscient authority.

Method Six

In the balancing act between being an ethnographer and an advocate, you cannot allow your ideological position as an advocate to distort or misrepresent ethnographic information. This will only weaken your position as an advocate and that of your consultants. You will be a stronger advocate by making an argument based on your commitment and field experience and claiming it as your own, rather than trying to force a connection between your argument and the data.

Illustration

Just as Joan does not feign objectivity through a disguised bias, she does not distort empirical information to suit her advocacy agenda. Joan is self-reflexive about paying attention to the different registers of *empirical fact, general description, theoretical and philosophical analysis,* and *political argument.* Although these registers are not always separate, as they often overlap and coincide with the others, it is useful to keep in mind their discrete distinctions and not to confuse what is an empirical fact with a politicized opinion. It is ethically problematic when the ethnographer is straightforward regarding his or her political position but distorts or falsifies empirical facts to make it fit that argument while presenting them as empirical or "true." *The reader must be able to decipher what is an empirical observation and what is a political claim.*

Method Seven

You will decide how you wish your ethnographic data to serve its advocacy purpose: as a published manuscript, reference for policy formation, public performance, resource for consultants and general public, or in some other form.

Illustration

Joan decided that she wanted her dissertation to serve multiple purposes relative to advocacy: (a) it would be published as a book for the enlightenment of students and scholars; (b) she would adapt her fieldwork data into a script for public performance and distribution that could be read and performed by advocates for arms regulation nationally and internationally and used as a source of persuasion and communication for policymakers; (c) the published script would include a general report of her fieldwork experience, including selected oral histories, for a wider distribution to the international population that may not have access to the scholarly book or the performance.

Case Two: Secrets of Sexuality and Personal Narrative

Trust, Confidentiality, and Informed Consent

- How is trust developed between myself and the subjects of the study?
- How do I adhere to the necessary steps in assuring confidentiality?
- How is informed consent legitimated?

The year came to an end. Robert had completed the final draft of his master's thesis and had given it to his committee members. Harry, Jim, and Raymond read a draft and gave their approval before Robert turned the final draft over to his committee, having incorporated some of the comments and concerns of the three. The defense date for his thesis was set, and Robert was looking forward to graduating and starting a new job on the West Coast for the HIV Hospice Network.

Four days before Robert was scheduled to meet with his committee to defend his thesis, Harry called him on the telephone. Harry told Robert that after thinking about the study for several days, he had changed his mind about consenting to having his narrative included. He felt compelled to pull his oral history out of the study and must now renege on his approval. Harry explained that he trusted Robert and felt that Robert took every precaution to protect his anonymity and confidentiality. However, as Robert had explained to him during the initial interview, there is never a *complete* guarantee that you will not be identified. He understood that, with the safeguards Robert took, it was unlikely he would ever be recognized in the study, but he felt he could no longer take the risk, even if it was a one percent chance he would be linked to the work. Harry went on to express how very, very sorry he was to back out at the last minute and jeopardize the year of research that it took Robert to complete the study. In fact, he felt "dreadful" about the "awful" position he was putting Robert in, especially since Robert was in the last stage of attaining his degree. Placing his own career aside, however, he could not risk the welfare of his wife and child if any of the details of the oral history were ever associated with him. Harry ended the conversation with sincere apologies and regret for disappointing Robert and imperiling his study; however, he had no choice but to consider, first and foremost, the interest of his family.

Robert hung up the phone; he was shocked and devastated. He did not understand. He had been working with Harry for over a year and there was never any indication that he was thinking about withdrawing from the study. Why would Harry call him at the last minute? Why didn't he give some indication before now of his concerns? In addition, Robert went to great lengths not only to use pseudonyms, but to also disguise all names, events, circumstances, and situations that may have led to any association with the three men. Robert remembered another incident that was very similar to his own in a study where the anthropologist Sue E. Estroff (1995) was awakened in the night by a phone call from an irate informant:

There is a kind of cold, quiet terror that comes with a telephone ring at 3 a.m. Almost always there is something to hear that one would rather not. And so it was that night—the confusion of sleep vanished in a second, replaced by nausea borne of fear. The voice I heard was almost chanting in rage and anguish. There was ridicule, too, and precision cuts at my fast-fading concepts of myself as a kind, careful, and just ethnographer. She had asked for a copy of the book I had written about her and the others. I gave it to her as a gift. She had just read what I had written about her ten years before. She was wounded by the images of herself in the past—psychotic, rambling, and charming. I had exploited her, used her, misunderstood everything, and was unmasked now, she said. Not the bright, "liberal," sympathetic researcher I claimed to be, but worse than the others for my self- and other deception. Furthered my career, made a name for myself, all at her expense. How could you? (By now I was asking this silently, along with her.) How could you come see me again, spend the whole day with me, like a friend, pretending to understand, to like me? (p. 78)

Robert remembered how, after receiving the call, Estroff was shaken and still "haunted" by the call seven years later as she recounted the incident in the article. Estroff poignantly questioned her ethical responsibility to the women and the nature of ethnographic authority and privilege in the probing and publication of other people's lives—of vulnerable lives. The woman had read Estroff's book ten years *before* the angry call, yet Estroff was deeply self-reflexive about the effects of her work and the woman's pain: "What responsibility did I have to protect her from the pain of recognizing herself in a prior state that later humiliated and undermined her well-being?" (p. 79). Estroff questioned her own privilege and the vulnerability of her informant: "It is a story about her, but my account is privileged. She has no access to a comparable forum in which to dispute or respond to my representation of her (except perhaps here, and still I intervene)" (p. 79). Estroff then asked the question that plagues us all: "Should I even be telling *this* story?" (p. 79).

Unlike Sue Estroff, Robert was stopped before the story got to the publisher. Perhaps he was saved. What if he had already published the work and Harry called him after the fact with charges of betrayal and deception? What if he gets a phone call in the middle of the night from Jim or Raymond next week, or next year, or ten years from now? Estroff is an experienced and principled ethnographer, and she works with great care and concern; yet that phone call still haunts her. . . . Robert was shaken.

After explaining the situation to his advisor, Professor Cunningham, Robert was asked to review his method of confidentiality. Professor Cunningham then asked, "Have you done all you can do to reassure Harry that you have followed the method and taken every step to safeguard his identity?"

"Yes," said Robert, "I spoke to him in great detail about the procedures I used to protect his privacy. But it didn't seem to matter to him."

"Well," said Professor Cunningham, "does Harry understand the full repercussions of withdrawing his oral history and what that would mean for you?"

"I didn't need to explain them to him because he already knows. We have been talking about the study for the past year."

"Have you met with Harry in person or was this conversation all over the telephone?"

"I spoke with him by phone," said Robert.

"You need to persuade Harry to meet with you in person. Talk to him face to face. This is not an all or nothing situation. You may possibly strike a compromise. Ask him if he has any suggestions for protecting his identity in such a way that would be almost impossible for anyone to identify his oral history. You may ask him if you can just use certain segments of his story with the understanding that the pseudonym and characterization of the narrator would serve to mask his personhood as completely as possible."

Robert took a deep breath. "I will call him now and try to set up a time to meet."

Method and Confidentiality

Method One

Discuss with your consultants in clear and comprehensible terms your feelings and attitude, as well as their own, in honoring anonymity and confidentiality as it relates to the project.

Illustration

Robert spoke with Harry, Jim, and Raymond during the initial interview and expressed his sensitivity to their concerns for anonymity. The men were already generally briefed on the study and safeguards for privacy from representatives of the organizations Robert had contacted. He shared his own experiences with them as a gay man who was closeted for many years until very recently. He then outlined in detailed steps the measures he would take to ensure their privacy.

Method Two

Reassure your consultants that the disclosure of information will be contingent on their permission and consent while mutually deciding what form of permission is more appropriate and compatible with the nature of your relationship and the field context.

Illustration

Robert asked each of the men which method of consent would be most comfortable for them. None of the men agreed to sign the informed consent form provided through Robert's university. Jim consented on the tape recorder, but Harry and Raymond felt more comfortable giving Robert verbal consent.

Method Three

Share with your consultants possible and exceptional situations where confidentiality and anonymity may demand disclosure and a breach of the original agreement. Explain what your efforts will be to safeguard and minimize such demands.

Illustration

Robert explained that in life and death situations disclosure may be necessary. It would also be necessary under court order. In these circumstances, he explained, it is a practice among qualitative researchers (a) to divulge as little information as required and (b) to request to be withdrawn, if possible, as a witness from the court proceedings. He went on to explain that in such circumstances the researcher will also request that all confidential information be placed under seal from public view.

Method Four

Explain the ethics policy and related mechanisms within your institution—university and/or funding agency—concerning privacy and protecting the rights of vulnerable populations or human subjects.

Illustration

Robert informed the men that privacy was a central concern in the nature of his work and that there were formal guidelines of ethical procedures established from various institutions and organizations within the academic community. He chose to cite specifically the ethical codes from anthropology and social work—the AAA and the NASW. He then explained the function and purpose of the IRB, including its policy and procedures.

Method Five

Reassure your consultants that you will not disclose identity or information considered private and confidential to anyone without their permission. This would include students and professional colleagues, as well as other participants in the study.

Illustration

Robert reassured the men that he would not discuss their identity with anyone, and he referred to specific examples of friends, students, colleagues, and coparticipants. He would not, even in the most casual and subtle of circumstances, divulge their identity. He also stated that he would not be careless in discussing or referring to them in public spaces, as well as in what might seem harmless environments, such as restaurants, hallways, banks, and elevators.

Method Six

Inform your consultants that in the case of your death or incapacitation their information remains safeguarded and will be either coded and locked or destroyed. Reassure them that you will honor their anonymity and confidentiality in the case of their death.

Illustration

Robert explained to the men that the data would be stored under lock and key, and if it were to be found, identifying information remains densely coded. He also explained that, after the publication of his manuscript, he would destroy or return specific information they requested.

Case Three: Community Theatre Conflict and Organization

Fairness, Critical Judgment, and Policy Implications

- How is fairness determined?
- How is critical judgment evaluated?
- How are policy implications considered in the study?

Nia was in a quandary. How should she represent what happened with the residents without denigrating them or making it appear as if their difficulty with the director was a racial issue? Was it a racial issue? How can she represent the profoundly important work of the director and the company while maintaining a critical view of their shortcomings? How can she include the residents' experience in her study and tell the truth about the problems without it having negative implications for the Urban Arts Exchange Program and future funding? If she did not include the residents' experience, would her ethnography be weakened by a significant omission?

Nia met with a friend who is an experienced ethnographer for guidance on how to proceed. After explaining her dilemma, Nia's friend smiled, chuckled a bit, and rolled back her chair. She told Nia that her dilemma was a classic one, and that she and many others who do fieldwork are faced with the same problem of varying extremes, where you meet an impasse between being a champion for the same subjects that you must simultaneously critique. Nia's friend then said, "I will share a technique with you that has always helped me in keeping the balance at times when it is absolutely necessary to do so and at other times letting the scale tip to one side or the other when balance is not the best or desired outcome."

"Over the years," the friend shared, "I have developed this technique into a method that I hope will be as helpful to you as it has been to me." She then went on to ask, "Have you heard of the four C's of criticism that require the researcher to probe? They are *clarity, conversation, contemplation,* and *consequences.*

Method and Criticism

Method One

When the study necessitates criticism of your consultants or friends, you may begin to *clarify* the nature of the problem. Move it out of the blurry space of ambiguity or "something doesn't feel right." Try as best you can to more specifically identify the "imperfection" or the "fly in the soup."

Illustration

Nia kept a detailed journal of her fieldwork. She noted and, when useful, sometimes deciphered between actions, attitudes, beliefs, and circumstances. In organizing what can be an overstimulation of meaning, information, and sensual experience, Nia was able to clarify and identify more easily certain problems. Identifying them and writing them down in the privacy of her journal enabled and freed her to question, probe, and even vent without constraint or insult. This allowed Nia to work out, process, and describe more concretely the ambiguity (or obscurity) of her initial impressions and observations of a possible fly in the soup.

Method Two

After you have identified the problem, you may ask yourself: Is my judgment right? Or do I have the right to judge? This *conversation* with yourself is the point of critical self-reflection, because you may decide you have been wrong. You reflect upon the problem(s) you have identified regarding your subjects through an effort toward genuine empathy. In other words, you try to achieve genuine empathy with your subject and, in doing so, you must also reflect on the problems or difficulties you may have with your subject. At this point, the conversation may move from being one you carry on with yourself to one conducted with a trusted or experienced listener, and finally with specific consultants. The conversation between you, your listener, and specific consultants should be based on questions, not statements.

Illustration

Nia discussed her concerns with her friend to guide her in articulating the problem she was observing, as well as to help her self-reflect upon the tensions between empathy and judgment. After gaining insight from the conversation with her friend, she spoke individually with the director, selected cast members, and one of the residents. She was careful not to cast the questions as interrogations, but as honest inquiries about how they might interpret specific intentions and actions, as well as the subject's behaviors and effects upon others in the company.

Method Three

After clarifying the problem, being self-reflexive regarding your judgment of the problem, and then engaging in meaningful conversations about the problem, you may then *contemplate* the necessity and purpose of your criticism. This contemplation requires a great deal of thought and deep circumspection regarding why you feel a critique of your subjects is required for the study and what function it will serve.

Illustration

At this point, Nia was certain that she must include the unfortunate experience with the residents, as well as the idiosyncrasies of the director that affected the residents' behavior. Her final decision was motivated by the purpose it would serve. She clarified the purpose with more precision. This involved a great deal of time and thought. She needed to resolve how to write critique so as not to denigrate or misrepresent, but to bring to light the complexity and the overall and deeply described experience with the company and all its productive challenges.

Method Four

After articulating the purpose and necessity of your critique, a consideration of the *consequences* of your work is in order. You may not be able to determine all the consequences, and you may wish to seek advice as you try to imagine what the consequences may be. Remember, there may be unintended consequences that may possibly undermine your intentions and purpose. It may be useful to think of what may be the *worst possible consequence*, and then judge how realistic such an outcome is. After considering the consequences, you may decide not to include your criticism, even after contemplating that necessity and purpose dictate that you should.

Illustration

Nia considered the consequences as she and her friend discussed a range of possibilities. After recognizing what some of the unintended consequences may be, she decided that she would not include a full description of the artist-in-residents as she had planned. She would omit from the study instances that, if interpreted from a particular perspective, would be used to jeopardize the city's Urban Art Program and place the company at an unfair and negative disadvantage. The success of the Urban Arts Program was ultimately more valuable relative to the lives it could positively affect than the ambition and success of her own study. Moreover, Nia felt that she needed to frame the incident in a manner that would not gratuitously denigrate, but would offer more viable solutions and responses when local organizations are faced with comparable problems.

Warm-Ups

1. What questions would you ask Joan, Robert, and Nia about their ethical dilemmas? Perform a mock interview and attempt to answer the questions both from their viewpoints and, if different, from your own.

2. How would specific ethical dilemmas change from one case study to the next? How would Joan's concern to sensationalize her consultants also be a factor for Robert? How would Nia's concern for public policy be a concern for Robert and Joan? How would the effects be discretely different in each project?

Suggested Readings

Alcoff, L. (1991). The problem of speaking for others. *Cultural Critique, 20,* 5–32.

Conquergood, D. (1988). Health theatre in a Hmong refugee camp. *The Drama Review, 32,* 174–208.

Estroff, S. (1995). Whose story is it anyway? Authority, voice, and responsibility in narrative of chronic illness. In K. S. Toombs, D. Barnard, & R. A. Carson (Eds.), *Chronic illness: From experience to policy* (pp. 78–103). Bloomington: Indiana University Press.

Hamera, J. (1996). Reconstructing Apsaras from memory: Six thoughts. In C. Ellis & A. Bochner (Eds.), *Ethnographic alternatives* (pp. 201–206). Walnut Creek, CA: AltaMira.

Hantzis, D. M. (1998). Reflection on "A dialogue with friends: 'Performing' the 'other'/self. In S. J. Dailey (Ed.), *The future of performance studies: Visions and revisions* (pp. 203–206). Washington, DC: National Communication Association.

Rabinow, P. (1986). Representations are social facts: Modernity and post-modernity in anthropology. In J. Clifford & G. E. Marcus (Eds.), *Writing culture* (pp. 234–261). Berkeley: University of California Press.

Read, A. (1993). *Theatre and everyday life: An ethics of performance.* New York: Routledge.

Smith, A. D. (1993). *Fires in the mirror: Crown Heights, Brooklyn, and other identities.* New York: Doubleday.

Strine, M. S. (1991). Critical theory and "organic" intellectuals: Reframing the work of cultural critique. *Communication Monographs, 58,* 195–201.

Tyler, S. (1986). Post-modern ethnography: From document of the occult to occult document. In J. Clifford & G. E. Marcus (Eds.), *Writing culture: The poetics and politics of ethnography* (pp. 122–140). Berkeley: University of California Press.

7

Performance Ethnography

The good news is that in recent decades there has been a remarkable constellation of thinking around performance. The "antitheatrical prejudice" notwithstanding, performance is now a powerful locus for research in the human sciences, a rallying point for scholars who want to privilege action, agency, and transformation.

—Dwight Conquergood, "Beyond the Text:
Toward a Performative Cultural Politics" (1998)

Performance has indeed, in the words of Dwight Conquergood (1998), brought about a "remarkable constellation of thinking" relating to the meanings and effects of human behavior, consciousness, and culture. These days, it seems one can hardly address any subject in the arts, humanities, and social sciences without encountering the concept of performance.

Performance has become a popular signifier expanding the definitions and assumptions of a range of social phenomenon. The power of performance is captured in the idea that human beings are naturally a performing species. Rather than *homo sapiens*, we more accurately resemble *"homo performans."* The oft-quoted passage by anthropologist Victor Turner (1985) has become a classic refrain in describing the significance of performance:

If man is a sapient animal, a tool making animal, a self-making animal, a symbolizing animal, he is no less, a performing animal, *Homo performans*, not in the sense, perhaps that a circus animal may be a performing animal, but in the sense that man is a self-making animal—his performances are, in a way, reflexive; in performance he reveals himself to himself. (p. 187)

If we accept the notion of human beings as *homo performans* and therefore as a performing species, performance becomes necessary for our survival. This is due to the belief that we come to simultaneously recognize, substantiate, and (re)create ourselves as well as Others through performance. Furthermore—in this process of recognition, substantiation, creation, and invention—culture and performance become inextricably connected and mutually formative. Performance becomes a ubiquitous force in our social and discursive universe. In accepting the deeper significance of performance, we must then try to set forth examples and bring some kind of order and clarification to its far-reaching uses and meanings. We must describe and decipher its multiple operations in order to comprehend it and recognize it, not simply for its own sake, but for what performance will teach us about our culture and ourselves.

In this chapter, we will order and decipher "the remarkable constellation of thinking" in the relationship between performance and ethnography through the following topics: (a) foundational concepts in performance and social theory, (b) the performance interventions of Dwight Conquergood, and (c) staging ethnography and the performance of possibilities.

Foundational Concepts in Performance and Social Theory

In this section, we will discuss selected foundational paradigms that connect ethnography and performance. These paradigms form core ideas out of which more detailed and complex examinations of performance are developed. This section serves as an introduction to theories of performance that is specifically directed to ethnographic projects and field research.

Performance as Experience

For me, the anthropology of performance is an essential part of the anthropology of experience. In a sense, every type of cultural performance, including ritual, ceremony, carnival, theatre, and poetry, is explanation and explication of life itself, as Dilthey often argued. Through the performance process itself, what is normally sealed up, inaccessible to everyday forth—Dilthey uses

the term Ausdruck, *"an expression," from* ausdrucken, *literally,
"to press or squeeze out." "Meaning" is squeezed out of an
event, which has either been directly experienced by the drama-
tist or poet or cries out for penetrative, imaginative understanding* (Verstehen). *An experience is itself a process, which "presses
out" to an "expression" which completes it.*

—Victor Turner, *From Ritual to Theatre* (1982a)

One important theoretical view of performance addresses the notion of
experience. This view asserts that experience begins from our uneventful,
everyday existence. Moving inconsequentially through the daily, colorless
activities of our lives, we flow through moments of ordinariness, nonreflec-
tion, and the mundane. We brush our teeth, ride the bus, wait in supermarket lines, and generally talk about the weather without excitement or
happenstance. But then something happens, and we move to moments of
experience. At this point, life's flow of uneventfulness is interrupted by a
peak moment that breaks through the ordinariness, and we think and consider what has just happened to us. We give feeling, reason, and language
to what has been lifted from the inconsequential day-to-day. We bring
experience to it.

The experience is received in consciousness and reflected upon: while
brushing our teeth this particular morning, we notice a gray hair growing at
the top of our head; while riding the bus, we meet an extraordinary person;
while in the supermarket line, the cake box jogs a childhood memory; and
while talking about the weather, we discover disturbing news. The mundane
becomes heightened when gray hair conjures thoughts of aging; when an
extraordinary person brings new insight; when the egg carton reminds us of
licking mother's cake pan; and when the rainy weather bring news of
tragedy and loss. Edward M. Bruner (1986) states,

> By experience we mean not just sense data, cognition, or in Dilthey's phrase, 'the
> diluted juice of reason,' but also feelings and expectations. . . . Lived experience,
> then, as thought and desire, as word and image, is the primary reality. (pp. 4–5)

"Feeling and expectation" that constitute experience now becomes the
potential for something more. It is from experience that expression may
now come forth. Turner (1982a) wrote that expressions are "the crystal-
lized secretions of once living human *experience*" (p. 17). Once an experience presses forward from the field of the mundane, it moves to expression;
it is no longer a personal reality, but a shared one. What we experience is
most often whatever needed to be expressed, whether through story,

gossip, or humor on the one end, or poetry, novels, or film on the other. The experience now made into expression is presented in the world; it occupies time, space, and public reality. Experience made into expression brings forth reader, observer, listener, village, community, and audience. In arriving at this third evolutionary stage of expression, we have arrived at the threshold of performance evolving from experience. Experience becomes the very seed of performance.

In understanding this view that emphasizes the performance of experience, we may then ask several questions: If performance begins with the rupture of the ordinary in our everyday, then can performance only be self-reflective, heightened, and therefore preceded by experience? Can performance ever be "just behavior," or do we always need that revelatory moment of experience? Can there be performance without bringing the ordinary into the extraordinary?

The movement just outlined, from quotidian ordinariness to reflective experience and ultimately to creative expression, is just one trajectory toward performance. It is true these moments that burst forth from everyday life into experience—then to expression and eventually into a full-blown performance—constitute the making of performance; however, there are other frameworks by which we may identify performance. Not all performance is necessarily based on individual experience or expression. Performance does not necessarily begin with experience; indeed, some argue that experience begins with performance. Conquergood (1986a) argues for this "reverse," saying that it is the "performance that realizes the experience" (pp. 36–37). Bakhtin (1981) affirms the precedence of performance:

> After all, there is no such thing as experience outside of embodiment in signs. It is not experience that organizes expression, but the other way around—expression organizes experience. Expression is what first gives experience its form and specificity of direction." (qtd. in Conquergood, 1986a, p. 85)

We will further explore the relationship between experience and expression, but now we turn to performance as an analytical framework for social patterns of behavior.

Performance as Social Behavior

> Cultures, I hold, are better compared through their rituals, theatres, tales, ballads, epics, and operas than through their habits. For the former are the ways in which they try to articulate their meanings.
>
> —Edward Bruner, *The Anthropology of Experience* (1986)

In performance as behavior, social life is constructed through an organizing metaphor of dramatic action, or what the social critic Kenneth Burke (1945) describes as *situated modes of action.* Burke (1966) invites us to ponder an important question: What does it mean and what does it entail when we interpret what people are doing and why they are doing it?

This is a question that can be applied to an infinite range of human actions. It is a question that demands consideration, contexts, and engagement. In asking the question, Burke (1945) opens the "dramas of living" while radically humanizing and historicizing it in his approach to an answer. Burke provides a dramatic paradigm comprising five key concepts in his attempt to answer the question—a pentad that is particularly relevant for critical ethnographers. His five key terms are *act* (which names what took place in thought or deed), *scene* (the background of the act, the situation in which it occurred), *agent* (the person or kind of person performing the act), *agency* (the means or instruments that were used in the act), and *purpose* (the aim or objective). Burke (1945) states,

> Men may violently disagree about the purposes behind a given act, or about the character of the person who did it, or how he did it, or in what kind of situation he acted; or they may even insist upon totally different words to name the act itself. But be that as it may, many complete statements about motives will offer *some kind* of answers to those five questions: what was done (act), when and where it was done (scene), who did it (agent), how (agency), and why he did it (purpose). (p. xvii)

Just as Burke employed elements of performance to analyze social patterns and behavior, the anthropologist Victor Turner (1982a, 1982b, 1985) is credited with making path-breaking contributions in ethnographic research for illuminating key performance dynamics that permeate social and cultural life.

Victor Turner left a rich and comprehensive body of work that is timeless and invaluable to those field researchers who are interested in the relationship between performance, culture, and ethnography (see Turner, 1982a, 1982b, 1985). Due to space and the focus of this text, I have not attempted to represent the immensity and complexity of Victor Turner's thinking. However, it is very important to introduce to the student of critical ethnography key concepts that constitute the foundation of his thinking.

Cultural Performance

The anthropologist Milton Singer (1984) first introduced the term *cultural performance*, stating that these kind of performances all possess a "limited time span, a beginning and an end, an organized program of activity, a set of performers, an audience, and a place and occasion" (xii). Cultural performances are therefore understood as more conventional forms of performance because they are framed by cultural conventions. They are consciously heightened, reflexive, framed, and contained. Cultural performances range from plays and operas to circus acts, carnivals, parades, religious services, poetry readings, weddings, funerals, graduations, concerts, toasts, jokes, and story telling. In all these examples, self-conscious and symbolic acts are presented and communicated within a circumscribed space. Meaning and affect are generated by embodied action that produces a heightened moment of communication.

Cultural performance inheres in what the ethnolinguist Richard Bauman (1977) calls "markings." It is framed by its content both within and outside the flow of life as lived, as well as by its distinct markings of beginnings and endings (Bauman, 1977). You cannot stumble into a cultural performance and be oblivious to it. You will pick up a book, witness a film, observe a wedding, or overhear an oral history and be unaware of stepping into a time and space in which thought and action are heightened, stylized, and set apart by symbolic or conventional indicators of a start and finish. These indicators—from "once upon a time" to curtain call, The National Anthem, film credits, or "The End"—are a few of the markers that are familiar to us.

One of the most immensely important characteristics of cultural performance articulated by Turner (1982a, 1982b, 1985) is how they reflect who we are and human behavior. It is said that cultural performances *show ourselves to ourselves* in ways that help us recognize our behavior, for better or worse, as well as our unconscious needs and desires. When we perform and witness cultural performances, we often come to realize truths about ourselves and our world that we cannot realize in our day-to-day existence:

> It might be possible to regard the ensemble of performative and narrative genres, active and acting modalities of expressive culture as a hall of mirrors, or better magic mirrors. . . . In this hall of mirrors the reflections are multiple, some magnifying, some diminishing, some distorting the faces peering into them, but in such a way as to provoke not merely thought, but also powerful feelings and the will to modify everyday matters in the minds of the gazers, for not one likes to see himself as ugly, ungainly, or dwarfish. *Mirror distortions of reflection provoke reflexivity* [italics added]. (1982a, p. 105)

Cultural performances are not only a reflection of what we are, they also shape and direct who we are and what we can become. Turner (1982a) states, "When we act in everyday life we do not merely re-act to indicative stimuli, we act in frames we have wrested from the genres of cultural performance" (p. 122).

Social Performance

In social performance, action, reflection, and intent are not marked as they are in cultural performances. Social performances are the ordinary, day-by-day interactions of individuals and the consequences of these interactions as we move through social life (Turner, 1982a, pp. 32–33). All these social performances are based upon a cultural script. Typically, the participants in social performances are not self-consciously aware their enactments are culturally scripted. Social performances become examples of a culture's or subculture's particular symbolic practices. These performances are most striking when they are contrasted against different cultural norms (e.g., greetings, dinning, dressing, dating, walking, and looking). Turner (1982a) ascribes social performances to any action that is formed, understood, and reiterated through cultural scripting. Eating a meal, shaking someone's hand, dressing for the beach, asking for a date, walking with a friend, speaking to a parent, or looking in the eyes of the person speaking to you are all very ordinary and "natural" to the flow of daily life. However, different cultures and subcultures may practice each of these actions in strikingly different ways. In some cultures, it is a common occurrence for men who are platonic friends to walk down public streets holding hands without there being any thought of a romantic or sexual involvement. There are cultures in which it is rude to look into the face of the person speaking to you. There are subcultures in the United States where a handshake and greeting in one community is a very different social performance from what one would do in another community.

Social performance is also elaborated on in the influential work of the sociologist Ervin Goffman. Goffman examined the characteristics of role-playing in social situations in his best-known work *The Presentation of Self in Everyday Life* (1959). Goffman emphasizes the various tasks and functions individuals assume as "roles" that carry with them scripted characteristics or "fronts" (e.g., settings, costumes, gestures, voice, appearances, and demeanor). These roles in everyday life are based upon the relationships between the performers and an audience. Such roles are public roles in what he calls "front-stage drama"—for example, a waiter and a customer, a teacher and students, a father and a child, as well as situations like the first date or the job interview. We perform the tasks or function of our roles before or "in front of" a particular audience. Goffman states that for every front-stage drama there is a backstage drama—the performance of the waiter, the school teacher, and the father out of the view of the customer, the students, the son and daughter, or "behind the scenes" of the date and the interview. For Goffman, performance can be defined as "all activity of an individual which occurs during a period marked by his continuous presence before a particular set of observers and which has some influence on the observers" (p. 22).

Social Drama

In social harmony, the working arrangements within a particular social unit are synchronized. When a social drama occurs, there is a schism or break in the synchronization. The social unit is disturbed and the parties involved are in disagreement. Turner (1982a) states, "Social life, then, even its apparently quietest moments is characteristically 'pregnant' with social dramas. It is as though each of us has a 'peace' face and a 'war' face, that we are programmed for cooperation, but prepared for conflict" (p. 11).

Turner (1982a) defines social drama using a four-phase structure: *breach, crisis, redressive action,* and *resolution.* In breach, there is an overt nonconformity and breaking away by an individual or group of individuals from a shared system of social relations, be it an African village, a political party, a family, or nation. In breach, the agreed-upon norm is violated (p. 38).

It is in the second stage of crisis that conflict becomes most apparent. The opposing forces are openly at odds; the masks are stripped away or magnified and the conflict escalates. In crisis, the breach has enlarged; it is made public. In the third stage, redressive action, a mechanism is brought forth to squelch the crisis from further disruption of the social system. This may be in the form of a mediator, of a judicial system, or of the opposing forces coming together themselves in an effort to resolve the crises. In the redressive phase, norms are suspended to make amends.

The final phase is resolution. It is here, according to Turner (1982a), where the "disturbed parties are reconciled and reintegrated back into their shared social system" (p. 198). The parties may reunite but with changes; or the other result is the recognition of a "legitimate and irreparable schism between the parties" which will separate them from the social system, and/or the parties may establish another social system (pp. 8–19). In reintegration, there is usually some kind of ritual act to mark the separation or a celebration of the union:

> The social drama concludes—if ever it may be said to have a "last act"—either in the reconciliation of the contending parties or their agreement to differ—which may involve a dissident minority in seceding from the original community and seeking a new habitat. . . . (Turner, 1982a, p. 10)

Structure and Antistructure

For Turner (1982a), performance rises out of the ever-shifting processes of culture (pp. 9–13). Turner's (1985) processual view describes culture as a never-ending phenomenon of "becoming" as opposed to "being" (pp. 178–181). Culture is never a finished product, but is a growing, changing organism; therefore culture is in constant creation, definition, and reflection of itself (Turner, 1985, p. 203). In the processes of cultural becoming, culture moves through phases of *structure* and *antistructure*. Turner (1982a) asserts that humankind "grows through anti-structure, and conserves through structure" (p. 114). Structure is order within systems (Turner, 1982a, p. 36). As a positive function, structure regulates and preserves culture, making its members feel safe, secure, and protected. Structure as a less positive function is "all that holds people apart, defines their differences, and constrains their action" (Turner, 1982a, p. 47). Turner (1982a) links structure with obligation, jurality, law, restraint:

> In people's social structure relationships they are by various abstract processes generalized and segmentalized into roles, statuses, classes, cultural sexes, conventional age-divisions, ethnic affiliations, etc. In different types of social situations they have been conditioned to play specific social roles. It does not matter how well or how badly as long as they "make like" they are obedient to the norm sets that control different compartments of the complex model known as the "social structure." (p. 46)

Antistructure, according to Turner (1982a) is the "dissolution of normative social structure, with its role-sets, statuses, jural rights and duties" (p. 28). The anthropologist Brian Sutton-Smith, in his conception of normative structure and antistructure, inspired Turner. Sutton-Smith states (1972),

> The normative structure represents the working equilibrium; the "anti-structure" represents the latent system of potential alternatives from which novelty will arise when contingencies in the normative system require it. We might more correctly call this second system the *protocultural* system because it is the precursor of innovative normative forms. It is the source of new culture. (pp. 18–19)

The "potential alternative" that antistructure nurtures is explored in Turner's (1982a, 1982b) discussion of the *liminal* and *liminoid*. Remarking on Sutton-Smith's assertion that antistructure generates creativity, Turner notes that what interests him in this formulation is that "liminal and liminoid situations" are "settings in which new models, symbols, paradigms, etc. arise—as seedbeds of cultural creativity . . ." (Turner, 1982a, p. 28). Turner has been criticized for his distinction between liminal and liminoid as he compares them to so-called tribal and advanced cultures. To examine the distinction between the concepts and the full range of their meanings requires a more detailed analysis than I offer here; however, as an overview for the student of critical ethnography, it is useful to apply the notion of the liminal and liminoid in your work.

Liminoid

In Turner's (1982a, 1982b, 1985) work, *liminoid* is a provocative term used to describe an individualized expression of creative and alternative expressions in industrialized societies, where varied leisure time activities and choices are more accessible than in agrarian or preindustrialized societies. The solitary artist *creates* the liminoid phenomena; the collectivity *experiences* collective liminal symbols. For Turner (1982a), this does not mean that the maker of

> liminoid symbols, ideas, images, etc., does so *ex nihilo*; it only means that he is privileged to make free with his social heritage in a way impossible to members of cultures in which the liminal is to a large extent sacrosanct. (p. 52)

Liminality

Turner (1982a, 1982b, 1985) contends that liminality is the state of being betwixt and between structures or situations. Members of liminoid societies are also generally referred to as being in states of liminality; however, Turner employed the term *liminoid* to industrialized societies to mark a distinction between them and nonindustrialized societies. However, societies that are considered liminal are not referred to as being *liminoid* in Turner's lexicon. Therefore, *liminoid* denotes a specific characteristic of materiality, whereas *liminality* is more generally used to describe the state of being neither here nor there—neither completely inside nor outside a given situation, structure, or mindset.

Relatively free of norms, guidelines, and requirements, liminality, for Turner, is the space of greatest invention, discovery, creativity, and reflection. It is in this state of liminality where we are at the threshold of systems, not stepping into the system to the right, nor the system to the left, but reflectively, creatively, or ceremoniously assessing both. It is also important to add that, while Turner (1982a) underscores the creativity invoked within liminal spaces, he also comments upon its destructive nature:

Liminality is, of course, an ambiguous state, for social structure, while it inhabits full social satisfaction, gives a measure of finiteness and security; liminality may be for many the acme of insecurity, the breakthrough of chaos into cosmos, of disorder into order, rather than the milieu of creative interhuman or transhuman satisfaction and achievements. Liminality may be the scene of disease, despair, death, suicide, the breakdown without compensatory replacement of normative, well-defined social ties and bonds. (p. 46)[1]

Liminoid/liminality as the state of creation and destruction—of the betwixt and between—and of being both and neither inside and/nor outside was captured earlier in Mikhail Bakhtin's (1981) idea of *carnival*: laws, prohibitions, and restriction that determine the structure and order of ordinary. That is, noncarnival life is suspended, and where it is suspended a space to defy the norms, invert the expected, embrace the playful, and form new and different human connections opens up. The carnival is "the place for working out, in a concretely sensuous, half-real and half-play-acted form, a *new form of interrelationships between individuals* [italics added], counter posed to the all-powerful socio-hierarchical relationships of noncarnival life" (Carlson, 1996, p. 28).

Communitas

Spontaneous *communitas* might be compared to a moment of utopian unity, in which human differences and hierarchies seem to fade into perfect cohesion. Communitas is the bond between individuals that is an intrinsic union beyond formal social bonds. Individual identities come together in a direct and immediate manner. Communitas is experienced as a communion of individuals as equals, where all racial, class, gender, or structural divisions are dissolved in the spontaneous and immediate feelings of communion (Turner, 1982a).

This inclusiveness, the antistructure of communitas, is not permanent; structure returns. Roles, status, and order can never be eliminated. It should also be understood that communitas encompasses three distinct and "necessarily sequential forms" (Turner, 1982a, p. 47): *spontaneous communitas, ideological communitas,* and *normative communitas.* Spontaneous communitas is a deep, direct, immediate, and total personal interaction that "has something magical about it" (p. 47). Ideological communitas is "a set of theoretical concepts which attempt to describe the interactions of spontaneous communitas" (p. 47). It is the search, "the centering of attention" on articulating and re-creating the nature of the magic. Normative communitas is "a subculture or group which attempts to foster and maintain relationships of spontaneous communitas on a more or less permanent basis" (p. 47).

Members of normative communitas are those persons having a substantive link, as in the sense of "comrades," and may include members of religious revivals, political rallies, disenfranchised groups, and so forth.

For Turner (1982a, 1982b, 1985), performance—whether cultural performance, social performance, or social drama—takes place under the rubric of structure or antistructure. Structure is all that which constitutes order, system, preservation, law hierarchy, and authority. Antistructure is all that which constitutes human action beyond systems, hierarchies, and constraints.

The Influences of Richard Schechner

In a discussion of Victor Turner, it is important to add the influence of performance theorist Richard Schechner (1973, 1985, 1998) on Turner's ideas, as well as to discuss Schechner's general contribution to performance ethnography. In a workshop lead by Turner and Schechner exploring the intersections between social and aesthetic drama, Turner commented that Schechner "persuaded [him] that co-operation between anthropology and theatrical people was not only possible but also could become a major teaching tool for both sets of partners" (qtd. in Carlson, 1996, p. 22). Carlson (1996) cites the 1973 special issue of *The Drama Review*, guest edited by Richard Schechner, which lists seven arenas in which performance theory and the social sciences overlap:

1. Performance in everyday life, including gatherings of every kind

2. The structure of sports, ritual, play, and public political behaviors

3. Analysis of various modes of communication (other than the written word); semiotics

4. The connection between human and animal behavior patterns, with an emphasis on plays and ritualized behavior

5. Aspects of psychotherapy that emphasize person-to-person interaction, acting out, and body awareness

6. Ethnography and prehistory—both of exotic and of familiar cultures

7. Constitution of unified theories of performance, which are, in fact, theories of behavior

In summary, the social critics discussed provide performance-oriented lenses for examining social action and patterns of human behavior that are especially helpful to the critical ethnographer. They contribute performance paradigms that identify and order the ambiguities, crises, and deeply felt problems that arise from human conflict ranging from the inner lives of individuals to the public lives of nations.

Performance as Language and Identity

What we will now add to the above discussion is a more detailed focus on the performative dimensions of language and the performative repetition of symbolic acts in the construction of identity. Just as we must attend to situated modes of action to unveil deep structures of intention and meaning, we must also attend to situated modes of language and the action generated from the words spoken. We begin here with the British philosopher J. L. Austin (1975) and his idea of speech-act theory. In 1955, Austin presented "How to Do Things With Words" for the William James Lecture Series at Harvard University. Austin's speech-act theory, set forth in 1955 and published later as a book, made an indelible impact on how we grasp the implications of language and its influence on human action. Briefly defined, a *speech-act* is the action that is performed when a word is uttered. For Austin, a performative utterance is not simply a statement that is true or false. To understand language as merely statements that describe, refer, or indicate based on accuracy and truth is much too narrow. Austin describes this view of language as mere statement as *constantive*, and argues that language has a function beyond the constantive. He states that language does more than describe; it also *does something* that makes a material, physical, and situational difference. For example, the words, "I promise to give him the message," "I pronounce you husband and wife," and "You are forgiven" all *do something in the world*. They create a particular reality. Language can bestow forgiveness, a blessing, freedom, citizenship, marriage, or a promise. Language *performs* a reality; therefore, for Austin (1975), language is not merely constantive, but *performative*.

Austin's student John R. Searle (1969) expands upon Austin's theory of performative utterance to assert not only that language is performative at certain heightened moments or ceremonial events that separate the performative from the constantive, but also that *all* language is a form of doing. Searle believes that whenever there is *intention* in speaking, there is also the performative. While Austin designates particular moments when words produce a speech-act—that is, when words are performed—Seale argues that whenever words are spoken with intention (and they almost always are), words are performative.

Jacque Derrida (1973, 1978, 1982), however, takes issue with Austin's and Searle's suggestion that a performative utterance creates a "doing" or a particular reality. Derrida's concern is that Austin did not recognize that language is always spoken within particular contexts and through certain identities, and therefore language is constantly producing the very reality to which it refers. Derrida argued against the notion that a performative utterance was aligned with a "presence" that was *original* and *unique* to a particular moment, and was therefore something done in that moment for the *first time*. For Derrida, the idea that a speech-act makes something happen within a particular present moment is to deny the fact of history and culture. Speech is citational; that is, what is spoken has been spoken many, many times before, and its effects are a result of its repetition and citation, not a result of a unique or present moment when words are uttered. Derrida's (1973) critique of speech-act theory is captured in the idea of a metaphysics of presence. For Derrida, all that we know and say is based upon what has gone before and what we have inherited from past actions. If something is done with words, it is because it has happened before and we know out of convention and custom to continue to do it.

The disagreement between speech-act theory and Derrida's metaphysics of presence tends to overlook what is useful about both arguments and what can be gained when we accept elements of both positions and see them as supplementary to one another rather than in opposition. What is important for critical ethnographers employing the analyses of Austin and Searle is that words are indeed performative and *do* have material effects. Obviously, they *do something in the world*; and that something is to reiterate (in terms of Derrida) speech, meaning, intent, and customs that have been repeated through time and that are communicative and comprehensible because they are recognizable in their repetition.

Note: Derrida and Deconstruction

- Deconstruction is a theory that posits that signifiers and signified are continually breaking apart and reattaching in new combinations; indeed, there is no fixed distinction between signifiers and signified.
- The deconstruction process is not only infinite, but also somehow circular: signified keeps transforming into signifier, and vice versa, and you never arrive at a final signified that is not a signifier itself.
- For Derrida (1973, 1978), the structure of the sign is determined by *trace*: One sign leads to another and so forth, indefinitely.
- Derrida (1973, 1978) labels "metaphysical" any thought system that depends on an unassailable foundation—an absolute or immutable truth claim.
- Derrida (1973, 1978) stresses the point that it is not enough simply to neutralize the binary opposition of metaphysics: Deconstruction invokes reversal and displacement. Deconstruction is not simply a strategic reversal of categories. Derrida's method consists of showing how the privileged term is held in place by the force of a dominant metaphor and not, as it might seem, by any conclusive logic.

- In deconstructionism, there is an abandonment of all references to a center, to a fixed subject, to a privileged reference, to an origin, to an absolute founding and controlling just principle.
- The deconstructionist method often consists of deliberately inverting traditional oppositions and marking the invisible concepts that reside unnamed in the gap between opposing terms.
- Deconstruction is an attempt to dismantle the logic by which a particular system of thought is grounded, as well as how a whole system of political structure and social control maintains its force.
- If there is a summarizing idea for deconstruction, it is the theme of the *absent center.* The postmodern experience is widely held to stem from a profound sense of ontological uncertainty.

Performativity

The feminist critic Judith Butler (1988, 1990, 1994), in her descriptions of performativity, further extends the examination of the performative. For Butler, performativity is understood as a "stylized repetition of acts" that are—like Derridian citation—"always a reiteration of a norm or set of norms," which means that the "act that one does, the act that one performs is, in a sense, an act that has been going on before one arrived on the scene" (Diamond, 1996, pp. 4–6). Butler employs performativity to mark gender identity in particular. Gender is recognized and embodied through very specific stylized acts that are repeated through generations to substantiate what it means to be male on the one hand and what it means to be female on the other. In other words, men are conditioned to act in certain ways, thereby making or constructing maleness, just as women have been conditioned to act in other ways, thereby constructing femaleness. Performativity in this sense becomes all at once a cultural convention, value, and signifier that is inscribed on the body—performed through the body—to mark identities.

Gestures, posture, clothes, habits, and certain distinctions, from the way one holds a cigarette to the manner in which one crosses one's legs, to the way one wears a hat—they all are performed differently depending on the gender, race, class status, and sexual orientation of the performer. How the body moves about in the world, and its various mannerisms, styles, and distinctions are inherited from one generation through space and time to another and demarcated within specific identity categories. Therefore, these performativities become the manifestation of gender, race, sexuality, and class. You have heard the saying, "Act like a man," or the stereotypes, "She acts like a boy," "He doesn't act black," "He acts like he's gay," or "She acts like she has no class." These expressions are common in the vernacular, because identity is performed, and to perform outside these inherited constructions is to break through these taken-for-granted and commonsense notions of what a specific identity is or should be. These performativities are engrained in the way we understand and order social behavior to the point that we often think it is not only natural, but *proper* and *as it should be*.

But what happens when performativity is disrupted? What happens when a boy acts like a girl? When a women acts like a man? When a black person does not act black? When an old person does not act old? Performativity is up for examination and reflection in cultural performance. What is taken for granted and goes unrealized within the everyday operations of the world is mirrored back in cultural performance, where "the urgent problems of our reality" (Turner, 1982a, p. 122) are witnessed, reinterpreted, and possibly undone.

Elin Diamond (1996) speaks to the politics of performance in the capacity for cultural performances to open up critical questions that penetrate the reiterations of performativity:

> When being is de-essentialized, when gender and even race are understood as fictional ontologies, modes of expression without true substance, the idea of performance comes to the fore. But performance both *affirms and denies this evacuation of substance*. In the sense that the "I" has no interior secures ego or core identity, "I" must always enunciate itself: there is not only performance of self, [but] an external representation of an interior truth. But in the sense that I do my performance in public, for spectators who are interpreting and/or performing with me, there are real effects, and meanings solicited or imposed that produce relations in the real. Can performance make a difference? A performance, whether it inspires love or loathing, often consolidates cultural or subcultural affiliations, and these affiliations might be as regressive as they are progressive. The point is, as soon as performativity comes to rest on *a* performance, questions of embodiment, of social relations, of ideological interpellations, of emotional and political effects, all become discussable. (p. 5)

Examinations of *performative, performativity,* and *metaphysics of presence* are helpful and relevant to critical ethnographers because they offer definitions for human action that shape and guide the roles, institutions, and values constituting our life worlds. The emphasis on performativity as citationality is helpful in understanding how identity categories are not naturally inherent or biologically determined, but rather how they are socially constructed within the meanings and values of politics and culture. This is a significant realization, because it beckons the call to change inequities. It places the responsibility to break through unfair practices upon our shoulders and forces us to reckon with the fact that these categories—and therefore the responses and practices based on these categories—are not a fact of life, but are based upon human behavior that we can change.

The description of performativity as citationality is a critical move, but, for many performance scholars, it is only *one* way of articulating performativity. Conquergood (1998) asks us to consider the deeper political implications when performativity is consistently reworked as citationality. We may understand performativity as citationality, but we may also understand performativity as having the capability of resistance. Just as performativity is an internalized repetition of hegemonic stylized acts inherited from the *status quo*, it can also be an internalized repetition of subversive stylized acts inherited by contested identities. Subversive performativity can disrupt the very citations that hegemonic performativity enacts. The postcolonial critic Homi Bhabha (1994) employs the performative as action that disturbs, disrupts, and disavows hegemonic formations (pp. 146–149).

Up to this point, we have discussed performance through the inquiries of Kenneth Burke (dramatic pentad), Victor Turner (performance anthropology), J. L. Austin (speech-act-theory), Jacque Derrida (metaphysic of presence), Mikhail Bakhtin (carnavalesque), and Judith Butler (performativity). Now we will turn to the work of Dwight Conquergood.

The Performance Interventions of Dwight Conquergood

No one has contributed more to the intersections between performance and ethnography than Dwight Conquergood (1982a, 1982b, 1983, 1984, 1986a, 1986b, 1988, 1989, 1991, 1992, 1997, 1998, 2000, 2000a). So many who are engaged in the work of performance and who are committed to the politics and ethics of ethnography find their source of inspiration in the intellectual insights and far-reaching activism of Dwight Conquergood. We will enter the corpus of Conquergood's work from four vantage points: (1) process and performance, (2) the body and scriptocentrism, (3) dialogical performance, and (4) cultural politics.

Process and Performance

Conquergood's early work (1982a, 1982b, 1983, 1984) is a critique of hard edge, positivist assertions of culture as a quantifiable, static, and absolute entity. Traditionally, researchers prided themselves on how accurately human behavior could be measured, managed, and manipulated

(Conquergood, 2002b). Conquergood places the emphasis on the "processes of becoming" in the changing and evolving dynamic of human relationships and creations. He asks us to move the focus of study from structures, patterns, and products that were so revered by positivist thinking to the yearnings, struggles, stories, tensions, symbols, and performances that produce and are produced by these structures, patterns, and products. Conquergood (1986a) reminds us that "meaning is in-between structures" and that "identity is conjectural and processual" (p. 36). It is these in-between meanings and conjunctural processes that generate, sustain, deconstruct, and reconstruct the very structures and patterns that positivist thinking attempts to quantify. Conquergood asks that we pay attention to the doing of identity and culture, as it is always made and remade within the matrices of varying histories, economies, and desires. Conquergood (1986) states,

> The ground-of-being of the autonomous Self is displaced by the *experience-of-becoming* a performing self that enacts its identities within a community of others. . . . Humanity as performer, rather than author, or her own identity, is always historically situated, culturally mediated, and intersubjectively constituted. (p. 6)

In this emphases on becoming, we turn from "spatialized products to temporal processes," understanding as we do that human beings are products and producers of culture in an ongoing and ever-changing process of creating the world around us and beyond us (Conquergood, 1986, p. 6).

The Body and Scriptocentrism

In the Western tradition, written expression has held a privileged place over bodily expression. Writing is valued within the higher realms of knowledge, cosmopolitanism, and civility. Conquergood (2002a, 2002b) dignifies the body by recognizing embodied practices as constituting knowledge, emotion, and creation. The body is more than appearances and a sensing organ that holds the mind and soul. An exclusive focus on writing negates the everyday expressions of orality and symbolic embodiment that pervade in cultural spaces often hidden and cast out from the center of writing. To attend to the performances of symbolic bodily practices is a radically democratic endeavor, because the body expresses itself writ large everywhere. Conquergood's (2002b) explication of the body informs critical ethnography in the following ways:

- Radical empiricism is an embodied mode of being together with Others on intersubjective ground. The aliveness of interactive engagement requires the touch, smell, sights, and sounds of physical, bodily contact free from the mediations of distance and detachment.

- *Coevalness* is the temporality of a shared experience in which bodies are present together in time. Bodies are bonded by the experience of a common time, and to negate the commonality of shared time is to negate the reality that particular bodies shared a particular space.

- Myths are composed of the stories we live by, whether they take the form of master narratives, sacred stories, or local resistance. Conquergood (1983) recalls, "Myths and narrative arts live in performance, not on the page" (p. 2). Myths circulate in and through the everyday through embodied practices and performances (as opposed to written stories) that we consciously and unconsciously reenact.

- Experience is known through embodied performance. Instead of the idea of experience pressing out to expression, we must remember that we know experience through the body. It is the embodied expression that organizes experience (Conquergood, 1982, p. 85).

Conquergood (2002b) argues that we can no longer privilege the written text over the expressive body, because to do so is to obscure the multiple sites, practices, and interventions that are variously in the margins, on the borders, and beyond the center of writing. He underscores that scriptocentrism resonates through the past and present forces of imperialism (2000, 2002a, 2002b).

Dialogic Performance

For Conquergood (1982), dialogical performance is an ethical imperative. It is through dialogue that we resist the arrogant perception that perpetuates monologic encounters, interpretations, and judgments. From the ethics discussion in Chapter 4, we will remember that dialogical performance embraces and complicates diversity, difference, and pluralism. Conquergood (1982) states,

> A commitment to dialogue insists on keeping alive the inter-animating tension between Self and Other. It resists closure and totalizing domination of a single viewpoint, unitary system of thought. The dialogical project counters the normative with the performative, the canonical with the carnavalesque, Apollonian rationality with Dionysian disorder. Instead of silencing positivism, the performance paradigm would strive to engage it in an enlivening conversation. Dialogicalism strives to bring as many different voices as possible into

the human conversation, without any one of them suppressing or silencing the other. (p. 11)

For Conquergood (1982a, 1983, 1988, 1989), the experience of becoming also means that, as a researcher, we must displace the primacy of seeing for a meaningful connection with listening. The traditional focus on seeing in the absence of profound listening is to *gaze out* at the Other as spectator, thereby risking a more dialogical meeting of *receiving in*. He calls on the critical ethnographer to move beyond the appearances that the exclusivity of sight holds to the deeper engagement with sound. Listening invites dialogue. As Conquergood (1982b) states, "The power dynamic of the research situation changes when the ethnographer moves from the gaze to the distance and detached observer to the intimate involvement and engagement of 'coactivity' or co-performance" (pp. 12–13). Dialogical performance means one is a coperformer rather than a participant-observer. It is to live in the embodied engagement of radical empiricism, to honor the aural/oral sounds that *incorporate* rather than *gaze over*.

Coperformance as dialogical performance means you not only do what subjects do, but you are intellectually and relationally invested in their symbol-making practices as you experience with them a range of yearnings and desires. Coperformance, for Conquergood (1982a, 1997, 2002b), is a "doing with" that is a deep commitment.

Cultural Politics

Conquergood's (1998, 2002a) explication of the politics of performance is of great importance to critical ethnography. I must mention that all of the concepts presented up to this point fall under the category of cultural politics. The corpus of Conquergood's work is never devoid of politics. I have included principles and paradigms under this topic that organize and address the distribution of power and modes of resistance. Conquergood's ideas on politics are presented in the following points with key excerpts from his writings.

Symbols and Images

Conquergood (1998) reminds us that "images and symbolic representations drive public policy" (p. 11). He goes on to state,

Symbols instill beliefs and shape attitudes that underpin social structures. The binding force of culture, by and large, is a web of symbols that enables people to control and make sense out of experience in patterned ways. . . . Images and symbolic representations drive public policy. (p. 11)

Transnational Narratives

The notion of territory in this era of globalization has taken on new and more expansive meanings. Moreover, the manner in which the local is affected by transnational communication and affiliations has problematized our understanding of the concepts of *community, nation,* and *identity.* Conquergood (2002b) states,

> According to Michel de Certeau, "what the map cuts up, the story cuts across" (1984:12). This pithy phrase evokes a postcolonial world crisscrossed by transnational narratives, Diaspora affiliations, and especially, the movement and multiple migrations of people, sometimes voluntary, but often economically propelled and politically coerced. In order to keep pace with such a world, we [can] not think of "place" as a heavily trafficked intersection, a port of call and exchange, instead of circumscribed territory. A boundary is more like a membrane than a wall. . . . Our understanding of local context expands to encompass the historical, dynamic, often traumatic, movements of people, ideas, images, commodities, and capital. It is not easy to sort out the local from the global: transnational circulations of images get reworked on the ground and redeployed for local tactical struggles. (p. 145)

Mimesis, Poiesis, Kinesis

The triad of *mimesis, poiesis,* and *kinesis* is one of Conquergood's (1998) most popular conceptualizations. He traces a three-tiered evolution of performance as political intervention, stating,

> The contours of this new analytic emphasis on process over product can be seen in the shifting meanings of the key word *performance* as it has emerged with increasing prominence in cultural studies. This semantic genealogy can be summarized as the movement from performance as *mimesis* to *poiesis* to *kinesis,* performance as imitation, construction, dynamism. (Conquergood, 1998, p. 31)

Mimesis is the mode where performance acts as a mirror or imitation of experience. Performance becomes a reflection of life, a simulation framed through dramatic convention or cultural convention. Citing social scientist Erving Goffman (1959) as an early proponent of the mimetic view of performance, Conquergood (1998) states that Goffman "studied the parts of social life that staged, clearly demarcated frontstage and backstage boundaries, and gave currency to notions of frames, role-playing, impression management, and benign fabrications" (p. 31). Although useful under very limited circumstances, this view of performance as primarily mimetic is incomplete. It focuses on surface and reinscribes the "Platonic dichotomy between reality and appearances, and thus reinforces the antiperformance prejudice" (Conquergood, 1998, p. 31).

Mimesis then moves to deeper levels of meaning and more consequential effects of human action in the form of poiesis. It is at the level of poiesis that the mirroring of mimesis is understood as the marking of meaning and effect. Poiesis reminds us that performance is a doing that actually denotes and connotes something beyond its appearance. We learn something from performance; it has an impression upon us. Conquergood (1982a) credits Victor Turner for opening the classic meaning of performance as mimesis to performance as poiesis in Turner's description of performance as "making not faking" (p. 93). Turner's (1985) notion of *homo performans*, in addition to the speech-act theory of J. L. Austin (1975), moves performance from simply being mimetic toward the higher realm of the poetic. When Austin distinguished the performative as the category of utterance that makes something happen—the idea that the utterance actually does something in the world—he contributed to the understanding of performance being more than simply theatrical.

Just as performance is more than simply mimetic, so it is also more than the poetic. From mimesis to poiesis, we now come to the culminating stage of kinesis. Kinesis is the point at which reflection and meaning now evoke intervention and change. The trajectory of performance, from the mirroring of mimesis to the enlightenment of poiesis, and finally to the intervention of kinesis, is a testament to the view of performance as a phenomenon that does not simply describe the world, but offers great possibility for changing it.

Conquergood (1998) cites the works of Michael Taussig (1993) on mimesis in terms of bringing the mimesis-poiesis-kinesis triad full circle. Taussig extends the possibilities of mimesis by offering alternative practices that use mimicry to subvert authority. Disenfranchised identities in differing locations and forms will mime the habits, gestures, and life customs of power-holders as a subversive act for various purposes. Mimicry in this instance become imitation for the purpose of intervention, acting in various capacities to bless the weak, mock the strong, protect the threatened, gain access to the inaccessible, and so forth.

Conquergood's emphasis on performance as kinesis is a kind of disruption that plays on the centrifugal force of decentering. Homi Bhabha (1994) uses the term *performative* to describe "action that incessantly insinuates, interrupts, interrogates, and antagonizes powerful master discourses" (p. 32). The trajectory from performance as mimesis to poiesis and finally to kinesis is particularly useful to qualitative researchers and ethnographers because it provides a means by which we may identify how human beings imitate each other in multiple and complicated ways while they are simultaneously generating meaning and resisting domestication. Moreover, it reveals how these performative actions are ripe with contestation, breakthroughs, and change. Conquergood (1998) states,

> Instead of construing performance as *transcendence,* a higher plane that one breaks into, I prefer to think of it as *transgression,* that force which crashes and breaks through sediment meanings and normative traditions and plunges us back into the vortices of political struggle—in the language of bell hooks as "movement beyond boundaries." (p. 32)

Performance as kinesis is the point of subversion that breaks through boundaries of domestication and hegemony. As critical ethnographers, this movement from mimesis, poiesis, and kinesis is another path in our endeavor to resist regimes of oppressive power structures.

Triads of Analysis and Activity

The overarching domain of performance is generally ordered through the triad of *theory, method,* and *event*: performance theory provides abstract analysis; performance method provides concrete application, and performance event provides an aesthetic or noteworthy happening. Although theory, method, and event are useful in ordering the unwieldy possibilities of performance, Conquergood (2002b) provides a more meaningful and productive set of triads, particularly for ethnography, in his triad of triads: (1) The I's, *imagination, inquiry,* and *intervention*; (2) the A's, *artistry, analysis,* and *activism*; and (3) the C's, *creativity, critique,* and *citizenship.* Conquergood (2002b) states,

> Performance studies is uniquely suited for the challenge of braiding together disparate and stratified ways of knowing. We can think through performance along three crisscrossing lines of activity and analysis. We can think of performance (1) as a work of *imagination,* as an object of study; (2) as a pragmatics of *inquiry* (both as model and method), as an optic and operation of research; (3) as a tactics of *intervention,* an alterative space of struggle. Speaking from my home department at Northwestern, we often refer to the three A's of performance studies: artistry, analysis, activism. Or to change the alliteration, a commitment to the three C's of performance studies: creativity, critique, citizenship (civic struggles for social justice). (2002b, p. 152)

Dwight Conquergood's body of work is essential for critical ethnographers who take on (a) culture as process; (b) expression and experience; (c) myth and orality; (d) radical empiricism, coperformance, and embodied practice;

(e) dialogical performance and questions of Otherness; and (f) cultural politics and performance interventions. Conquergood has conducted field-work with Hmong refugees in Ban Vinai, Thailand; Palestinian refugees in the Middle East, Gaza Strip; inner-city gang members on the south side of Chicago; and with organizations and communities across the United States to end the death penalty. Conquergood's activist scholarship provides us with a model for critical performance ethnography grounded in Lugones's (1994) world traveling and loving perception.

In the next section, we will turn to theoretical questions in staging fieldwork.

Staging Ethnography and the Performance of Possibilities[2]

In this section, we will examine the political and social implication of what it means to stage our fieldwork data. Translating from the field to the stage presents several theoretical and ethical questions. In this section, we will discuss staged, cultural performances—what I shall call a *performance of possibilities*—based on ethnographic data from the specific spheres of (a) the subjects, whose lives and words are being performed; (b) the audience, who witnesses the performance; and (c) the performers, who embody and enact the data.

In a performance of possibilities, the possible suggests a movement culmi-nating in creation and change. It is the active, creative work that weaves the life of the mind with being mindful of life, of merging the text with the world, of critically traversing the margin and the center, and of opening more and dif-ferent paths for enlivening relations and spaces. A performance of possibilities raises several questions for the ethnographer: By what definable and material means will the subjects themselves benefit from the performance? How can the performance contribute to a more enlightened and involved citizenship that will disturb systems and processes that limit freedoms and possibilities? In what ways will the performers probe questions of identity, representation, and fairness to enrich their own subjectivity, cultural politics, and art?

We will turn now to these questions as each relates to subjects, audience, and performer.

The Subjects

The means by which the subjects themselves benefit from the performance are explored by examining the arenas of voice, subjectivity, and interroga-tive field. By voice, I do not simply mean the representation of an utterance, but the presentation of a historical self, a full presence that is in and of a particular world. The performance of possibilities does not accept "being heard and included" as it focus, but only as its starting point; instead, voice is an embodied, historical self that constructs and is constructed by a matrix of social and political processes. The aim is to present and represent subjects as made by and makers of meaning, symbol, and history in their full sensory and social dimensions. Therefore, the performance of possibilities is also a performance of voice wedded to experience and history.

Moreover, whether one likes the performance or not, one cannot completely undo or (un)know the image and imprint of that voice (inside history) upon their own consciousness once they have been exposed to it through performance. Performing subversive and subaltern voices proclaims existence, within particular locales and discourses, that are being witnessed—entered into one's *own* experience—and this witnessing cannot be denied. The subjects themselves benefit from this proclamation through the creation of space that gives evidence not only that "I am here in the world among you," but more importantly that "I am in the world under particular conditions that are constructed and thereby open to greater possibility."

How, then, does all this benefit the subjects? Human desire implores that we be listened to, apprehended, engaged, and free to imagine in and with worlds of Others. This idea of existence and self is further illustrated in Nisa, a !Kung woman speaking to the anthropologists Margorie Shostake (1983) as she expresses the fear of the disappearances of her stories: "I'll break open the story and tell you what is there, this like the others that have fallen out onto the sand, I will finish with it, and the wind will take it away" (p. 233). That we are all social beings who live in a world where others necessarily constitute the self reflects Mikhail Bakhtin's (1981) words, "Nothing is more frightening than the absence of an answer" (p. 111). The nature of Bakhtin's answer is a profound giving back that affirms we are real to others (and to ourselves) and that we are not alone.

This is not to argue that we do not have a self (or a soul) that generates its own will, action, and meaning ("I think therefore I am"), but that the self is reciprocally joined to other selves (or souls) for its own being and creations ("I am because we are, and we are because I am"). This acknowledgement of subjects within experience, relative to the social world, is just the beginning; a deeper connection is necessary that now takes us a step further into the realm of subjectivity.

Subjectivity

Subjectivity requires that we delve more deeply into the desires resonating within the locations of the Other. It is the move beyond the *acknowledgment* of voice within experience to that of *actual engagement.* Audience and performer must now engage the material and discursive world of the Other. Because subjectivity is formed through a range of discursive practices— economic, social, aesthetic, and political—and meanings are sites of creation and struggle, subjectivity linked to performance becomes a poetic and polemic admixture of personal experience, cultural politics, social power, and resistance. We witness subjects as they work for and against competing discourses and social processes in the quest for security and honor in their locations. The acknowledged Others become subjects when the audience and performers actually identify with the substance of who they are, where they are, and what they do. We have entered, albeit symbolically and temporarily, into their locations of voice within experience. Through performance, we are placed, subject to subject, in that contested space while, as the feminist critic bell hooks (1990) describes, oppressed "people resist by identifying themselves as subjects by defining their reality, shaping new identity, naming their history, telling their story" (p. 43).

The performance strives to communicate a sense of subjects' worlds in their own words; it hopes to amplify their meanings and intentions to a larger group of listeners and observers. These listeners and observers are then affected by what they see and hear in ways that motivate them to act and think in ways that now beneficially affect (directly and indirectly) either the subjects themselves or what they advocate. At this point, the audience moves from the performance space to the social world or the interrogative field.

Interrogative Field

The interrogative field is the point at which the performance of possibilities aims to create or contribute to a discursive space where unjust systems and processes are identified and interrogated. It is where what has been expressed through the illumination of voice and the encounter with subjectivity motivates individuals to some level of informed and strategic action. The greatest benefit to subjects is for those who bear witness to their stories to interrogate actively and purposefully those processes that limit their health and freedom. I do not mean to imply that one performance can rain down a revolution, but one performance can be revolutionary in enlightening citizens to the possibilities that grate against injustice.

The Audience

How the performance will contribute to a more enlightened and involved citizenship is another question from the performance of possibilities.

Creating performances in which the intent is largely to invoke interrogation of specific political and social processes means that in our art we are consciously working toward a cultural politics of change that resonates in a progressive and involved citizenship. To regard the audience as citizens with the potential for collective and involved action and change is part of the foundation upon which a performance of possibilities is based. Toni Morrison (1994) underscores the symbiosis between art and politics:

> I am not interested in indulging myself in some private, closed exercise of my imagination that fulfills only the obligation of my personal dreams—which is to say yes, the work must be political. It must have that as its thrust. That's a pejorative term in critical circles now: if a work of art has any political influence in it, somehow it's tainted. *My* feeling is just the opposite: If it has none, it is tainted. The problem comes when you find harangue passing off as art. It seems to me that the best art is political and you ought to be able to make it unquestionably political and irrevocably beautiful at the same time. (p. 497)

Where the intent is both "the political and irrevocably beautiful," art assumes responsibility for political effectiveness and communicates the principle that we are all part of a larger whole and are therefore radically responsible to each other for all of our individual selves. Linda Alcoff (1991) describes a web in which our social practices are made possible or impossible by agents and events that are spatially far from our own body and that, in turn, can affect distant strangers: "We are collectively caught in an intricate, delicate web in which each action I take, discursive or otherwise, pulls on, breaks off, or maintains the tension in many strands of a web in which others fined themselves moving also" (p. 20). A performance of possibility strives to reinforce to audience members the web of citizenship and the possibility of their individual selves as agents and change makers.

Intersubjectivity

Striving toward an enlightened and involved citizenship also means that, although formerly the focus was on subjectivity relative to the subjects, the focus must now move to *intersubjectivity* relative to the audience. Because performance asks the audience to travel empathically to the world of the subjects and to feel and know some of what they feel and know, two life-worlds meet and the domain of outsider and insider are simultaneously demarcated and fused. I have an identity separate from the subject, and the performance clearly illuminates our differences. In the space of the performance, I am outsider; in the space of the world, these positions are more likely switched: I am insider and the subject is the outsider. While I see that I am an outsider to the subject's experience, the performance ironically pulls me inside.

I am now in the midst of a profound meeting. Do I remain here at the margins of the meeting, or is the performance beautiful enough and political enough to compel me to travel more deeply inside the mind, heart, and world of the subject? In this ability to travel across worlds, two identities meet, engage, and become something more. Maria Lugones (1994) describes this process of intersubjectivity: "The reason why I think that traveling to someone's 'world' is a way of identifying with them is because by traveling to their 'world' we can understand *what it is to be them and what it is to be ourselves in their eyes* [italics added]. Only when we have traveled to each other's 'worlds' are we fully subjects to each other" (p. 637). Performance becomes the vehicle by which we travel to the worlds of subjects and enter domains of intersubjectivity that problematize how we categorize who is *us* and who is *them*, and how we see *ourselves* with other and different eyes.

As I argue that action beyond the performance space is of essential benefit to the subjects, so it is to audience members as well. Ideally, as an audience member consciously reenters the web of human connectedness and then travels into the life-world of the subject, where rigid categories of insider and outsider transfigure into an intersubjective experience, a path for action is set. Action, particularly new action, requires new energy and new insight. In the performance of possibilities, when the audience member begins to witness degrees of tension and incongruity between the subject's life-world and those processes and systems that challenge and undermine the world, something more and new is learned about how power works. The question is to what extent these life-worlds are threatened and, in turn, resist being captured in the space and time of performance. The audience, however, as involved citizens who are both disturbed and inspired, may seek the answer long after the final curtain. This is a *pursuit of possibility,* a gift of indignation and inspiration, passed on from the subject to the audience member. The performance of possibilities expects the audience member to continue, reaffirmed, or at least to begin honing his or her skills toward world traveling. In the performance of possibilities, both the performers and audience can be transformed: They can be themselves and more as they travel between worlds.

The performance ambitiously hopes to guide members of the audience and to equip them for the journey with empathy and intellect, passion and critique. There are creative tensions at the borders between self and Other, yet the performance hopes to challenge them to become witness, interlocutor, subversor, and creator.

The Performers

One of the initial challenges for a performer is the identity of the subjects. In this meeting with identity, the performer is confronted with questions: How is identity formed and what constitutes it? How can performance defer to the ways in which identity changes, transforms itself, and multiplies? Since the performer is transported slowly, deliberately, and incrementally at each rehearsal and at each encounter toward the knowledge and life-world of the subject, the performer is creatively and intellectually *taking it all in*, internalizing and receiving partial maps of meaning that reflect the subject's consciousness and context. This receptiveness, however, is never completely without the generative filter of the performer's own knowledge and location. The process of being transported, of receiving meanings and generating meanings, is a more intimate and potentially a more traumatic engagement for the performers than for the audience members, because the transportation is mentally and viscerally more intense than traveling to the world of Others. It is making those worlds your home place. The performer is not only *engaged*, but also strives to *become*. For the performer, this is an endeavor not only to live in an individual consciousness shaped by a *social world*, but also to live in that social world as well. Of course, by "living in that social world," I do not mean literally changing your address. I do, however, mean that the performer must first seriously research all the crucial elements that encompass a cognitive map of the social, economic, cultural, and political practices that constitute that world. Moreover, the performer must be committed—doing what must be done or going where one must go—to experience the felt-sensing dynamic of that world: its tone-color—the sights, sounds, smells, tastes, textures, rhythms—the visceral ethos of that world.

In personal narrative performances, particularly of contested identities, performers are not only performing the words of subjects, they are performing the subjects' political landscapes. Cultural studies scholar Lawrence Grossberg (1994) calls this "spatial territorialisation"; he writes, "Places and spaces, of people, practices, and commodities, describes this political landscape. It is in this sense that discourse is always placed, because people are always anchored or invested in specific sites. Hence, it matters how and where practices and people are placed, since the place determines from and to where one can speak (or act)" (p. 20). Identity is then constituted by identification with certain cultural practices and connected to creation, empowerment, and belonging. At the same time, identity is contingent upon how these practices and locales change over time. Identity is definable yet multiple, contested yet affirmed, contextual yet personal, a matter of difference and a matter of identification.

As the performer is being transported into domains both of spatial territorialization and of the subject's consciousness, we understand this process is always partial, contingent, and relative. While some performers more than others struggle through the complicated tensions between trauma and transformation, any move toward transgression is dangerous without taking on the serious questions of identity conjoined with representation. Performance becomes the vehicle by which a representation is manifest and through which identity is presented; therefore, representation of the Other is a value-laden construction of signification within a specific context. Representation and identity are largely mediated through the performer's body—what it does and says in performance space. Therefore, in the performance of possibilities, we understand representation as first and foremost a responsibility. We are responsible for the creation of what and who is being represented; we are representing the represented, and our representing most often carries with it political ramifications far beyond the reach of the performance. Again, because "how a people are represented is how they are treated" (Hall, 1998, p. 27), the act of representation is also an act of material consequences. The body politic responds to individuals and communities by the way they understand them, which is itself based upon a complex configuration of discourses and experiences, none of which is more profound than how these lives enter their consciousness through representations in cultural performances.

In a performance of possibilities, moral responsibility and artistic excellence culminate in an active intervention to break through unfair closures, remake the possibility for new openings, and bring the margins to a shared center. The performance of possibility does not arrogantly assume that we exclusively are giving voice to the silenced, for we understand that they speak and have been speaking in spaces and places often foreign to us. Nor are we assuming that we possess the unequivocal knowledge and skills to enable people to intervene in injustice—or that they have not been intervening through various other forms all the time.

We understand that in performing the contested identities of subjects that there must be caution and politics. We are involved in an ethics guided by caution and a strategy informed by cultural politics. We are not recklessly speaking to and against one location, but to our very endeavor and ourselves. We are involved with the "opening the self" work of breaking, with the grandest dialogic possibility of remaking.

Warm-Ups

1. Discuss the social dramas that have an impact on your life both personally and on a broader (inter)national scale. How do they both adhere to and diverge from Turner's (1982a, 1982b, 1985) paradigm?

2. What is the value of understanding ethnography through a performance paradigm?

3. What are the most memorable cultural performances you have experienced and how did they affect you?

4. How would you use performance in your research?

Notes

1. From *Ritual to Theatre: The Human Seriousness of Play*, by Victor Turner. Copyright © 1982 Victor Turner and PAJ Publications. Reprinted by permission of PAJ Publications.

2. This section, "Staging Ethnography and the Performance of Possibilities," is used with permission from the National Communication Association. Reprinted from Madison, D. Soyini. "Performance, Personal Narratives, and the Politics of Possibility." 1988. In Dailey, Sheron J. (Ed.), *The Future of Performance Studies: Visions and Revisions*. Washington, DC: National Communication Association. 276–286.

Suggested Readings

Bell, E. (1998). Accessing the power to signify: Learning to read in performance studies. In S. J. Dailey (Ed.), *The future of performance studies: Visions and revisions* (pp. 57–59). Washington, DC: National Communication Association.

Bowman, R. (1998). Performing social rubbish: Humbug and romance in the American marketplace. In D. Pollock (Ed.), *Exceptional spaces: Essays in performance and history* (pp. 121–141). Chapel Hill: University of North Carolina.

Case, S.-E., Brett, P., & Foster, S. L. (Eds.). (1995). *Cruising the performative: Interventions into the representation of ethnicity, nationality, and sexuality.* Bloomington: Indiana University Press.

Fabian, J. (1990). *Power and performance.* Madison: University of Wisconsin Press.

Fine, E C., & Speer, J. H. (1989). A new look at performance. *Communication Monographs, 44,* 374–389.

Fusco, C. (1994). The other history of intercultural performance. *The Drama Review, 38,* 143–167.

Jackson, S., & Davis, T. (2004). *Professing performance.* Cambridge, UK: Cambridge University Press.

Kirby, M. (1975). On political theater. *The Drama Review, 19,* 129–135.

Phelan, P. (1993). *Unmarked.* London: Routledge.

Pineau, E. L. (1998). Performance studies across the curriculum: Problems, possibilities, and projections. In S. J. Dailey (Ed.), *The future of performance studies: Visions and revisions* (pp. 128–135). Washington, DC: National Communication Association.

Schechner, R. (1998). What is performance studies anyway? In P. Phelan & J. Lane (Eds.), *The ends of performance* (pp. 357–362). New York: New York University Press.

Taft-Kaufman, J. (1985). Oral interpretation: Twentieth-century theory and practice. In T. W. Benson (Ed.), *Speech communication in the twentieth century* (pp. 158–165). Carbondale: Southern Illinois University Press.

Taussig, M. (1993). *Mimesis and alterity: A particular history of the senses.* New York: Routledge.

8

It's Time to Write

Writing as Performance

For me and most of the other writers I know, writing is not rapturous. In fact, the only way I can get anything written at all is to write really, really shitty first drafts. . . .

—Anne Lamott, *Bird by Bird* (1998)

But the foremost reason I write might at first strike you as petty. I write for revenge—that time-honored but somewhat clichéd motivation. Living well isn't the best revenge, I can tell you from experience. Writing well, on the other hand, is.

Revenge against apathy, against those who are not interested in listening to the voices that surround them—wife, husband, brother, daughter, father, friend or nameless traveler.

Revenge against the bullets of assassins, against the wild forces that trample the earth, against the terror and tragedy that is in every life.

Revenge against the Devil and, pardon the blasphemy, revenge against God, for slaughtering us in the crossfire of their eternal quarrel."

—Bob Shacochis, "Writing for Revenge" (2001)

I remember when a colleague phoned to say that one of her graduate students had completed his fieldwork almost a year earlier, but still was not able to sit down and begin writing. She felt he had put off the writing for too long, finding every excuse not to write. Having made several attempts to get him to write, she was becoming more and more concerned with his procrastination. My colleague asked if I could suggest books or sources that she might recommend to help him get started writing.

I remember another occasion when one of my brightest students and most skilled fieldworkers sat across from me in my office utterly frustrated: "*Soyini, writing is such a pain! It is actually depressing. I love fieldwork, but the thought of sitting down and trying to write it all up is such a burden! Where do I begin? There is just too much to write about. I experienced so much in the field. Yet, when I sit down to write, it takes me forever to just get that first sentence written. Nothing seems to make sense. It takes me forever to really get flowing with my writing and even then I'd rather be anywhere than sitting down trying to put words together on a page.*"

My only concern in sharing these two anecdotes is that most of my students may think I am writing about them. Writing is a baneful charge for too many of us. This chapter is a synthesis of some of the most effective writing methods that I have discovered over the years. But more importantly, the chapter augments these methods by recognizing the performative aspects of what it means to write. Hopefully, understanding writing through the lens and metaphor of performance might be a soothing balm for the pains of writing.

Getting Started: In Search of the Muse

Writing comes more easily when you have something to say.

—H. L. Goodall, Jr., *Writing the
New Ethnography* (2000)

Never sit down to write until you know what you're going to say.

—Kenneth Atchity, *A Writer's Time* (1986)

Forget talent! If you have it fine. Use it. If you don't have it, it doesn't matter. As habit is more dependable than inspiration, continued learning is more dependable than talent.

—Octavia Butler, *Blood Child and Other Stories* (1996)

Research Questions and Statement of Purpose

There are very few gifted individuals who can sit down with no plan in their head, but with the will to write, and suddenly craft pages and pages of thoughtful, engaging, and lucid sentences. Particularly if the writing follows the form of an essay and especially if we are writing ethnographic accounts, we must have a clear notion of what it is we want to say *before* we begin to write. Most of us, even the best writers, will flounder and become hopelessly frustrated if we do not have a loosely formed sequence of ideas to draw from. Staring at a blank page is the first step, and it is often the hardest step to overcome, but you can take that step with a lot more ease by knowing the very bare essentials or the raw ideas of what you want to write about. Goodall's (2000) words are simple and true: Before you begin remind yourself, *Writing comes more easily when you have something to say.* And, please remember, knowing what you want to say is the best cure for writer's block! (Goodall, 2000; Rubin & Rubin, 1995; Wolcott, 2001). Now, you might ask yourself," What is it I want to say?"

The Muse Map and the Road Map

The road map, or what I like to call the *muse map*, becomes a sort of list that comprises all you want to say and the order in which you want to say it. The muse map is the bare bones of what you are about to write. It can serve as informant, guide, and catalyst, keeping your writing going when your mind goes blank or when thoughts start to jumble. It also transforms the intimidating glare of the blank page from an absent space to a playing field for jotting down words and playing with ideas. The muse map overlooks the absent space and welcomes the expressive irreverence of the playing field. In the playing field, you lay words to the page playfully—without the need for perfection, permanence, or propriety—only to free your first ideas with as much confidence and joy as possible so they can live whimsically on the page until more and others come along. Remember, a really, really shitty first draft is okay!

Creating Your Muse Map

You begin with your notes or your coded data (see Chapter 2), which comprise the raw material of your field notes and theoretical paradigms.

From your notes, you further refine and order your themes and concepts forming annotated topics or descriptive units that may take the form of major topics, subtopics, and, if necessary, sub-subtopics. Please, do not write your paper directly from your notes before you create your muse map unless your notes are already synthesized into main points and ordered.

Although not exactly the same, your muse map resembles the format of a formal outline, an idea tree, a series of clusters, or an annotated list of primary and secondary ideas. Your muse map is different from these, however, because you will experiment with a format or combination of formats. Moreover, you are learning through the process of reviewing, delimiting, and sequencing ideas. You are jotting down the map that is unfolding on a separate sheet of paper or on a computer. The muse map is not identical to the conventional outline format, because you are designing it to your specific needs. You may include small drawings and symbols to signal certain ideas; you may use your own style of shorthand, or color code certain points for emphasis. Feel free to keep it simple or go for the detail. More detail helps if you need more direction and guidance as you write; however, less detail is better if more direction feels too overbearing or restricting. Make the map you need to keep the writing going and focused.

Enjoy how much you are learning and feel confident in the clarity the process fosters. The point is that you must feel unrestricted in creating the most effective means of delimiting your morass of notes so that you may then list and order your ideas. Whatever format is most comfortable for you is fine. What is most important is that *you get the essential ideas—the bare bones—down on paper and place them in a sequence and an order*. Keep in mind OED—that is, remember to *order essential ideas*. This is all the muse map is about: It constitutes the very core ideas of your writing project and the sequence in which you wish to present them.

Writing your muse map is a process. As you are deciding what bare bones you want to include and are then grouping them and placing them in order (very much like coding and logging data, discussed in Chapter 2), you are, of course, jotting it down. I usually begin the basic draft of my map by writing in long hand with a yellow pad and pencil. Then, I type it out on the computer and print it out. It takes time, but the muse map is perhaps the most important step in the writing process. It truly is the bones of the final written product, but, more important, it becomes the muse that keeps the ideas and the writing flowing.

If you feel the term *muse map* is a bit too New Age, let it go. I only conjure it up so you may think about what a muse does performatively. But, if *muse map* feels a bit silly, you can always go back to the term *outline* and imagine your outline as your muse (or not). I happen to call this process the *muse map* rather than an *outline* or a *road map*, not because it is so drastically different in form or content from a conventional outline, but because performatively and psychologically the muse map *does* something different.

It conjures the mythic meaning of the muse and performs the function of that guiding force, keeping the ideas and the words flowing, counteracting the dread of the absent space and writer's block. *Muse map* reminds me that this "outlining" is more than just outlining; it is a learning process whereby I inscribe, creatively and idiosyncratically, for my own needs, the essence of my ideas in an order and priority that will keep my writing going. More to the point, the muse map might stop the writing and inspire it to change and go in another direction entirely.

Schedules and Time Management

> *Discipline is the key to all that follows, the bedrock of productive writing. Talent is not a rare commodity. Discipline is. It requires determination more than self-confidence, the commitment of your will to the dream.*
>
> —Kenneth Atchity, *A Writer's Time* (1986)

The most brilliantly constructed muse map in the world and the most gifted writer on the planet will fall completely short of the mark without *time, organization,* and *deep discipline,* or what I like to call my best friend TODD. Some of the best talents have lost great opportunities and missed important deadlines, because they did not know how to manage their time. They cannot seem to get organized. The time management and organization required to complete ethnographic writing are fueled by deep discipline.

Deep discipline is not simply being disciplined for fear of being punished, or being disciplined because it is your duty or because it is the right thing to do. This is discipline and it is good and fine—we all need it and have it in varying degrees—but it is not *deep* discipline. Deep discipline is more substantive: you are disciplined because you have a guiding, inner purpose that motivates you to make certain choices over other choices. Enacting this purpose is a priority that not only demands certain sacrifices, but also inspires them. Deep discipline is always accompanied by a level of self-determination and the pleasure that comes with the feeling of having direction and self-control. One of the perks of deep discipline (and discipline) is the wonderful ability to create habit. At those moments when purpose and deep discipline are challenged, we can always rely on the habit that discipline created. I remember Octavia Butler saying at a writer's conference that "Habit is more dependable than inspiration."

Keeping in mind the importance of TODD in the completion of your writing project, I have also listed important time management techniques that will help you as you achieve TODD:

- Set goals with the determination to keep them. Don't kill yourself: Set realistic goals that are achievable. If your goals place unreasonable demands upon you, it is more than likely that you will become discouraged.

- Prioritize and create a master list of things to do. Keep in mind what is most important. Think in terms of what *must* be done, what *should* be done, and what *could* be done.

- From your master list, create a list for the month, the week, and the day. The combination of lists helps to prioritize your things to do, but it also helps organize the time needed to do those things.

- Remember, prioritize! Learn the Jelly Bean lesson. I remember seeing this demonstrated by Stephen Convoy on television many years ago. You have three glass containers: One container is filled with jellybeans, another is filled with three large rocks, and the third is empty. You must fit the empty container with both the rocks and the jellybeans. The rocks represent what is most important to you—that is, your goals. The jellybeans represent what is not so important—that is, watching television, shopping, cleaning the house, Internet surfing, the telephone, and so forth. Now, you are asked to place the jellybeans in the large empty jar. After all the jellybeans are emptied into the jar you are then asked to place the rocks. All the jellybeans are in the jar, but there is no room in the jar for the rocks. Indeed, you can barely fit one rock into the jar. Then, you are asked to empty the jar and place the rocks in first. After placing all three rocks inside the jar, you are now asked to put the jellybeans inside the jar. Most of the jellybeans fit inside the jar with all the rocks. Is this lesson pretty obvious? First things first!

- Schedule tasks for high energy and prime body rhythm times. There really are times of the day when the body and mind are better at certain tasks than other times. Listen to your body and try to schedule your work around its rhythms. For me, writing is best in the morning and proofreading my work is better later in the day.

- Develop a routine: Designate tasks on specific days and times. Routines do not always have to be dull and repetitive. They can enhance productivity and energy, as well as provide a sense of direction and self-confidence.

- Proportion your efforts to the worth of the tasks and create a time-line. This was a very important lesson that I learned the hard way. So many of us "sweat the small stuff": Don't waste a lot of time and effort on items that are not a priority. Give them the least amount of effort in order to complete them so you can free your time for what is most important.

- Assign deadlines to priorities to keep them from becoming emergencies. Self-imposed deadlines require you to complete a task before it becomes an emergency and so are one of the best stress relievers invented.

- Avoid procrastination by dividing tasks into small units. Procrastination can imprison us, because we are trapped into worrying about what is not yet done. If you are faced with a large task, do a bit at a time each day or throughout the day. Peck away until the job gets done.

- Always identify what is the right thing to do! There are a lot of distractions and seductions, but before you are tempted to go with you friends to the mall or stay up later than you should, ask yourself, "Is this really what I need to be doing?"

- Do one thing at a time. Multitasking is fine, and some of us are more skilled at it than others, but if you can, please try as best you can to do one thing at a time. Doing so creates better quality work, and, moreover, is gentler on the body and mind.

- Take advantage of hidden time and wait time. Most all time management tips include this point. There is a great deal of "unused" time that can be used in completing certain tasks. Waiting can be turned into a really productive time.

- Just say "No!" This sometimes takes courage, but you have a right and an obligation to yourself and your goals to say "no" sometimes. With practice, it really does get easier.

- Do it, delegate it, or dump it! Decide which of these options is best based on what you think is really worth doing. If you can dump it, you should. If you can delegate it, then do so without guilt. If it is worth doing and only you can do it, then do it.

- Review and plan at night or first thing in the morning. This helps set the day without the mushy feeling of not being sure what you need to do or how to begin your day.

Remember: Be self-determined and stay the course!

First Draft and Free Writing

After you have completed your muse map, it is time now to start writing. With your muse map as your director and guide, start placing ideas on the page. As each idea lands on the page, you are elaborating, joining, and transitioning from one idea to the next. You are *not stopping to think or deliberate* about what you are writing. You have already done that when you made your muse map. You are *not stopping to correct, check, or perfect* your writing. If you feel you must stop to think or correct, take *only a few seconds* to get yourself in order, then start writing again. But remember— stop only if you feel you absolutely must and immediately start writing again.

In the words of writer Natalie Goldberg (1990), "*Keep your hands moving!*" (p. 3). This might be very difficult and feel unnatural to you if you have the inclination or have formed the habit to stop frequently to read over and correct your writing. But resist it as best you can and keep the hand moving. One technique to help you keep going is to use question marks or dashes when you get stuck trying to think of the right word or even the right phrase. Instead of stopping to think of the word or to properly craft the phrase, write or type a question mark keeping the overall flow of your ideas uninterrupted. You will notice that when you feel you can't capture the right word or phrase and you skip over it (with a question mark or a dash), you complete that section and you come back to the missing word. It will come to you. It is generally the case that when the words do not come to mind immediately, if you keep going they will come to you later on (right after you read the passage, or in few hours or days). Skip the parts that would interrupt your thinking and that would keep your hand from moving. It is a matter of filling in the blanks. Rest assured, the right word will come to you.

The purpose in keeping the hand moving is not to be in the frustrating position of creating ideas *and* editing them at the same time. Let the editor in you rest for a while and let the playful creator free to express itself on the playing field of the page. Let it truly be *free* writing. Harry F. Wolcott (2001) states,

> Writers sometimes referred to as "bleeders" follow the opposite of freewriting. I do not know the origin of the term, although it brings to mind an observation attributed to sports journalist Red Smith: "There's nothing to writing. All you do is sit down at a typewriter and open a vein." Bleeders are methodical. Their approach reflects a combination of confidence and command about writing, along with some personal qualities (hang-ups?) about having everything just right. They worry over each sentence as they write. They do not press ahead to the next sentence until the present one is perfected. . . . If you recognize the bleeder tendency in yourself, and you cannot imagine romping through an early draft and subsequently discarding material with abandon, then perhaps a tightly detailed outline (or Table of Contents) is sufficient to get you started on the slow-but-steady production of a first draft. (pp. 26–27)

Wolcott also adds that, when the writing is not coming forth, he will turn from the keyboard and take out his yellow notepad and ballpoint pens to get the words down on paper.

The Anxiety of Writing:
Wild Mind and Monkey Mind

That big sky is wild mind. I'm going to climb up to that sky straight over our heads and put one dot on it with a Magic Marker. See that dot? That dot is what Zen calls monkey mind or what western psychology calls part of conscious mind. We give all our attention to that one dot. So when it says we can't write, that we're no good, are failures, fools for even picking up a pen, we listen to it.

—Natalie Goldberg, *Wild Mind:*
Living the Writer's Life (1990)

Natalie Goldberg (1990) equates our struggle to write with the battle between wild mind and monkey mind. Wild mind in Western psychology is understood as the *unconscious*. But Goldberg sees wild mind as much larger than the unconscious: It is the big sky and all that surrounds us, from our dreams and desires to everyone we ever met or wanted to meet; it is all our experiences and imagined experiences; it is "mountains, rivers, Cadillacs, humidity, plains, emeralds, poverty, old streets in London, snow, and moon" (Goldberg, 1990, p. 32). Wild mind is everything. However, monkey mind is that small dot in the big sky of wild mind. Monkey mind is consumed by control, and it rules by constraint, admonishment, and judgment. Monkey mind is always chiding us and demanding restraint. Monkey mind abhors the daring, the beauty, and the magnanimity of wild mind. "So our job as writers," according to Goldberg, "is not to diddle around our whole lives in the dot but to take one big step out of it and sink into the big sky and write from there" (p. 33).

Wild mind and monkey mind are at battle when we free write. We turn to wild mind to keep the hand moving on the playing field of the page, but we feel the pressure of monkey mind trying to take control by correcting us, second guessing our first thoughts, and telling us we are dumb or the writing isn't good enough. Goldberg (1990) suggests, "Let everything run through us and grab as much as we can of it with a pen and paper. Let yourself live in something that is already rightfully yours—your own wild mind. . . . Can you do this? Lose control and let wild mind take over? It is the best way to write. To live, too" (p. 34).

Continents, Islands, and the Editor

Kenneth Atchity (1986) provides us with another metaphor that captures the tension between the freedom of wild mind and the constraint of monkey mind in the form of three spheres: *continents, islands,* and *the editor.* The continent of reason, according to Atchity, is the "rational part of the mind, the logical and conventional part we all share in common" (p. 6). The continent is a "more efficient thinking machine" than the islands, which are the many elements of "intuitive consciousness, those countless idiosyncratic centers of perception that are different for each of us" (p. 6). When we begin to write, the continent of reason begins to form sentences, but the many intuitive islands of the mind don't like it; they think, "It's a ridiculous way to start your story—too weak!" (p. 6). The islands reject what reason has written, and "the islands have a million better ideas and each and every one of them starts thinking about better sentences" (pp. 15–16). At this point, the battle between the continent of reason and the multitude of islands begins. As the many islands express all their many different ideas against the continent of reason, another part of the mind, which Atchity describes as the *managing editor,* now appears on the scene. He states,

> As the day wears on, ideas from the strongest islands begin announcing themselves to that part of your mind I call "the Managing Editor." The rational mind has programmed the intuitive islands to reject its arbitrary decision because it knows what the islands have to say is likely to be more powerful than anything it can come up with through sheer intellectualizing. (pp. 6–7)

Atchity (1986) asserts, "Learning to write is learning your own mind" (p. 14). His illustration of the islands, continent, and editor, like Goldberg's wild mind and monkey mind, animates the psychology of writing by giving graphic characterizations to the working of the mind. "The islands of consciousness are free floating and changeable. . . . A new island can be formed instantly from a new impression. . . . Individuality and originality are island characteristics," writes Atchity (p. 15). The continent of reason "is relatively stationary and immovable . . . the Continent is the consciousness of society and culture, and is constructed by our education" (p. 15). The Continent is slower and more deliberate than the impressionable islands, because it must "search its warehouse of memory to find a category to which to relate the new impression so that it can use that new impression in dealing with the world outside the mind" (p. 15). As the Continent is motivated by reason and structure, the islands are energized by originality and the polyvocality of their individual impressions.

Atchity's (1986) and Goldberg's (1990) metaphors are versions of Turner's (1982a, 1982b, 1985) structure and antistructure doing battle in the writer's mind. The centripetal and centrifugal, the wild and the monkey, are in rousing competition. No wonder writing for some is a frustrating and sometimes painful experience. Again, in Atchity's words:

The interaction of islands and Continent—the tension between them—causes the productive energy identified with the Editor's creative awareness. Once it has been formed from the island-Continent tension (and the acceptance of that tension as the neutral stat of things), the Managing Editor focuses like a spinning laser beam to illuminate activities on the islands and on the Continent, moving slowly or quickly depending on the writer's energy level. . . . Writing is the Editor's ordering of materials from all the islands into the language and structure of the Continent, managing the analytical mind to have it organize images from the non-analytical mind. No wonder writing causes anxiety. (pp. 15–16)

In summary, the following points may serve as helpful reminders as you approach your writing project.

- Remember TODD: Develop a schedule and block out time to write.
- Know what you want to write before you start and create your muse map.
- Let your muse map be your prompter and guide in keeping the hand moving.
- With your muse map as your springboard and safety net: lose control and play.
- Honor wild mind and try not to heed the controlling impulse of monkey mind: Try not to stop, think, or correct punctuation, grammar, or spelling.
- If you get stuck trying to think of le mot juste, skip it, type in a question mark, and keep writing.
- If you get stuck writing larger sections or transitions, move away from the computer. Treat yourself to a change of scenery (go to a café or a park) and then get out your writing pads and pencils.
- When you have employed the services of the muse map—transformed empty pages to playing fields—take a break. Congratulate yourself for having completed the hardest draft of all, the first draft.
- After your lovely break, come back, put on your editor's cap, and begin crafting your work.
- Reading your drafts out loud, as you complete each section, is one of the best methods to truly "realize" what you have written and notice what needs more work.

Writing as Performance and Performance as Writing

Because of you I have listened to others. I have performed in writing, sometimes in writing, sometimes instead of in talking, touching, and staging, our narrative rites.

—Della Pollock, *Telling Bodies*
Performing Birth (1999)

In Della Pollock's path-breaking essay "Performing Writing" (1998), she defines performative writing as (a) evocative, (b) metonymic, (c) subjective, (d) nervous, (e) citational, and (f) consequential. This section draws primarily from Pollock's important contribution to performative writing and serves to extend her six components of performative writing through the interactive characteristics of the relational, evocative, and the embodied, and concludes by reiterating Pollock's idea of the consequential.

Performative Writing as Relational

Understanding performative writing as something relational means you are writing for an audience of readers and you *care* about them. You are invested in them, because you are hoping that what you write makes a difference to them and that it makes some kind of contribution. You want your words to matter to your audience. In performative writing, you want your readers to come away with something they did not feel or know before they read your words. Your writing is an offering, because you care about what they receive from your writing and how they receive it. Performative writing is relational because it is generous. You consciously extend yourself to your readers. You want them to take in your words without it being complicated for the sake of being complicated.

What I mean here is that writing that is hard to read or writing that is hard for the sake of being difficult is not smart writing. Making the writing complicated doesn't necessarily make it more substantive. You should not unnecessarily overwork or overburden your readers for the purpose of proving yourself smarter than them. It is more important that your readers grasp and encounter your writing than it is for them to be impressed by how deep or brilliant you are. This does not mean that simplicity is always a virtue either. Sometimes keeping it simple is really just simplistic thinking. In performative writing, there is virtue and beauty in the complex if it is purposeful and not gratuitous or self-indulgent. Complexity can be the most generous offering, because it demands growth, challenges the expected, and disturbs the complacent. Relational writing means that you find the very difficult balance between the necessity for simplicity and the necessity for complexity because you are offering your words to Others and you care about what it does *for* them.

Performative writing emphasizes the relational. This does not, however, mean that all writers should claim the relational as a quality of their work. Some writers will argue that they write for themselves and for the passion that enlivens their own being. They argue that they write from the center of their individual heart, soul, and life-world, in which the reader is welcome to share. They write with the conviction that they will be true to their own voice, and the readers will then enter as a result of that truth.

Performative writing emphasizes the relational dynamic between writer and reader in a spirit of caring about the dialogic and communicative quality of the connection. This does not mean that the performative writer must repress his or her own unique voice or soul to appease the reader. Nor does it mean that the performative writer *only* writes *for* the reader, or that every word or idea is focused on what the reader might think, but we do not fixate on our own individuality either.

Performative writing as a relational act means we do not write purely as individuals. We live in a world with Others, and their imprint is upon who we are and what we write. Mikhail Bakhtin (1984) states,

> Everything that pertains to me enters my consciousness, beginning with my name, from the external world through the mouths of others (my mother, and so forth), with their intonation, in their emotional and value-assigning tonality. I realize myself initially through others: from them I receive words, forms, and tonalities for the formation of my initial idea of myself. . . . Just as the body is formed initially in the mother's womb, a person's consciousness awakens wrapped in another's consciousness. (p. xx; qtd. in Goodall, 2000, p. 140)

An example of how performative writing both affirms and complicates Bakhtin's (1984) words in the way we realize as well as lose ourselves and the Other is illustrated in the performative writing of performance scholar Judith Hamera (1996, 1997, 2002). The following passage, from Hamera's (2001) ethnographic study on virtuoso dance, discusses how the relational simultaneously encompasses dancer, audience, ethnographer, and the ethnographer's ability to write about it all. In this essay, Hamera describes how she is remade through the dancer and the dance, and discusses the challenge of what this means when the ethnographer must grapple with language and discourse to bring that embodied presence to the page:

> Roxanne told me that she and Oguri dance out of what she called a strange obligation, and unpeaceful obligation, because she said, they took it seriously when a member of their audience told them she never came in with a problem their dances couldn't solve. I find this ironic because I never come in with a discursive, representational solution that these dances couldn't make problematic.
>
> The issue is this: Roxanne is a dancer of enormous grace and power but Oguri overwhelms. His body, his movement vocabulary, his ethos are almost excessively present. He is always almost too much there and not, or not only, because of the choreography or mise-en-scene. His work is beautiful, terrifying, "at the limits of the possible" (Barthes, "Romantic Song," 286). His excess of

presence, and my joy and anxiety in the face of it, leave me searching for language up to the task of representing, not only the dance, but how I am remade through it. How was he better, and what was he better at, and how can I tell you? And in the search for the ways to tell you, I lost his body to language. (p. 236)

Performative Writing as Evocative

Seeing performative writing as an evocative act means that what is written down in words is now lifted from the page into a more sensuous awareness. In the sentiment of Norman Denzin (2001, 2003), performative writing enacts as it describes. What is described becomes evoked through detail, sensuality, and verisimilitude into another felt-sensing presence (Bacon, 1979). The readers enter this new presence through the guiding hand of the writer because they have been given enough information and enough inspiration to make a metaphorical leap from the page to a fusion of imaginations: The writer's imagination evokes the reader's, and words are not just words anymore, flat on a page, but are now images woven through meaning. Performative writing is evocative because it is a braiding of poetry and reportage, imagination and actuality, critical analysis and literary pleasure. Pollock states (1998),

> Performative writing is evocative. It operates metaphorically to render absence present—to bring the reader into contact with "other worlds," to those aspects and dimensions of our world that are other to the text as such by re-marking them. Performative writing evokes worlds that are other-wise intangible, unlocatable: worlds of memory, pleasure, sensation, imagination, affect, and in-sight. (p. 80)

Performative writing renders absence present by evolving a world of meaning upon which the reader may now enter. Performative writing defies monologism; it is an inherently dialogic endeavor. A collaboration of imaginations between reader and writer in evoking a world that is Other and wise is illustrated in the work of Dwight Conquergood. A scene is evoked from Conquergood's (1988) fieldwork in Thailand: Through his performative writing, he brings the camp to us in a quintessential moment that captures the history of dislocation, struggle, and transnational politics that is metaphorically contained in one woman's song:

> A Hmong widow walks to a crossroad in Camp Ban Vinai, surveys the scene, and then settles herself on a bench outside the corner hut. Bracing her back against the split-bamboo wall, she begins to sing. At first softly, as if to herself,

she sings a Hmong Khy txhiaj (folksong). Aware of a gathering audience, she raises her voice to fill the space around her. She sings a lamentation, carving her personal anguish into a traditional expressive form. With exquisitely timed gestures, she strips and peels with one hand the branch of firewood she holds in the other. Tears stream down her face as she sings about the loss of her husband, her children, her house, her farm, her animals, and her country. She sings of war, and flight, and breaking, and of a time when she was wife and mother in the Laotian village where silver neck-rings were worn. She punctuates each refrain by tossing away a sliver that her strong fingers have torn from the wood she holds across her lap as if it were a child.

The sad beauty of her singing attracts a crowd. She never makes eye contact but acknowledges the crowd's presence in her spontaneously composed verses, subtly at first, and then more confidently. She is both lamenting and entertaining. With nothing left to tear away, she makes the final toss of the last splinter, rises, and begins to sway with the rhythm of her song. People set out food for her. I give her the few ath I have in my pocket. Her face still wet, she breaks into a broad smile. Strange laughter interrupts her otherwise balanced verses. (p. 174)[1]

Performative Writing as Embodied

Performative writing as something embodied means the evocations of "Other-wise" worlds are not disembodied creations (Pollock, 1998). Writing has been considered a marriage between the imagination and intellect. In performative writing, we recognize that the *body* writes. Critical ethnography adheres to radical empiricism: the intersection of bodies in motion and space. Meanings and experiences in the field are filtered and colored through sensations of the body—that is, through body knowledge. If we accept that knowledge has infinite origins and forms, we are able to accept knowledge from and of the body. Body sensation as body knowledge is not to be equated solely with the sensational or feelings of arousal, though it certainly includes these elements. Rather, body sensation as body knowledge comprises *impressions* and *interpretive meaning*. Body knowledge is the emotion and cognition of physical pain: blazing heat burning the skin, hunger that dulls the senses, grotesque smells that sicken the stomach. As physical pleasure, it is the night breeze caressing the skin, the delicious taste of a communal feast, the alluring smell of locally made body oils. Because these knowledges of the body are embedded with meanings that filter and guide our experiences in the field, they will obviously inform and influence what we write. We write *from* our body and we write *through* our body.

In writing from our body, we are writing from the memories (and field notes!) of our embodied space and impressions in the field. When we are writing through our bodies we move to the space and the *act* of putting words down on a page. In writing through our body, the act of writing becomes the enactment of an embodied voice. In performative writing, the reader is not taking in disembodied ideas and images from a cognitive word machine or an omniscient knower. In performative writing, words are inhered by a subject with a voice. To state that there is a subject and a voice is to state that there is a body. There has been a great deal of discussion over the notion of *voice* in writing: "finding your voice," "honoring your voice," "listening to your voice," and so forth. Goodall (2000) states,

> Voice is *the personal rhetorical imprint of who we are and what we write.* Singularly and multiply, voice is the *sound* of a character *speaking.* Voice sums the way in which prose communicates a writer's vocal range and tone, her or his sensitivities to the nuances and passions of spoken language, and the essential *phenomenological essence* of what is being said. Voice is the sound of the ethnographic world being *called* into being. It is a pattern of heard recognitions, and of differences, that convey to readers the self that is textually constructing other and contexts. (pp. 139–140)

The performance artist and scholar E. Patrick Johnson (2003) enacts embodied writing with a clear presence of voice in his description of a gay nightclub:

> Inside, my friends and I squeeze down the staircase and descend into the sea of bodies onto the dance floor. There is barely enough room to breath, let alone move, every inch of the space is filled with bodies—every body imaginable. Clearly, the body is on display: There are drag queens in skintight hot pants and platform shoes. There are "butch" men donning their black leather jackets, lining up along the wall like two by fours holding the structure together. There are "queens" dressed in black chiffon blouses unbuttoned to their navels and tight black jeans, who are constantly pursing their lips while looking over the tops of their retro "cat-eye" shades; there are older men (in this context anyone over 45) sitting on bar stools, dressed conservatively in slacks and button-up shirts sipping their scotch and sodas while looking longingly at the young bodies sauntering across the dance floor. The hip-hop contingent is sprinkled throughout the club in their baggy jeans, ski caps, sneakers, and black shades, some sucking on blow pops while others sip Budweiser's. And there are those like me and my friends who are dressed in designer jeans (Calvin Klein) and tight, spandex muscle shirts, performing middle class (acting bourgeoisie)—as if we actually have two nickels to rub together! (p. 104)[2]

Performative Writing as Consequential

Performative writing is consequential because it inheres in performance as a contested concept that "crashes and breaks through sedimented meanings and normative traditions and plunges us back into the vortices of political struggle" (Conquergood, 1998, p. 32). Performative writing is conducive to critical ethnography because it embraces political struggle and is not ashamed of its politics and advocacy (Agger, 2002; Denzin, 2001). Della Pollock (1998) states,

> As the effect of social relations and as a mode of cultural, historical action, performative writing throws off the norms of conventional scholarship for an explicit, alternative normativity. It operates by a code of reflexive engagement that makes writing subject to its own critique, that makes writing a visible subject, at once making it vulnerable to displacement by the very text/performances it invokes and shoring up its capacity for political, ethical agency. As performance, as writing that stipulates its own performativity, performative writing enters into the arena of contest to which it appeals with the affective investment of one who has been there and will be there at the end, which has a stake in the outcome of the exchange. The writing/subject puts his/her own status on the line . . . in the name of mobilizing *praxis*, breaking the discursive limits of the emperor's stage, and invigorating the dynamics of democratic contest in which the emperor and his new clothes (or lack thereof) are now continually refigured. (p. 96)

The following example of performative writing as a consequential act is taken from my fieldwork in Ghana (Madison, in press). I'm writing performatively about the relationship between globalization and poverty in the global South:

> The human body is indeed a wonder. In its beauty it is a miracle. The beautiful body can heal itself in mysteries beyond science. In marvelous precision the beautiful body can inhere remarkable strength, speed, and endurance past its own expectation. . . . The Other bodies, the loathsome bodies—the dirty body, the disfigured body, the sick body, the body that smells of refuse, the body that oozes, excretes and cannot shelter its waste, the body where matter is grotesquely "out of place" emitting itself in public view—are the bodies that wrenching poverty engenders and breeds in its abominable lack.
>
> For much of the global South, specifically Africa, dirt is a contentious symbol. Blackness, dirt, and disgust are perennially linked. It is within designated locales where we only see dirty people having dirty children with dirty clothes and dirty faces. We see them living in dirty spaces on dirty roads filled with all kinds of dirty things. We know that dirt is to be gotten rid of, but do we remember that when water is inaccessible dirt dwells? Do we remember that dirt braces disease when sanitation systems are not effectual, or existent? Dirt is a stigma and an effect of many of the world's poor. It is both imagined and real. Dirt resides when poverty annuls the time and resources to attend to it, and when global machinations neglect its relief. Dirt and the political economy

are insidious partners. Dirt is a fact of material and political conditions but it is too often cast as a moral flaw . . . This village, these people and the 2,800 million people who live on less than $2 a day and comprise 46% of the world's population are 2,800 million stories of epoch injustices. . . . The heat is blazing . . . I look at Patience sitting beside me. I ask her to take a photograph with the village women we have been talking with all day before we leave to go back to the city. . . .[3]

Warm-Ups

1. Place four different and ordinary objects on the floor or a table—they can be any kind of objects that you find in the room. Arrange them together. Now, write about them. Describe in great detail their appearance, their arrangement, and their function.

2. Write a story describing what you did yesterday from the beginning of the day until you went to sleep. How can you write the yesterday story so that it would be interesting to read and hear?

3. List what you consider the joys or the difficulties (or both) of writing ethnographic accounts.

Notes

1. Reprinted with permission from the publisher from Dwight Conquergood, "Health Theatre in Hmong Refugee Camp: Performance, Communication, and Culture." *TDR/The Drama Review*, 32:3 (T119-Fall 1988), pp. 174–208. © 1988 by New York University and the Massachusetts Institute of Technology.

2. Reprinted with permission from the publisher from E. Patrick Johnson, "Strange Fruit: A Performance about Identity Politics." *TDR/The Drama Review*, 47:2 (T178-Summer 2003), pp. 88–116. © 2003 by New York University and the Massachusetts Institute of Technology.

3. Excerpted from author's essay "My Desire Is for the Poor to Speak Well of Me" to be published in D. Pollock (Ed.), *Remembering: Performance and Oral History* (forthcoming). New York: Palgrave/St. Martin's Press.

Suggested Readings

Atchity, K. (1986). *A writer's time: A guide to the creative process, from vision through revision.* New York: Norton.
Crapanzano, V. (1977). On the writing of ethnography. *Dialectical Anthropology, 2,* 69–73.

Elbow, P. (1981). *Writing with power: Techniques for mastering the writing process*. New York: Oxford University Press.

Ellis, C., & Bochner, A. P. (Eds.). (1996). *Composing ethnography*. Walnut Creek, CA: AltaMira.

Goldberg, N. (1988). *Writing down the bones*. New York: Bantam.

Goldberg, N. (1990). *Wild mind: Living the writer's life*. New York: Bantam.

Goodall, H. L. (2000). *Writing the new ethnography*. Boston Way, MD: AltaMira.

Madison, D. S. (1999). Performing theory/embodied writing. *Text and Performance Quarterly, 19,* 107–124.

Pelias, R. J. (1999). *Writing performance: Poeticizing the researcher's body*. Carbondale: Southern Illinois University Press.

Pollock, D. (1998). Performing writing. In P. Phelan & J. Lane (Eds.), *The ends of performance* (pp. 73–103). New York: New York University Press.

Van Maanen, J. (1988). *Tales of the field: On writing ethnography*. Chicago: University of Chicago Press.

9

The Case Studies

Case One: Staging Cultural Performance

Cultural performances, I contend, do not just happen. Instead, they make things happen that would not have happened in that way, to that extent, in that place, at that time, or among those persons had the cultural performances not taken place. This is the work of performance.

—Kirk W. Fuoss, *Striking Performances/Performing Strikes* (1997)

Joan had conducted fieldwork for more than two years in West Africa. The first stage of her fieldwork had come to an end, and it was time to begin preparation for the second stage—the public performance, there on the ground of her field research. From her fieldwork data, Joan would adopt a performance she hoped would communicate a sense of the subjects' life-worlds and amplify their meanings, contexts, and intentions to a larger group of listeners, observers, and coperformers.

The performance would serve as a testament to the dedication and commitment of her consultants and as a way of giving something back to them before she was to leave and return home to the United States. Joan felt it was time to end the interviews and the first stage of fieldwork, because the seminal questions that guided her study had been addressed. Although newer questions evolved throughout various processes of discovery, these new questions would be part of the performance. Joan also recognized something very important in the ethnographic enterprise: She recognized that a story was forming, an argument, a narrative that now had a life of its own. It had its own form and content; that is, a unity of location had evolved with its own message and purpose. This field story, comprising the range of interviews, performances, field notes, and cultural products, became the response to her most urgent questions. Now it was time to end the fieldwork and stage the story.

Why Did Joan Choose to Adopt and Direct a Cultural Performance From Her Fieldwork?

1. Joan wanted to communicate to a larger public and to a far-reaching distance—from village to the city—the need for arms regulation, and she wanted to make known the work of those who were sacrificing their lives and livelihoods for global justice and their cause.

2. She wanted to serve as a translator for people who would not otherwise have access to discourses surrounding globalization and proliferation in terms that would be relevant to their lives.

3. She wanted to appeal to the emotions. Performance, as an artistic form, appeals to the emotions, as well as the logic of reason. She felt she could present a moving portrayal that would join humor, passion, and reason, offering the audience a way into an empathic connection with the material reality of the subjects—a matching between the inner world of the fieldwork with the inner lives and emotion of the audience. The cultural critic Walter Benjamin (1968) states, "The story teller takes what he tells from experience—his own or that reported by others. And he in turn makes it the experience of those who are listening to his tale" (qtd. in Langellier & Peterson, 2004, p. 5).

4. She wanted the performance to serve as a force for advocacy. The performance would get the message across and it would form something like Alcoff's (1991) web, reaching out to build more alliances and comrades for the cause.

How Did Joan Translate Her Fieldwork to the Stage? What Was Her Process?

1. Joan read through her field notes and listened to the interview tapes several times until themes and contrasting and comparing threads and lines of inquiry began to emerge.

2. Joan began to group the notes and tapes in piles. Each pile had a thematic title, and under the titles that were placed upon each pile was a list of the individual interviews and field note entries.

3. After each pile had been marked and listed and the themes had been clearly developed, Joan reviewed the categories of themes and made the necessary changes. It was during this stage that she spent time rearranging specific listings and switching certain themes. When Joan finally settled on an arrangement, she was ready for the next step.

4. Joan began to place the piles in a sequence, just as she had in the thematic stage. She shifted and experimented with the sequence. It was during the sequencing stage that she ordered and reordered the piles until she was satisfied with the flow of the data. She was building the narrative structure by arranging and juxtaposing interviews, literary excerpts, journal notes, musical selections, and stage movements.

What Stage Techniques Did Joan Adapt?

Joan decided to stage the fieldwork using several different techniques.

Dramatic Reading

Joan used dramatic readings—dramatically reading the written words from a text using the range of the human voice and the dramatic frame of the stage or scene. A dramatic reader is the effective storyteller who brings his or her listeners into the world of the text being read. Dramatic reading as a device is also successful in providing a visual image of physically holding a book, thereby connoting the profound experience of what it means to read and enter the world of a text and be transformed by it.

Images and Stage Pictures

Stage pictures sculpt the performers' bodies into forms and movements to create abstract images from ideas like *freedom, justice, dream,* or *possibility,* and transform their bodies into three-dimensional conceptual pictures. Joan adapted Augosto Boal's (1979, 1995) idea of Image Theatre. Adrian Jackson (2002) states,

> Image Theatre is a series of exercises and games designed to uncover essential truths about societies and cultures without resort, in the first instance, to spoken language—though this may be added in the various "dynamisations" of

the images. . . . The frozen image is simply the starting point for a prelude to the action, which is revealed in the dynamisation process, the bringing to life the image and the discovery of whatever direction or intention is innate in them. At its simplest, the idea underlying this is that "a picture paints a thousand words." . . . Images work across languages and culture barriers and, as Boal shows, frequently reveal unexpected universalities. Also, working with images, sculpting rather than talking, can be more democratic, as it does not privilege more verbally articulate people. (pp. xix–xx)

Representational Scenes

Representational scenes present the illusion of an ethnographic present that represents remembered moments in the field as they occurred, creating the illusion that the audience is not present (often known as "the fourth wall") and that a so-called real-life encounter is being enacted on stage as the audience eavesdrops.

Presentational Scenes

In presentational scenes, performers acknowledged the presence of the audience. Turning again to the performance work of Augusto Boal (1979, 1995), during rehearsals Joan adapted a rendition of what Boal defines as the "joker." The performers enacted a scene or image as a question that is offered to the other performers. The joker introduces the scene and provides background information, if necessary. The scene abruptly ends in the middle and is presented as an incomplete idea. The joker asks the other performers to provide several endings for the scene. Each ending is then performed until the performers collaboratively settle on one or a combination of endings.

Long's Four Evaluations

Joan adapted the four-point evaluation schema of the director and performance scholar Beverly W. Long (1987). The four points include *reporting, evoking, enacting,* and *arguing.* The range of fieldwork data and the performative interpretations of specific voices and scenes that evolved were enacted and evaluated against these levels:

• Reporting—The performer enunciates sounds and words "translating printed symbols into human speech" (Long, 1987, p. 4). The demeanor is similar to that of an objective journalist reporting the events of a story. The emphasis in this category is on the "denotative power of fixed words"

(Long, 1987, p. 4). Long emphasizes that here "performance as reporting situates meaning and authority in the literary text" (p. 4).

- Evoking—During the performance, the performer moves from the denotative to the more connotative. *Expression* and *re-creation* enter into the performance where the performer "actively, but subserviently, participates as mediator . . . offering to an audience one humanized recreation of the literature's complex structure of sound, sense, and feeling" (Long, 1987, pp. 5–6).

- Enacting—The performer now enters into the spheres of experiencing, embodying, matching, and actualizing. Long (1987) states that "the performer seeks to match, to become as much as one can an Other, to experience as if for the first time, whatever the text's speaker experiences. The act aims to blur those distinctions we might make between performer and text" (p. 7).

- Arguing—The performer now moves from the text to that of commenting, questioning, judging, and critiquing. At the level of argument, the performer now becomes the performer as critic. This does not simply mean that the performer finds fault with the text or critiques it in a conventional sense. Rather, the performer as critic *explores* what can be remarked and recreated to augment and to question the text:

> In addition to exposing embedded ideology, performance as critique can also lift, as it were, a possible overlooked or neglected aspect of the literary work— perhaps the contraries and oppositions. . . . Performance as commentary or judgment exists in the present but recalls a shared past with the literary work and anticipates a future when the literature and whatever world it is now a part of cannot be viewed in exactly the same way as before (Long, 1987, pp. 8–9).[1]

Did Joan Encourage a Collaborative Process in Directing the Performance?

1. The performers and Joan as the director developed the themes from the fieldwork data together. They discussed and negotiated among themselves, sharing viewpoints and ideas regarding the inclusion, arrangements, order, and purpose of the themes.

2. During the rehearsal process, all participants shared in leading the warm-ups and developing the blocking and stage pictures. It was during this stage that themes, ideas, situations, and encounters in the field data were discussed in more detail and made into tangible movements and scenes. The collaborative process invites the best ideas from each performer and joins

them together forming an integration of elements to shape a scene. When there is a disagreement, the director assures that each viewpoint is discussed respectfully, until a consensus is reached. If consensus is not possible, then the director may encourage a compromise where viewpoints may merge in some fashion or the group may vote, or the director makes the final decision.

3. In collaborative performance, it is a good idea for each participant to contribute their feelings and ideas by bringing tangible items of interest that represent for them a meaningful connection to the performance—for example, photographs, newspaper clippings, poetry and prose, music, or any artifact that will evoke discussion and further responses toward the performance and its purpose. During the rehearsal process, Joan encouraged the performers, if they wished, to read their journal entries that have particular relevance or insight.

Could Joan Have Employed a More Collaborative Approach?

The collaborative approach is a powerful learning experience. It also builds a sense of camaraderie and shared respect and responsibility. It is through collaboration that all participants are creators in a mutual journey of discovery and invention. The essence of collaboration is the deeply humanizing reciprocity of different individuals working through the complications and challenges of a problem in which the force is the interactive relationship they holds for and with each other. However, the directed approach is also a powerful learning experience. The skilled director inspires participation through his or her vision of the project and through a democratic process of mutual consideration and respect in the attainment of that vision. The directed project is not so much authoritarian as it is a guided path open to suggestions on the various methods and ideas in traveling along the path. The essence of a directed performance is the illumination of knowledge and skills offered through the generosity and attentiveness of relevant experience and a committed vision.

Whether to choose collaborative performance or a directed performance depends on several factors: (a) the nature of the project; (b) the needs and experience of the performers; (c) the disposition, skills, and goals of the director; and (d) the time required to complete it. Joan chose a combination of collaboration and direction. She had a clear purpose or vision in mind, but was open to suggestions. Joan intended to serve as an advocate through specific directing choices while open to a mutually formative process within the parameters of her vision.

Case Two: Oral History and Performance

The telling of the story is a performance. As a human communication practice, performing narrative combines the performative "doing" of storytelling with what is "done" in the performance of a story.

—Kristin M. Langellier and Eric E. Peterson,
Story Telling in Daily Life (2004)

Robert chose a performance-centered approach in the analysis and interpretation of the three oral histories. He felt that a performance-centered transcript of the in-depth interviews would capture the fuller range of their communicative interaction by including nonverbal signs and verbal nuances. Robert wanted to capture the "how" of the said as well as the "what." Over one year of interviewing the three men, Robert experienced many deeply important hows—the intonation, inflection, rhythm, volume, and tone of voice, all were ripe with performance and meaning. He wanted to capture as best he could those moments.

The oral histories of the three men reflected their struggle for identity, their need for belonging, and their yearnings to live without secrets or threat. He understood these narratives were acts in themselves of substantiating personhood and providing the freedom to name and rename what they were to others and to themselves. Robert realized that for the men to narrate their lives was for them to engage in Myerhoff's (1982) idea of a *definitional ceremony*. It was one of the few moments when they were free of the secret they held and liberated to reflect and express their dreams. The performance approach provided a means by which emotion and affect were honored and reflected through poetic transcription.

What Is Poetic Transcription?

In poetic transcription, words are not in isolation from the movement, sound, and sensory dimensions that enrich their substance. Words are placed on a page in poetic form to include these performative dimensions of the speaker. The narrative event is a *gestalt*; therefore, in documentation, the intent is to represent as authentically as possible its range of meanings. Elizabeth Fine (1984) points to the artistry in voice and body: "A performance of verbal art is something more than words. Each of us has, at one time or another, sat under the spell of a performer, conscious of the artistry of voice and body" (p. 1).

In presenting oral narratives as "more than just words," Fine's (1984) analysis of channels helps the ethnographer capture the integrity of the original performance and pinpoint specific aspects of these performance channels. These channels include the *visual, tactile, olfactory,* and *aural* aspects of oral narratives. The visual channel calls for an awareness of performance in relationship to motion (kinesics), objects (artifact), and space (proxemic). The tactile and olfactory channels are concerned with the sensual dynamics of touch and smell. And the aural is composed of linguistic and paralinguistic dimensions. The concern in an analysis of channels here is the mutual importance of *how* something is said along with *what* is said in a performance utterance.

As poetic transcription aims to capture the multidimensional nature of the narrative event, it also offers an alternative to the prose text. The performance-centered text embraces the personal utterances of the performer through a poetic text, where words are placed symbolically in relation to how they are uttered. In striving to recapture the aural experience of performance, contemporary ethnographers may translate the active voice in a more meaningful and poetic manner. These scholars translate beyond the good syntax and the spelling eye of a prose writer (Tedlock, 1983). They embrace style and dramatic poetry with lines of varying lengths, positioning words and phrases that project the rhythm, tone, and personality of the human voice. Dennis Tedlock (1983) states,

> We have punctuated our visible text according to the rising and falling contours of oratorical periods and shaped its lines and stanzas according to the stops, and starts of dramatic timing, we have begun to free ourselves from the inertia, from the established trajectory, of the whole dictation era, an era that stretches (in the west) all the way back to the making of the Homeric texts. We have begun to construct an *open text . . .* a text that forces even the reading eye to consider whether the peculiarities of audible sentences and audible lines might be good speaking rather than bad writing. . . . It is a brilliant stroke of practical poetics that enhance the audible impact of this one particular story. (p. 7)

Robert found Tedlock's concept of "practical poetics" to be a challenging endeavor. It required concentrated listening to and observance of the various channels. Robert also considered what to include or exclude, so as not to overburden the narrative with too many symbols and descriptions. The next step for Robert was to describe in words the tone, attitude, and drama of the performance. In listening to the tape recordings, each word on paper must capture the pitch, range, volume, and timing of the performer's living voice. The recordings were played again to check for accuracy and to delete symbols that might distract from the flow of the narrative. The recordings were played and replayed, checked and rechecked for accuracy and meaning.

Robert also decided that he would merge Fine's (1984) performative channels with significant meanings. In other words, the *meanings* of certain words determined line breaks. Not only were the breaks determined by focusing on the replication or authenticity of the narrative, but the breaks also served to emphasize the significance of narrative content. As a model for poetic translation that considered both performance channels and internal meanings, Robert turned to the ethnographic work of communication studies scholar Bernadette Marie Calafell (2004). In this excerpt, Calafell listens to Mario as he speaks to her of his isolation as a Latino in North Carolina:

Much like the characters in *The Greatest Performance*, through our imagined pasts, renegotiated memories, and spaces of identification we created a sense of community in the space. Together we created Aztlan . . . even in North Carolina:
  [Mario speaking to Calafell]

> *Because my parents are the immigrant generation,*
> *I have all these . . .*
> *different selves*
> *There are times when I like to hang out with people who*
> *are Mexican and speak Spanish.*
> *But I always . . .*
> *When I was here by myself,*
> *I always felt like there was a part of me that*
> *was ignored.*
> *You know, and a part of me . . . that*
> *I couldn't talk to anyone else about*
> *and*
> *when I met your friend*
> *I was so happy.*
> *I was like, "Oh my God!"*
> *And we talked and talked and this and that and*
> *even though she wasn't Chicano*
> *I felt like we understood each other in a way*
> *And then when she told me she had a friend in the same*
> *program*
> *Who was Chicana*
> *I was like waiting for you to call me and*

then when you finally DID
and
we went out to dinner
we were talking about Cherrie Moraga . . . and other people
we
knew of
. . . the Chicano scholar canon I guess
And we didn't have to be explaining,
"You know
. . . Chicano means this_____"
I mean it was just awesome.
You know.
It was cool.
It really transformed my space.
And you know, all this shit happened and all that
but at the same time
I negotiate my spaces
. . . like you are my Chicano space.
This right now is my Chicano space.
Sometimes I still go to Mexican space,
I found like right now I am a very balanced situation
and
you continue to form part of that balance with
those other people
Who have impacted my life here. (pp. 188–189)[2]

For Robert, poetic transcription embraced the fuller presence of his narrators and the implications of their embodied telling. The process of translation from "performance to print" (Fine, 1984) was more than documenting experiences, it was presenting his multilayered engagement with three men who trusted him to represent them.

What Analytical Tool Did Robert Employ?

Robert was inspired by the work of Kristin M. Langellier and Eric E. Peterson (2004) in his analysis of the oral histories. He employed their concepts of (1) *embodiment*, (2) *situated constraints*, (3) *discursive regularities*, and (4) *legitimation/critique* as a method of interpreting the meanings, functions, and implications of the three oral histories.

1. Narrative as *embodied* emphasizes the living presence of bodily contact. Bodies are within touch, not simply representing, displaying, or portraying a past moment (Langellier & Peterson, 2004). Nor are bodies being mediated by technologies, but they are together within a space of direct bodily communion with all its ramifications and effects upon the story and the event.

2. Narrative as *situated* concerns the material conditions in which the narratives occur: History, power, language, culture, and so forth generate particular "stories, to particular performances of stories, and to particular performance practices" (Langellier & Peterson, 2004, p. 18). To recognize the situatedness of narratives is to focus on how environment both restricts and enables the stories they surround.

3. Narrative as *discursive regularities* attends to four concerns. First, it examines what is considered meaningful and what is considered meaningless, as well as "what belongs to the narrative and what does not, what contributes to understanding and what does not" (Langellier & Peterson, 2004, p. 19). At another level, we are concerned with how "it is possible to classify types of discourse by locating gradations of repetition and sameness . . . the internal formation of discourse through classification, ordering, and distribution" (Langellier & Peterson, 2004, p. 19). At a third level of discursive regularities, we are concerned with the speaking subject and "what qualifies someone to tell a story . . . to speak for herself or himself from the 'authority of experience,' or to speak for others as an expert" (Langellier & Peterson, p. 20). Finally, the concern "is a critical effort to discuss the conditions of discourse that frame what can be said, what can be understood, and what can be done in storytelling" (Langellier & Peterson, p. 20). In this final aspect of discursive regularity, the concern is not with what a story means, but how meaning is formed in the first place and how it is, in itself, a point of struggle.

4. Narrative as *legitimation/critique* recognizes that oral histories or performing narratives have the power of kinesis; that is, narrative has the power to expose, break open, and revise unjust systems. Langellier and Peterson (2004) state,

> The danger of performing narratives is that by doing something in and with a discourse that is neither uniform nor stable, we risk changing the bodily practices and material conditions in which they are embedded: what is done can be undone. As discourse, performing narrative "transmits and produces power; it reinforces it, but also undermines and exposes it, renders it fragile and makes it possible to thwart it." (p. 25)

Did Robert's Theoretical Analysis Threaten to Diminish the Living Voices and Perspectives of His Narrators?

Robert recognized two very different views regarding narrative analysis: the thick description of the researcher's analysis, on the one hand, and the oral history standing alone on its own merit, unimpeded by any interpretation by the outside voice of the researcher or interpreter, on the other. There are valid arguments on both sides of the divide. Some general reasons given why oral history should stand alone without interpretive analysis include the following:

- Oral history legitimates the narrator's or subject's own words and interpretation without the need of a "higher" authority. Analysis by researchers only adheres to a power imbalance where dominance and privilege get the last word and must be included, thereby centering the attention on themselves in every story, even when it is not about them.

- To interpret an interpretation is redundant and only distracts and diminishes the vibrancy and power of the oral history.

- The interpretation or analysis of the researcher is always derivative of the researcher's subjectivity, biases, and the knowledge regimes under which he or she was trained, and it is therefore prey to misinterpretation, misrepresentation, and false claims.

- Interpretation disallows the readers from deriving their own interpretation by having the analysis imposed upon them by the researcher.

The other side of the argument stresses the importance of the researcher's analysis in interpreting oral history:

- Analysis honors the oral history by focusing a shining light upon the meanings already inherent within. Analysis is not meant to (dis)place the narrative, but to illuminate it for the reader.

- Analysis engages the narrative even more, creating a more compelling read by acknowledging the inherent implications and possibilities, thereby acknowledging its rich texture and ambiguities, as well as demonstrating the multiplicity of implications in a single experience. This is not redundancy, but it is a discovery of new and more layers.

- In interpretation, the researcher acknowledges his or her positionality. Their subject position is communicated to the reader in the process of illuminating these histories and within the objectives of interpretation. This can be done without making it a story about the researcher or masking the researcher's identity in the guise of objectivity. Positionality refutes the idea that an oral history appears on a page in pure form without the mediation of a subjective researcher.

- Analysis invites the reader to enter more layers. Also, there are moments in the oral history when gestures, words, or phrases carry added significance as well as contradictory moments that are only witnessed through the presence of the researcher. As a result of this witnessing, the researcher notes these dimensions and draws upon their implications.

Case Three: The Fieldwork of Social Drama and Communitas

> *The act of creation itself is cast as a consequence of responsible living . . . constructing the work of art as a metaphysical product of social response-ability is an inventive and useful way of insuring group trust and cohesion around a central mission, albeit one that each . . . understands differently.*

> —Judith Hamera, "Dancing Other-Wise: Ethics, Metaphysics, and Utopia in Hae Kyung Lee and Dancers" (2004)

The artists-in-residence programs had come to an end. The residents left the company to get back to their own theatre group on the other side of town. The company was looking forward to planning the next theatre season and beginning a fresh start, having learned many lessons from all the trouble and strife caused by the visitors.

Everything was going well for the company and the new year that was approaching was going to be stronger than ever: More participants than ever before signed up for the educational skills workshop; several new members from the community volunteered to help with the after school program; and the performance company was about to produce a new play by one of the company members based on the life of Daisy Bates, the courageous but little-known civil rights activist. All the programs were operating successfully, until one day the director received a letter stating that their funding had been cut due to the "lack of success" and "compliance" with the city's artist-in-residence project. The letter also indicated that the company could appeal, and it set a date for a representative to appear before an appeals committee. What happened next became of great interest to Nia in her fieldwork study of the company. What unfolded evolved into a classic social drama that also ended in a magical, compelling moment of communitas.

When Did the Breach Occur?

The company had received funding from the city since it was first established; therefore, it was generally understood they would appeal. When the company had been denied funds in the past, their appeals were always accepted. However, the company director decided to interrupt the expected and change the usual way of operating. She took the stand that the company should no longer depend on city funding and that all support should come from the community and donors who believed in the self-determination and autonomy of the company. Nia observed a breach at two levels: (1) the breach by the city artist-in-residence project when the decision was made, after many years of support, to cut the funding, and (2) the breach by the director, who decided the company would now take a new and more challenging path of financial independence against those who felt the company should appeal.

At both levels, the usual way of doing things had been disrupted. However, Nia focused on the breach created by the director. She wondered if a crisis would erupt within the company, growing into a full-scale social drama and creating polarized sides between those who supported the decision of the director and those who did not. Nia watched very closely and anticipated the repercussions from the breach.

How Did the Crisis Evolve?

In the fashion of a social drama, the deviation from the *status quo* left members split on the issues of whether to side with the way things had always been or to side with change. Nia examined the developing crises through the following stages:

1. Upon hearing the decision not to appeal, members began to narrate and define the director's decision from various perspectives that added more layers and dimensions to the decision. What the director decided, how she decided it, and why she made the decision were communicated and circulated throughout the company—interpretations of the decision were forming on both sides from varying viewpoints. The breach was now made known, and the story of the decision was becoming embellished and public.

2. As the breach was made public and interpreted, members began to form their own opinions and judgments through conversations and debates among themselves.

3. As the breach was narrated between and among company members, disagreements began to arise with greater intensity. The more the breach was

discussed and given value, the more adamant members stood on their side of the issue. Members were now invested in their positions, emotionally and politically. Nia observed that a schism had developed among competing views: those who agreed with the director, those who did not, and those who understood both sides of the issue. The crises erupted into more than the director's decision that disrupted the *status quo*. The crisis stage defined a specific problem, but then fueled the issue into greater proportions. The issue of government funding cut very deeply. Governmental funding became a highly polarized issue. Full community support became a utopian vision for some and an impossibility for others. The crises stage represented an age-old contention over grass roots independence. Both sides articulated their own narratives of attack, defense, and justification. Neither would budge; resentment and anger surfaced.

What Form Did Redressive Action Take?

Understanding that the crisis stage required some form of intervention in order to save the company from splitting apart, Nia witnessed and recorded the unique manner in which redressive action took place through the added dimensions of communitas. The judicial function and mediation from outside the circle of contestation took the form of the Board of Directors. The mechanism for redress comprised members of the Board, community members, supporters of the arts, and art practitioners who were committed to the viability of community theatre.

A special meeting was called to function as a space of redress; it would serve as an opportunity for further narration of all the issues. Each point of view was heard with its full justification and logic. It was during this stage of redress when the very nature of contention was made clear and more deeply considered. The redressive stage was to be the platform for *reflection*.

Questions were raised and addressed on both sides for the purpose of resolving the crisis: Is it economically possible for community organizations to support themselves without government funding? Do artists truly enjoy freedom of expression when the government is funding them? As the company and audience are composed of taxpayers and citizens, does the government have a responsibility to support community arts initiatives?

In the redressive stage, the mechanism of intervention is understood to be a higher order for resolving the crises. Therefore, company members must agree with the decision of the board. Trust was necessary in the understanding that the board members were fair and just and that they held the best interest of the company at heart. As the questions were raised and the responses deliberated, the company would ultimately abide by the decision of the board. Nia realized that compliance with the decision of the board was based on trust, unlike the redressive action of a legal courtroom, which is primarily based on law with the threat to discipline and punish. A person may trust and believe in the law, but he or she must certainly obey or face legal consequences. In the case of the company, the Board of Directors held no legal jurisdiction over the members. It was trust, the feeling of belonging and a commitment to the goals of the company more than fear, or even shame, that must outweigh the crisis and that must eventually lead to resolution.

The stage of redress, in which the positions on each side were narrated, contemplated, and evaluated, had finally come to a resolution. The judgment was made, and the crisis was settled. Now, all the members could come back together as a company and continue with their work under new conditions, or those dissatisfied with the decision could leave the company and form their own.

How Did Communitas Invoke Reintegration?

The Board of Directors meeting is a biannual gathering. Each meeting ends with a closing ritual comprising the lighting of candles, a collective reading of the company's mission statement, and a selection from one of the performances the company produced for that year. Because this was a special meeting to resolve the crisis in the company, the board felt it necessary to include more performative elements to the ritual, hoping to emotionally repair the rift and recover the feeling of camaraderie.

Nia observed that the ritual served two very important functions: first, it reconfirmed the members' commitment to the mission of the company; second, it inspired a feeling of renewal and unity among all those present. The rituals were a vital part of the meetings, and at this particular meeting Nia was more than an observer: Like everyone present, she became a coperformer in a quintessential moment.

Although those company members who were on the opposing side of the decision were greatly disappointed and expressed their discontent with the board, they complied with the decision for the sake and survival of the company. After the decision was made and the closing ritual began with the lighting of candles and the reading of the mission statement, one of the board members began to speak. What emanated from this moment evolved into spontaneous communitas.

One of the board members, Mr. Perkins, began to tell the story of how Abena, the director of the theatre, founded the company. Most everyone in attendance knew the general history of how the company started: the date, the first building where the theatre was housed, the reason it was started, and that a group of committed community members under Abena's lead formed the company in the living room of her small apartment on the South Side. This was the official history that everyone knew. However, the history that was about to be told was a different history. On the occasion of the meeting, the company had never before been under such internal turmoil. The severity of the crises motivated Mr. Perkins to remember the details of a little-known history.

As he began to recount the story, he talked about the struggles and strife of the old neighborhood and how Abena dedicated her life to fulfill her dream of building an art center in the neighborhood that would bring the community together. It would be a creative and enlivening haven from the problems and confusion outside. It would be a place where people could realize their own value in their ability to make meaningful and beautiful art. It would be a place where they could ask questions and make demands about their lives and what they wanted their lives to be through creating art. It would not be an escape from the neighborhood, but it would embrace and live fully within the borders of the neighborhood by remaking and reperforming the stories and lives of neighborhood people. The theatre would be a space where all that was dramatic and staged would not come from fiction and plays, but from the everyday oral histories and narratives of neighborhood people themselves. It would come from the scripts of their real-life stories. Abena wanted a theatre for the community where community people could reach into the hearts and minds of one another through the magic of performance and realize who they were to themselves, who they were to each other, and who they could become. This was her dream, and as Mr. Perkins spoke and as the story unfolded, it seemed that all the listeners were meeting Abena again for the very first time through memory.

As he ended his story, Ali, one of the master drummers, picked up his drum and carried it to the center of the room and began drumming very softly. Ali played as a gesture to honor and give thanks for this new history. The other drummers present at the meeting brought their drums and formed a circle. The drummers now played with great volume and speed. The sound reverberated throughout the theatre. The drummers began to chant and everyone followed. The rhythm of the drum and the chanting voices brought everyone to their feet, moving to the music and clapping their hands. The performers all gathered around the drummers and began dancing. As the dancers and drummers performed, everyone sang and chanted to a song led by Ali. The clapping was now rising with even greater excitement as bodies, young and old, moved and swayed to the thundering drums, chanting voices, and dancing performers. Everyone was living in the story that had just been told with mythic joy and communion. The drummers began repeating words from the story, and everyone joined in forming a new rising rhythm to the whirling energy vibrating throughout the room: "Abena's strength is her dream!" "Abena!" "Abena!" "Where there is no art, there is no life!" The room was filled with tears and laughter. Everyone was caught in this flow of energy and robust excitement. They were all, for this moment, living inside this excess of communal performance and spontaneous communitas. They were all suspended within the space and time of collective performance.

Warm-Ups

1. How might the performance paradigms for each case study be applied differently among them all and how might they be combined?

2. What performance concepts would you employ in your projects and how would you apply them?

3. List specific themes or concepts that reoccur in your fieldwork. With a group of three or more people, create a series of abstract images for the themes and concepts, as though your bodies were made of clay and you were creating a sculpture of the theme or concept. Give each stage picture a name. Keep in mind Boal's idea of image theatre as you work through the assignment. Be creative, adding movement, sounds, and words to your sculpted stage picture.

Notes

1. Courtesy of Beverly Long. Reprinted from "Performance as Doing: A Reconsideration of Evaluating Performed Literature," 1987. In Bacon, Wallace A., ed. *Festschrift for Isabel Crouch: Essays on the Theory, Practice, and Criticism of Performance*. Las Cruces, NM: New Mexico State University.

2. Copyright 2004 from "Disrupting the Dichotomy: 'Yo Soy Chicana/o?' in the New Latina/o South" by Bernadette Marie Calafell. In *The Communication Review*, 7. Reproduced by permission of Taylor & Francis, Inc., http://www.taylorand francis.com.

Suggested Readings

Boal, A. (1995). *The rainbow of desire: The Boal method of theatre and therapy* (A. Jackson, Trans.). New York: Routledge.

Corey, F. C. (1998). The personal: Against the master narrative. In S. J. Dailey (Ed.), *The future of performance studies: Visions and revisions* (pp. 249–253). Washington, DC: National Communication Association.

Dailey, S. J. (1998). *The future of performance studies: Visions and revisions.* Washington, DC: National Communication Association.

Drewal, M. T. (1992). *Yoruba ritual: Performers, play, agency.* Bloomington: Indiana University Press.

Fuoss, K. W. (1997). *Striking performances/performing strikes.* Jackson: University Press of Mississippi.

Hill, R. T. G. (1997). Performance and the "political anatomy" of pioneer Colorado. *Text and Performance Quarterly, 17,* 236–255.

Jenkins, M. M. (1998). Personal narratives changed my life: Can they foretell the future? In S. J. Dailey (Ed.), *The future of performance studies: Visions and revisions* (pp. 264–271). Washington, DC: National Communication Association.

Johnson, E. P. (2001). "Quare" studies, or (almost) everything I know about queer studies I learned from my grandmother. *Text and Performance Quarterly, 15,* 122–142.

Kershaw, B. (1992). *The politics of performance: Radical theatre as cultural intervention.* New York: Routledge.

Legel, L., & Warren, J. T. (Eds.). (in press). *Casting gender: Women and performance in intercultural contexts.* New York: Peter Lang.

Lockford, L. (1998). Emergent issues in the performance of a border transgressive narrative. In S. J. Dailey (Ed.), *The future of performance studies: Visions and revisions* (pp. 214–220). Washington, DC: National Communication Association.

Paget, M. (1990). Performing the text. *Journal of Contemporary Ethnography, 19,* 136–155.

Park-Fuller, L. (2000). Performing absence: The staged personal narrative as testimony. *Text and Performance Quarterly, 20,* 20–42.

Pellegrini, A. (1997). *Performance anxieties: Staging psychoanalysis, staging race.* New York: Routledge.

Pollock, D. (1990). Telling the told: Performing "like a family." *Oral History Review, 18*(2), 1–36.

Richards, S. L. (1995). Writing the absent potential: Drama, performance, and the canon of African-American culture. In A. Parker & E. K. Sedgwick (Eds.), *Performativity and performance* (pp. 64–88). New York: Routledge.

Smith, A. D. (1993). *Fires in the mirror: Crown Heights, Brooklyn, and other identities.* New York: Doubleday.

Spry, T. (1998). Performative autobiography: Presence and privacy. In S. J. Dailey (Ed.), *The future of performance studies: Visions and revisions* (pp. 254–263). Washington, DC: National Communication Association.

Stucky, N. (1993). Toward an aesthetics of natural performance. *Text and Performance Quarterly, 13,* 168–180.

Weisman, J. (1973). *Guerilla theater.* Garden City, NY: Anchor.

References

Agger, B. (2002). *Postponing the postmodern: Sociological practices, selves, and theories.* New York: Rowman & Littlefield.

Alcoff, L. (1991). The problem of speaking for others. *Cultural Critique, 20,* 5–32.

Althusser, L. (1969). *For Marx* (B. Brewster, Trans.). London: New Left Books.

Althusser, L. (1970). *Reading capital* (B. Brewster, Trans.). London: New Left Books.

American Anthropological Association. (1998, June). *Code of ethics of the American Anthropological Association.* Retrieved October 15, 2004, from http://www.aaanetorg/committees/ethics/ethcode.htm

American Anthropological Association. (1995, May). *Commission to review the AAA statement on ethics final report.* Retrieved October 16, 2004, from http://www.aanet.org/committees/ethics/ethrpt.htm

American Folklore Society. (n.d.). Documentation of informed consent. *Statement of the American Folklore Society on research with human subjects.* AFS Position Statements: Human subjects and ethnographic research. Retrieved October 16, 2004, from http://www.afsnet.org/aboutAFS/humansubjects.cfm/

Amnesty International. (1948, December 10). *Universal declaration of human rights.* Retrieved October 16, 2004, from http://web.amnesty.org/pages/aboutai-udgr-eng

Amnesty International, IANSA, & Oxfam. (1999). Shattered lives: The case for tough international arms control. *Control Arms.* Retrieved October 14, 2004, from http://www.controlarms.org/documents/arms_report_full.pdf

Appiah, K. (1992). *In my father's house: Africa in the philosophy of culture.* London: Methuen.

Aquinas, T. (1947). *The summa theologica* (Fathers of the English Dominican Province, Trans.). New York: Benziger Brothers.

Ashby, W. (1997). *A comprehensive history of western ethics.* New York: Prometheus Books.

Ashcroft, B., Griffiths, G., & Tiffin, H. (1998). *Key concepts in post-colonial studies.* London: Routledge.

Atchity, K. (1986). *A writer's time: A guide to the creative process, from vision through revision.* New York: Norton.

Austin, J. L. (1975). *How to do things with words.* Cambridge, MA: Harvard University Press.

Bacon, A. W. (1979). *The art of interpretation*. New York: Holt, Rinehart & Winston.

Bakhtin, M. (1981). *The dialogic imagination* (C. Emerson & M. Holquist, Trans.). Austin: University of Texas Press.

Bakhtin, M. (1984). *Problems in Dostoevsky's poetics* (C. Emerson, Ed. & Trans.). Minneapolis: University of Minnesota Press.

Barthes, R. (1975). *The pleasure of the text* (R. Miller, Trans.). New York: Hill & Wang.

Barthes, R. (1987). *Criticism and truth* (K. Keuneman, Trans.). Minneapolis: University of Minnesota Press.

Barthes, R. (1988). *The semiotic challenge* (R. Howard, Trans.). New York: Hill & Wang.

Bauman, R. (1977). *Verbal art as performance*. Rowley, MA: Newbury House.

Beauvoir, S. de (1952). *The second sex* (H. M. Parshley, Trans.). New York: Knopf.

Benjamin, W. (1968). *Illuminations*. New York: Schocken.

Bentham, J. (1988). *The principles of morals and legislation*. New York: Prometheus.

Bhabha, H. K. (1994). *The location of culture*. New York: Routledge.

Blumer, H. (1969). *Symbolic interactionism: Perspective and method*. Berkeley: University of California Press.

Boal, A. (1979). *The theatre of the oppressed* (C. A. McBride & M.-O. L. McBride, Trans.). New York: Theatre Communication Group.

Boal, A. (1995). *The rainbow of desire: The Boal method of theatre and therapy* (A. Jackson, Trans.). New York: Routledge.

Boas, F. (1928). *Anthropology and modern life*. New York: Norton.

Boas, F. (1931). *The mind of a primitive man*. New York: Macmillan.

Bonnett, A. (1997). Constructions of whiteness in European and American anti-racism. In R. D. Torres, L. F. Mirron, & J. X. Inda (Eds.), *Race, identity, and citizenship: A reader* (pp. 200–218). Oxford, UK: Blackwell.

Bruner, E. M. (1986). Experience and its expressions. In V. Turner & E. M. Brunner (Eds.), *The anthropology of experience* (pp. 3–30). Urbana: University of Illinois Press.

Burke, K. (1945). *A grammar of motives*. Englewood Cliffs, NJ: Prentice Hall.

Burke, K. (1966). *Language as symbolic action: Essays on life, literature, and method*. Berkeley: University of California Press.

Butler, J. (1988). Performative acts and gender constitution: An essay in phenomenology and feminist theory. *Theatre Journal, 40,* 519–531.

Butler, J. (1990). *Gender trouble: Feminism and the subversion of identity*. New York: Routledge.

Butler, J. (1994, Summer-Fall). More gender trouble: Feminism meets queer theory [Special Issue]. *Differences, 6.*

Butler, O. E. (1996). *Blood child and other stories*. New York: Seven Stories Press.

Calafell, B. M. (2004). Disrupting the dichotomy: "Yo soy chicana/o?" in the new latina/o south. *The Communication Review, 7,* 175–204.

Carby, H. V. (1997). White women listen! Black feminism and the boundaries of sisterhood. In R. Hennessy & C. Ingraham (Eds.), *A reader in class, difference, and women's lives* (pp. 110–128). New York: Routledge.

Carlson, M. (1996). *Performance: A critical introduction*. London: Routledge.

Carspecken, P. F. (1996). *Critical ethnography in educational research: A theoretical and practical guide*. New York: Routledge.

Case, S.-E. (Ed.). (1990). *Performing feminisms: Feminist critical theory and theatre*. Baltimore: John Hopkins University Press.

Clark, L., & Kingsolver, A. (2000, November). *Briefing paper on informed consent*. Retrieved October 16, 2004, from http://www.aaanet.org/committees/ethics/bp5.htm

Conquergood, D. (1982a). Communication as performance: Dramaturgical dimensions of everyday life. In J. I. Sisco (Ed.), *The Jensin lectures: Contemporary communication studies* (pp. 24–43). Tampa: University of South Florida Press.

Conquergood, D. (1982b). Performing as a moral act: Ethical dimensions of the ethnography of performance. *Literature in Performance, 5*(2), 1–13.

Conquergood, D. (1983). A sense of the other: Interpretation and ethnographic research. In I. Crouch & G. Owen (Eds.), *Proceedings of the Seminar/Conference on Oral Traditions* (pp. 148–155). Las Cruces: New Mexico University Press.

Conquergood, D. (1984). Point at issue: The center which holds. *Literature in Performance, 5*(1), 86–88.

Conquergood, D. (1986a). Between experience and meaning: Performance as paradigm for meaningful action. In T. Colson (Ed.), *Renewal and revision: The future of interpretation* (pp. 26–59). Denton, TX: Omega.

Conquergood, D. (1986b). Performing cultures: Ethnography, epistemology, and ethics. In E. Siembeck (Ed.), *Miteinander Sprechen and Handelm: Festschrift fur Hellmut Geissner* (pp. 55–66). Frankfurt, Germany: Scriptor.

Conquergood, D. (1988). Health theatre in a Hmong refugee camp. *The Drama Review, 32,* 174–208.

Conquergood, D. (1989). Poetics, play, process, and power: The performative turn in anthropology. *Text and Performance Quarterly, 9,* 82–88.

Conquergood, D. (1991). Rethinking ethnography: Cultural politics and rhetorical strategies. *Communication Monographs, 58,* 179–194.

Conquergood, D. (1992). Ethnography, rhetoric, and performance. *Quarterly Journal of Speech, 78,* 80–97.

Conquergood, D. (1997). Street literacy. In J. Flood, S. B. Heath, & D. Lapp (Eds.), *Handbook of research on teaching literacy through the communicative and visual arts* (pp. 334–375). New York: Macmillan.

Conquergood, D. (1998). Beyond the text: Toward a performative cultural politics. In S. J. Dailey (Ed.), *The future of performance studies: Visions and revisions* (pp. 25–36). Washington, DC: National Communication Association.

Conquergood, D. (2000). Rethinking elocution: The trope of the talking book and other figures of speech. *Text and Performance Quarterly, 20,* 325–341.

Conquergood, D. (2002a). Lethal theatre: Performance, punishment, and the death penalty. *Theatre Journal, 54,* 339–367.

Conquergood, D. (2002b). Performance studies: Interventions and radical research. *The Drama Review, 46,* 145–156.

Davis, C. A. (1999). *Reflexive ethnography: A guide to researching selves and others.* London: Routledge.

Denise, T. C., Peterfreund, S. P., & White, N. P. (1996). (Eds.), *Great Traditions* (8th ed., pp. 199–218). Belmont, CA: Wadsworth.

Denzin, N. K. (1997). *Interpretive ethnography: Ethnography practices for the 21st century.* Thousand Oaks, CA: Sage.

Denzin, N. K. (2001). *Interpretive interactionism* (2nd ed.). Thousand Oaks, CA: Sage.

Denzin, N. K. (2003). *Performance ethnography: Critical pedagogy and the politics of culture.* Thousand Oaks, CA: Sage.

Derrida, J. (1973). *Speech and phenomena.* Evanston, IL: Northwestern University Press.

Derrida, J. (1978). *Writing and difference* (A. Bass, Trans.). Chicago: University of Chicago Press.

Derrida, J. (1982). *Margins of philosophy* (A. Bass, Trans.). Chicago: University of Chicago Press.

Dewey, R. E., & Hurlbutt, R. H. (1997). *An introduction to ethics.* New York: Macmillan.

Diamond, E. (Ed.). (1996). Introduction. *Performance and cultural politics* (pp. 1–2). New York: Routledge.

Dyson, M. E. (2003). *Open mike: Reflections on philosophy, race, sex, culture and religion.* New York: Basic Books.

Dyson, M. E. (2004). *The Michael Eric Dyson reader.* New York: Basic Books.

Estroff, S. (1995). Whose story is it anyway? Authority, voice, and responsibility in narrative of chronic illness. In K. S. Toombs, D. Barnard, & R. A. Carson (Eds.), *Chronic illness: From experience to policy* (pp. 78–103). Bloomington: Indiana University Press.

Fetterman, D. A. (1998). *Ethnography* (2nd ed.). Thousand Oaks, CA: Sage.

Fine, E. C. (1984). *The folklore text: From performance to print.* Bloomington: Indiana University Press.

Fine, G. A. (1993). Ten lies of ethnography: Moral dilemmas of field research. *Journal of Contemporary Ethnography, 22*(3), 267–294.

Fine, M. (1994). Dis-stance and other stances: Negotiations of power inside feminist research. In A. Gitlin (Ed.), *Power and methods* (pp. 13–55). New York: Routledge.

Frankenberg, R. (1993). *The social construction of whiteness: White women, race matters.* Minneapolis: University of Minnesota Press.

Frazer, J. G. (1900). *The golden bough: A study in magic and religion* (2nd ed.). London: Macmillan.

Freud, S. (1927). *The ego and the id* (J. Riviere, Trans.). London: Hogarth Press and the Institute of Psychoanalysis.

Freud, S. (1963). *Dora: An analysis of a case of hysteria* (P. Rieff, Ed.). New York: Macmillan.

Freud, S. (1980). *The interpretation of dreams* (Reissue ed.). New York: Avon.

Frye, M. (1983). *The politics of reality: Essays in feminist theory.* Trumansburg, NY: The Crossing Press.

Fuoss, K. W. (1997). *Striking performances/performing strikes.* Jackson: University Press of Mississippi.

Fuss, D. (1989). *Essentially speaking: Feminism, nature, and difference.* New York: Routledge.

Glesne, C. (1999). *Becoming qualitative researchers: An introduction.* New York: Longman.

Goffman, E. (1959). *The presentation of self in everyday life.* Garden City, NJ: Doubleday.

Goldberg, N. (1990). *Wild mind: Living the writer's life.* New York: Bantam.

Goodall, H. L. (2000). *Writing the new ethnography.* Boston Way, MD: AltaMira.

Gorden, R. L. (2003). Dimensions of the depth interview. *American Journal of Sociology, 62,* 158–164.

Gramsci, A. (1977). *Selections from political writings, 1910–1920* (Q. Hoare, Ed.). London: Lawrence & Wishart.

Gramsci, A. (1978). *Selections from political writings, 1921–1926* (Q. Hoare, Ed.). London: Lawrence & Wishart.

Gramsci, A. (1994). *Letters from prison.* (R. Rosenthal, Trans.). New York: Columbia University.

Greimas, A. J. (1983). *Structural semantics: An attempt at a method* (D. McDowell, R. Schleifer, & A. Velie, Trans.). Lincoln: University of Nebraska Press.

Grossberg, L. (1994). Bringing it all back home: Pedagogy and cultural studies. In G. Girous & P. McLaren (Eds.), *Between borders: Pedagogy and the politics of cultural studies* (pp. 1–25). New York: Routledge.

Guillaumin, C. (1999). "I know it's not nice, but . . .": The changing face of "race." In R. D. Torres, F. L. Miron, & J. X. Inda (Eds.), *Race, identity, and citizenship: A reader* (pp. 39–64). Oxford, UK: Blackwell.

Habermas, J. (1971). *Knowledge and human interests* (J. J. Shapiro, Trans.). Boston: Beacon.

Hall, J. (1998, September). You must remember this: Autobiography as social critique. *Journal of American History,* pp. 439–465.

Hall, S. (1992). What is this "black" in black popular culture? In G. Dent (Ed.), *Black popular culture* (pp. 21–33). Seattle, WA: Bay Press.

Hall, S. (Ed.). (1997). *Representation: Cultural representation and signifying practices.* London: Sage.

Hamera, J. A. (1996). Reconstructing Apsaras from memory: Six thoughts. In C. Ellis & A. Bochner (Eds.), *Ethnographic alternatives* (pp. 201–206). Walnut Creek, CA: AltaMira.

Hamera, J. A. (1997). Critical theoretical perspectives on *The Storytellers.* In S. Mason & E. van Erven (Eds.), *Edgy Storytellers* (pp. 112–120). Utrecht, The Netherlands: Atlantic/International.

Hamera, J. A. (2001). I Dance to You: Reflections on Irigaray's *I Love to You* in Pilates and virtuosity. *Cultural Studies, 15*(2), 229–240.

Hamera, J. A. (2002). An answerability of memory: Saving Khmer (classical) dance. *The Drama Review, 46,* 65–85.

Hamera, J. A. (2004, Summer). Dancing other-wise: Ethics, metaphysics, and utopia in Hae Kyung Lee and dancers. *Modern Drama, 47*(2), 290–307.

Hartigan, J., Jr. (1997). Establishing the fact of whiteness. In R. D. Torres, L. F. Miron, & J. X. Inda (Eds.), *Race, identity, and citizenship: A reader* (pp. 183–199). Oxford, UK: Blackwell.

Hegel, G. W. F. (1956). *The philosophy of history.* New York: Dover.

Heidegger, M. (1961). *An introduction to metaphysics* (R. Manheim, Trans.). New York: Doubleday.

Heidegger, M. (1962). *Being and time* (J. Macquarrie & E. Robinson, Trans.). New York: Harper & Row.

Hennessy, R., & Ingraham, C. (1997). *Material feminism: A reader in class, difference, and women's lives.* London: Routledge.

Hobbes, T. (1996). *Leviathan.* Oxford, UK: Oxford University Press.

hooks, b. (1990). *Yearnings.* Boston: South End.

Hord, L. F., & Lee, J. S. (Eds.). (1995). *I am because we are: Readings in black philosophy.* Amherst: University of Massachusetts Press.

Hume, D. (1985). Of the dignity or meanness of human nature. *Essays: Moral, political, and literary.* Indianapolis, IN: Liberty Press. Retrieved October 20, 2004, from http://www.class.uidaho.edu/mickelsen/texts/Hume%20Treatise/hume%20treatise2.htm#PART%20III

Husserl, E. (1999). *The essential Husserl: Basic writings in transcendental logic* (D. Welton, Ed.). Bloomington: Indiana University Press.

Ingraham, C. (1997). The heterosexual imaginary: Feminist sociology and theories gender. In R. Hennessy & C. Ingraham (Eds.), *A reader in class, difference, and women's lives* (pp. 276–290). New York: Routledge.

Jackson, A. (2002). Introduction. In A. Boal, *Games for actors and non-actors* (pp. xxii–xxvii). New York: Routledge.

Jackson, J. L. (2001). *Harlemworld: Doing race and class in contemporary Black America.* Chicago: University of Chicago Press.

Jameson, F. (1991). *Postmodernism, or the cultural logic of late capitalism.* Durham, NC: Duke University Press.

Johnson, E. P. (2003). Strange fruit: A performance about identity politics. *The Drama Review, 47,* 88–116.

Jung, C. G. (1981). *The archetypes and the collective unconscious* (Vol. 9 of *Collected Works of C. G. Jung*). Princeton, NJ: Princeton University Press.

Jung, C. G. (1997). *Man and his symbols* (Reissue ed.). New York: Dell.

Kant, I. (1947). *The fundamental principles of the metaphysics of ethics* (T. A. Kingsmill, Trans.). London: Longmans, Green.

Kant, I. (1991). *Political Writings* (H. B. Nisbet, Trans.). New York: Cambridge University Press.

Kinchloe, L. J., & McLaren, P. (2000). Rethinking critical theory and qualitative research. In N. K. Denzin & Y. S. Lincoln (Eds.), *Handbook of qualitative research* (2nd ed., pp. 279–313). Thousand Oaks, CA: Sage.

King, M. L., Jr. (1994). Facing the challenge of a new age. In R. A. Long & E. W. Collier (Eds.), *Afro American writing: An anthropology of prose and poetry* (pp. 557–568). University Park: Penn State University Press.

Lacan, J. (1966). *Ecrits: A selection* (A. Sheridan, Trans.). New York: Random.

Lamott, A. (1998). *Bird by bird: Some instructions on writing and life.* New York: Pantheon.

Langellier, K. M., & Peterson, E. E. (2004). *Story telling in daily life: Performing narrative.* Philadelphia: Temple University Press.

Levinas, E. (1987). *Time and the other* (R. A. Cohen, Trans.). Pittsburg, PA: Duquesne University Press.

Levinas, E. (1996). *Emmanuel Levinas: Basic writings* (R. Bernasconi, S. Critichley, & A. Peperzak, Eds.). Bloomington: Indiana University Press.

Lofland, J., & Lofland, L. H. (1984). *Analyzing social settings: A guide to qualitative observation and analysis.* Belmont, CA: Wadsworth.

Long, B. (1987). Performance as doing: A reconsideration of evaluating performed literature. In W. A. Bacon (Ed.), *Festschrift for Isabel Crouch: Essays on the theory, practice, and criticism of performance* (pp. 21–32). Las Cruces: New Mexico State University.

Loomba, A. (1998). *Colonialism/postcolonialism.* London: Routledge.

Lugones, M. (1994). Playfulness, "world"-travelling, and loving perception. In D. S. Madison (Ed.) *The woman that I am: The literature and culture of contemporary women of color* (pp. 626–638). New York: St. Martin's.

Luong, H. V. (2001, October 26–28). *Briefing paper on the impact of material assistance to study population.* Prepared for American Anthropological Association Committee on Ethics. Retrieved October 16, 2004, from http://www.aaanet.org/committees/ethics/bp3.htm

Lyotard, J.-F. (1984). *The postmodern condition: A report on knowledge.* Minneapolis: University of Minnesota Press.

Machiavelli, N. (1914). *The Prince* (N. H. Thomson, Trans.). New York: P. F. Collier & Son.

Machiavelli, N. (1985). *Discourses* (L. J. Walker & B. Crick, Trans.). New York: Viking.

Madison, D. S. (1988). Performance, personal narratives, and the politics of possibility. In S. J. Dailey (Ed.), *The future of performance studies: Visions and revisions* (pp. 276–286). Washington, DC: National Communication Association.

Madison, D. S. (in press). My desire is for the poor to speak well of me. In D. Pollock (Ed.), *Remembering: Performance and oral history.* New York: St. Martin's.

Magee, B. (2001). *The story of philosophy.* London: Dorling Kindersly.

Malinowski, B. (1926). *Crime and custom in savage society.* New York: Harcourt Brace.

Malinowski, B. (1945). *The dynamics of culture change: An inquiry into race relations in Africa.* New Haven, CT: Yale University Press.

Marx, K. (1976). *Capital: Vol. 1. A critique of political economy* (B. Fowkes, Trans.). New York: Penguin.

Marx, K. (1977). *Early writings.* New York: Penguin.

Marx, K. (1983). Theses on Feuerbach. In E. Kamenka (Ed.), *The portable Karl Marx* (pp. 155–158). New York: Penguin.

Marx, K., & Engles, F. (1999). *The communist manifesto* (J. Toews, Trans.). New York: St. Martin's.

McClintock, A. (1994, Winter). The angel of progress: Pitfalls of the term "post-colonialism." In F. Barker, P. Hulme, & M. Iverson (Eds.), *Colonial discourse/ postcolonial theory* (pp. 253–266). Manchester, UK: Manchester University Press.

Mead, G. H. (1938). *The philosophy of the act.* Chicago: University of Chicago Press.

Merleau-Ponty, M. (1962). *Phenomenology of perception* (C. Smith, Trans.). London: Routledge & Kegan Paul.

Merleau-Ponty, M. (1969). *Humanism and terror* (J. O'Neill, Trans.). Boston: Beacon.

Mill, J. S. (1910). *Letters of John Stuart Mill* (H. S. R. Elliot, Ed.). London: Longmans, Green.

Mill, J. S. (1997). *The subjection of women.* New York: Dover.

Minh-ha, T. T. (1989). *Woman, native, other.* Bloomington: Indiana University Press.

Minnich, E. K. (1986). *Conceptual errors across the curriculum: Towards a transformation of the tradition* (Memphis Research Clearinghouse and Curriculum Integration Project). Memphis, TN: Memphis State University, Center for Research on Women.

Mohanty, C. T. (1984). Under western eyes: Feminist scholarship and colonial discourses. In P. Williams & K. Chrisman (Eds.), *Colonial discourse and post-colonial theory: A reader* (pp. 196–220). New York: Columbia University Press.

Moran, D. (2000). *Introduction to phenomenology.* London: Routledge.

Morrison, T. (1994). Rootedness: The ancestor as foundation. In D. S. Madison (Ed.), *The woman that I am: The literature and culture of contemporary women of color* (pp. 492–497). New York: St. Martin's.

Murillo, E. G., Jr. (2004). Mojado crossing along neoliberal borderlands. In G. W. Noblit, S. Y. Flores, & E. G. Murillo, Jr. (Eds.), *Postcritical ethnography: An introduction* (pp. 155–179). Cresskill, NJ: Hampton.

Myerhoff, B. (1982). Life history among the elderly: Performance, visibility, and re-membering. In J. Ruby (Ed.), *A crack in the mirror: Reflexive perspective in anthropology* (pp. 99–117). Philadelphia: University of Pennsylvania Press.

National Association of Social Workers. (1999). *Code of ethics.* Retrieved October 15, 2004, from http://www.naswdc.org/pubs/code/code.asp

Nkrumah, K. (1966). *Neocolonialism: The last stage of imperialism.* New York: International.

Nkrumah, K. (1968). *Dark days in Ghana.* London: Lawrence & Wishart.

Nkrumah, K. (1969). *The struggle continues.* London: Panaf Books.

Noblit, G. W., Flores, S. Y., & Murillo, E. G., Jr. (Eds). (2004). *Postcritical ethnography: An introduction.* Cresskill, NJ: Hampton.

Norman, R. (1997). *The moral philosophers* (2nd ed.). Oxford, UK: Oxford University Press.

Ong, W. (1982). *Orality and literacy: The technologizing of the word*. London: Methuen.

Outlaw, L. (1995). Philosophy, ethnicity, and race. In L. F. Hord & J. S. Lee (Eds.), *I am because we are: Readings in black philosophy* (pp. 304–328). Amherst: University of Massachusetts Press.

Pala, A. (1977). Definitions of women and development: An African perspective. *Signs: Journal of Women in Culture and Society, 9,* 9–13.

Patton, M. (1990). *Qualitative evaluation and research methods* (2nd ed.). Newbury Park, CA: Sage.

Plato. (1909). *The apology of Socrates* (B. Jowett, Trans.). New York: P. F. Collier & Son. Retrieved October 20, 2004, from http://www.eastern.edu/academic/trad_undg/honors_college/readings/apology_g.pdf

Plato. (1999). *Great dialogues of Plato: Vol. 1. Complete texts of* The Republic, Apology, Crito, Phaido, Ion, *and* Meno. New York: Signet.

Plato. (2000a). *A guided tour of five works by Plato: Euthyphro, Apology, Crito, Phaedro (Death scene, Allegory of the cave)* (3rd ed., C. Biffle, Ed.). New York: McGraw-Hill.

Plato. (2000b). *The republic* (B. Jowett, Trans.). Retrieved October 20, 2004, from http://classics.mit.edu/Plato/republic.html

Pollock, D. (1998). Performing writing. In P. Phelan & J. Lane (Eds.), *The ends of performance* (pp. 73–103). New York: New York University Press.

Pollock, D. (1999). *Telling bodies performing birth: Everyday narratives of childbirth*. New York: Columbia University Press.

Radcliffe-Brown, A. R. (1958). *Method in social anthropology: Selected essays*. Chicago: University of Chicago Press.

Rawls, J. (1999). *Theory of justice* (Reissue ed.). Cambridge, MA: Belknap Press.

Robinson, D., & Garratt, C. (1999). *Introducing ethics*. Cambridge, UK: Icon Books.

Rollins, J. (1985). *Between women: Domestics and their employers*. Philadelphia: Temple University Press.

Rousseau, J. J. (1762). *The social contract: Or, principles of political right* (G. D. H. Cole, Trans.). Public Domain. Retrieved October 20, 2004, from http://www.constitution.org/jjr/socon.htm

Rubin, H. J., & Rubin, I. S. (1995). *Qualitative interviewing: The art of hearing data*. Thousand Oaks, CA: Sage.

Sartre, J.-P. (1973). *Existentialism and humanism* (P. Mairet, Trans.). London: Methuen.

Sartre, J.-P. (1993). *Being and nothingness* (H. E. Barnes, Trans.). New York: Washington Square.

Saussure, F. (1959). *Course in general linguistics* (W. Baskin, Trans.). New York: Philosophical Library.

Schechner, R. (1973). Performance and the social science. *The Drama Review, 17,* 5.

Schechner, R. (1985). *Between theatre and anthropology*. Philadelphia: University of Pennsylvania Press.

Schechner, R. (1998). What is performance studies anyway? In P. Phelan & J. Lane (Eds.), *The ends of performance* (pp. 357–362). New York: New York University Press.

Scholte, J. A. (2000). *Globalization: A critical introduction*. New York: St. Martin's.

Schwandt, T. A. (1997). *Qualitative inquiry: A dictionary of terms*. Thousand Oaks, CA: Sage.

Searle, J. R. (1969). *Speech acts: An essay in the philosophy of language*. Cambridge, UK: Cambridge University Press.

Shacochis, B. (2001). Writing for revenge. In M. R. Waldman (Ed.), *The spirit of writing: Classic and contemporary essays celebrating the writing life* (pp. 14–16). New York: Penguin.

Shome, R. (2003). Space matters: The power and practice of space. *Communication Theory, 13,* 1, 39–56.

Shome, R., & Radha, S. H. (2002). Postcolonial approaches to communication: Charting the terrain, engaging the intersections. *Communication Theory, 12,* 3, 249–270.

Shostake, M. (1983). *Nisa: The life and words of a !Kung woman*. Cambridge, MA: Harvard University Press.

Singer, M. (1984). *Man's glossy essence: Explorations in semiotic anthropology*. Bloomington: Indiana University Press.

Small, S. (1999). The contours of racialization: Structures, representations and resistance in the United States. In R. D. Torres, L. F. Miron, & J. X. Inda (Eds.), *Race, identity, and citizenship: A reader* (pp. 47–64). Malden, MA: Blackwell.

Solomos, J., & Back, L. (1999). Marxism, racism, and ethnicity. In R. D. Torres, L. F. Miron, & J. X. Inda (Eds.), *Race, identity, and citizenship: A reader* (pp. 65–78). Malden, MA: Blackwell.

Spellman, E. (1988). *Inessential woman: Problems of exclusion in feminist thought*. Boston: Beacon.

Spinoza, B. de. (1999). *The ethics (Ethica ordine geometrico demonstrata)* [E-book]. Project Gutenberg. Champaign, IL: R. H. M. Publication.

Spivak, G. C. (1988). Can the subaltern speak? In C. Nelson & L. Grossberg (Eds.), *Marxism and the interpretation of culture* (pp. 271–313). Urbana: University of Illinois Press.

Spradley, J. P. (1979). *The ethnographic interview*. New York: Holt, Rinehart & Winston.

Strine, M. S. (1991). Critical theory and "organic" intellectuals: Reframing the work of cultural critique. *Communication Monographs, 58,* 195–201.

Sutton-Smith, B. (1972, December 1). *Games of order and disorder*. Paper presented at a symposium on Forms of Symbolic Inversion, American Anthropological Association, Toronto, Canada.

Taussig, M. (1993). *Mimesis and alterity: A particular history of the senses*. New York: Routledge.

Taylor, P. W. (1978). *Problems of moral philosophy: An introduction to ethics* (3rd ed.). Belmont, CA: Wadsworth.

Tedlock, D. (1983). *The spoken word and the work of interpretation*. Philadelphia: University of Pennsylvania Press.

Thomas, J. (1993). *Doing critical ethnography*. Newbury Park, CA: Sage.

Torres, R. D, Miron, L. F., & Inda, J. X. (1999). *Race, identity, and citizenship: A reader*. Oxford, UK: Blackwell.

Turner, V. (1982a). *From ritual to theatre: The human seriousness of play*. New York: Performing Arts.

Turner, V. (1982b). Performing ethnography. *The Drama Review, 26,* 33–35.

Turner, V. (1985). *On the edge of the bush: Anthropology as experience*. Tucson: University of Arizona Press.

Wagner, G. E. (2000, November). *Briefing paper on remuneration to subject populations and individuals*. Prepared for American Anthropological Association Committee on Ethics. Retrieved October 16, 2004, from http://www.aaanet.org/committees/ethics/bp2.htm

Walker, A. (2003). *In search of our mother's gardens*. Orlando, FL: Harcourt Brace.

Warren, K. J. (2003). *Nature and women's rights: An ecofeminist philosophical perspective on women's rights and gender discrimination*. Paper presented at the Oxford Round Table, Oxford University, Oxford, UK.

Watkins, J. (2000, November). *Briefing paper on consideration of the potentially negative impact of the publication of factual data about a study population on such population*. Prepared for American Anthropological Association Committee on Ethics. Retrieved October 16, 2004, from http://www.aaanet.org/committees/ethics/bp4.htm

Weedon, C. (1987). *Feminist practice and poststructuralist theory*. Oxford, UK: Blackwell.

West, C. (1991). *The ethical dimensions of Marxist thought*. New York: Monthly Review.

Wolcott, H. F. (2001). *Writing up qualitative research*. Thousand Oaks, CA: Sage.

Wood, J. T. (2005). *Gendered lives: Communication, gender, and culture* (6th ed.). Belmont, CA: Wadsworth.

Young, R. J. C. (2001). *Postcolonialism: An historical introduction*. Oxford, UK: Blackwell.

Index

About the Author

 **D. Soyini Madison**'s published works focus on performance ethnography and the intersections between gender and critical race theory. Her teaching centers on myth and popular culture, performance ethnography, the performance of literature for social change, and the political economy of performance. She is a former Fulbright Scholar, where she held visiting lectureship at the University of Ghana at Legon. She is also a recent recipient of a Rockefeller Foundation Fellowship in Bellagio, Italy, where she worked on her current project focusing on staging/performing local debates surrounding human rights and traditional religious practices and on how these debates are influenced by the global market and national development. She has also taught performance ethnography at the graduate level for 14 years.